A. S. MAKARENKO

A BOOK
FOR PARENTS

*

A. S. MAKARENKO

A BOOK
for
PARENTS

Fredonia Books
Amsterdam, The Netherlands

A Books for Parents

by
A. S. Makarenko

ISBN: 1-58963-937-5

Reprinted from the 1954 edition

Fredonia Books
Amsterdam, The Netherlands
http://www.fredoniabooks.com

"A BOOK FOR PARENTS WAS WRITTEN
IN CO-OPERATION WITH MY WIFE
GALINA STAKHIEVNA MAKARENKO

A. Makarenko

Chapter One

*P*ERHAPS this book is too daring?

In moulding their children, modern parents mould the future history of our country and, consequently, the history of the world as well. Can I shoulder the burden of so tremendous a subject? Have I the right or the courage to tackle even its main problems?

Fortunately, no such daring is required of me. Our Revolution has its great books, but it has even more great deeds. The books and deeds of the Revolution—these are the teachers of the new man. Every thought, every movement, every breath of our life vibrates with the glory of the new citizen of the world. Is it possible not to sense that vibration, is it possible not to know how we should educate our children?

But there is also a humdrum side to our life, and this humdrum side gives rise to a complicated set of trivialities. Amid the trivialities one is apt to lose sight of the man. It happens sometimes that our parents seek the truth among these trivialities, forgetting that ready to their hand lies the great philosophy of the Revolution.

To help parents look about them, to help them think, to open their eyes—such is the modest aim of this book.

Our youth is a world phenomenon which defies comparison, a phenomenon whose greatness and significance we are, perhaps, incapable of comprehending. Who gave it birth, who taught it, educated it, entrusted it with the cause of the Revolution? Whence came these tens of millions of craftsmen, engineers, airmen, combine-operators, commanders, scientists? Can it be that we, we old people, created this youth? But when? How did we fail to notice it? Was it not we who grumbled at our schools and universities, grumbled, more often than not, unthinkingly, for want of something better to do; was it not we who considered our People's Commissariats for Education only fit to be grumbled at? And meanwhile the family seemed to be creaking at every joint, more chilled by emotional currents than warmed by love. And anyhow there was no time. We built, we fought, then built again, and we are still building now, we do not down tools for an instant.

But look! In the incredible vastness of the Kramatorsk workshops, in the immense expanse of the Stalingrad Tractor Works, in the Stalino, Makeyevka and Gorlovka mines, in aeroplanes, in tanks, in submarines, in laboratories, over microscopes, above the wastes of the Arctic, at every possible kind of steering gear and regulator, at entrances and exits—everywhere there are tens of millions of new, young and terribly interesting people.

They are modest. Some of them are not very refined in their conversation, sometimes their humour is rough. . . . There is no denying that.

But they are the masters of life, they are calm and confident; unhesitatingly, without hysterics and posing, without boastfulness and without complaining, at absolutely unforeseeable speed—they are doing the job. And just show them one of the sights, which even we are already beginning to forget about, such as, for instance: "*N. A. Pastukhov & Sons. Engineering Works*"—and you will be surprised at the subtle humour of their reactions!

And against the background of this historical miracle, how barbaric seem family "catastrophes" which ruin the relationship between father and children and the happiness of the mother, which break down and destroy the characters of the future men and women of the U.S.S.R.

In our country there must be no childhood catastrophes, no failures, no percentage, not even a hundredth per cent, of defective goods! And yet in some families things do go wrong. Rarely is it a catastrophe, sometimes it is an open conflict; far more often the conflict is secret: not only do parents fail to see it, they fail to see any of its portents.

In a letter received from a mother, I read:

"We have only one son, but it would be better if we had none.... This awful, indescribable misfortune has made us old before our time. It is not only sad, it is painful and distressing to watch a young man going further and further downhill when he could be among the best. After all, youth nowadays means happiness and joy!

"Every day he is killing us, steadily and persistently killing us by his conduct, by everything he does."

The father's appearance is not very attractive: his face is broad, unshaven, lop-sided. He is slovenly: there are hen feathers or something on his sleeve; one feather has even stuck to his finger; the finger is gesticulating over my inkstand, and so is the feather.

"I am a worker ... understand? I work ... and I teach him.... Ask him if that's not so. Well, what have you got to say: did I teach you or didn't I?"

On a chair by the wall sits a boy of about thirteen, handsome, dark-eyed, grave. Without flinching, he looks his father straight in the eye. In the boy's face I can read no feelings, no expression but calm, cold attention.

The father waves his fist, his distorted face going purple.

"The one and only, eh? Robbed me and left me ... with nothing but what I stand up in!"

His fist lunges towards the wall. The boy blinks, then resumes his coldly serious examination of his father.

The father falls back tiredly into his chair, drums with his fingers on the table, and looks round, completely at a loss. An upper muscle in his cheek twitches rapidly, deformed by an old scar.

He lowers his big head and spreads his arms despairingly.

"Take him somewhere.... Well ... I failed. Take him...."

He says this in a defeated, pleading voice, but suddenly he gets excited again, and again brandishes his fist.

"But how can it be? I was a partisan. Look at me... that was a Shkuro sabre... split my head open! For their sake, for yours!"

He turns towards his son and thrusts his hands into his pockets. Then he speaks with that extreme pathos which comes only from the lips of a dying man:

"Misha! How could you?! My only son!..."

Misha's eyes remain cold, but suddenly his lips move, some momentary thought shows itself for an instant and vanishes.

I see that these two are enemies and will remain enemies for a long time, perhaps for life. Their characters have clashed over some trifle or other, in some dark corner of the soul instincts have been aroused, temperaments fired. An unexpected explosion is the usual culmination of careless treatment of character—this father, of course, used the rod. And the son rose up against his father, free and proud—it was not for nothing that his father fought with the Shkuro gang! That was how it started. Now the father is driven frantic—and his son?

I looked at Misha sternly and said quietly:

"You'll go to the Dzerzhinsky Commune! Today!"

The boy straightened up on his chair. Real bonfires

of joy flamed in his eyes, and the room seemed to grow brighter. Misha did not say anything, but leaned back in his chair and directed his new-born smile straight at the Shkuro scar and tormented eyes of his father. And only then did I read in his smile implacable, unconcealed hatred.

The father sadly lowered his head.

When Misha left with the inspector, the father asked me, as if he were addressing an oracle:

"Why have I lost my son?"

I made no answer. Then the father asked:

"Will it be all right for him there?"

Books, books, books up to the ceiling. Well-loved names on splendid binding. An enormous writing-table On the table—more books, a monumental sarcophagus of an inkstand, sphinxes, bears, candlesticks.

This study bubbles with life; the books do not merely stand on the shelves, they rustle in people's hands; newspapers do not merely lie about among the cushions on the divan, they are spread out and read; here events are knowledgeably discussed and come to life. Through the tobacco smoke one has glimpses of bald pates, elaborate coiffures, shaven chins, American moustaches and amber cigarette-holders; and behind horn-rimmed spectacles eyes glisten with the fine dew of wit.

In the spacious dining-room tea is served, tea which is not rich old-fashioned samovar tea, not tea to be drunk, but refined tea, tea which is almost symbolic, an occasion for china, lace table-napkins and the severe beauty of the ascetic biscuit. Slightly languid, a little naive, the exquisitely auburn-haired hostess conducts the tea-party with her pampered, manicured hands. Tea is attended by a merry flock of names of artistes and ballerinas, mischievous short stories and light-hearted episodes from life. Well, and if a snack is served with the tea and the smiling host makes two or three rounds with the decanter? Then after tea the company will go back into the study, light up again, squash the newspapers on the divan, loll on the cushions and, throwing back their heads, roar with laughter over the latest funny story.

Is there anything wrong with that? Who knows? But among these people there is always a wide-eyed, twelve-year-old Volodya running to and fro, rather thin and pale, but an energetic lad. When for some reason a hitch occurs in the smooth flow of anecdotes, Daddy "serves up" Volodya—just a tiny portion of him. In theatrical parlance this is called an "entr'acte."

Daddy draws Volodya on to his knee, tickles the back of Volodya's head and says:

"Volodya, why aren't you in bed?"

Volodya replies:

"And why aren't you there?"

The guests are delighted. Volodya lowers his eyes to Daddy's lap and smiles shyly—guests like it better that way.

Daddy pats Volodya on any suitable spot and asks:

"Have you finished *Hamlet* yet?"

Volodya nods.

"Did you like it?"

This time, too, Volodya is not at a loss, but now shyness is out of place.

"Pooh, not much! If he's in love with that ... um ... Ophelia, why don't they get married? They just dawdle along and you have to read and read!"

A fresh burst of laughter from the guests. From a corner of the divan somebody's cosy bass adds the necessary spice: "He doesn't want to pay alimony, the rogue!"

This time Volodya laughs too, so does Daddy, but the appropriate funny story has already taken the stage: "Do you know what the priest said when he was told to pay alimony?"

"End of entr'acte." Volodya is rarely served up as part of the programme—Daddy realizes that Volodya is pleasant only in small doses. Volodya does not like such a system of doses. He runs to and fro among the crowd, passes from one guest to another, tags on even to strangers and fishes intently for a chance to make a sortie, to show himself off, to raise a laugh from the guests and to exalt his parents.

At tea Volodya's ringing voice suddenly breaks into a story.

"She's his mistress, isn't she?"

Mother throws up her hands and exclaims:

"Did you hear him say that? Volodya, what are you saying?!"

But on Mother's face, together with a certain degree of false surprise, are written involuntary delight and pride; she takes this boyish freeness as evidence of talent. In the general list of elegant bric-à-brac Volodya's talent is also acceptable: Japanese cups, little knives for lemon, napkins and—such a wonderful son.

In the midst of their trivial and foolish vanity the parents are unable to look closely into their son's character and see there the first signs of their future family troubles. Volodya has a very complicated look in his eyes. He tries to make them into innocent childish eyes—that is "by special request," for his parents; but in those very same eyes glitter sparks of insolence and habitual falsehood—that is for himself.

What kind of a citizen will he make?

Dear parents!

You sometimes forget that in your family there is a person growing, a person for whom you are responsible.

Do not console yourselves with the idea that this is no more than a moral responsibility.

There may come a moment when you will lose heart and spread out your arms in bewilderment, and then, perhaps, you will mutter to quieten that very same sense of moral responsibility: "Volodya was such a wonderful boy! Simply everyone was delighted with him."

But will you never understand who is to blame?

However, catastrophe may not occur.

The moment comes when parents first feel there is something slightly wrong. Then this feeling deepens, that there is something really unhealthy in what they had thought was their happy family. For a time the worried parents submit to this, whisper unhappily to each other in the bedroom, but maintain their dignity in public, pretending that all is well and no tragedy has occurred, for the outward appearance of the family is wholesome enough.

The parents act just like all producers of shoddy goods: the latter are offered to society as the proper article.

When the first little "child" trouble occurs in your family, when you see in your child's eyes a little animal, as yet small and weak but already hostile, why do you not look back, why do you not set about reviewing your own conduct, why are you too weak-minded to ask yourself: Have I, in my family life, acted like a Bolshevik?

But I am sure you are looking for an excuse ...

A man in spectacles, with a short red beard, a rubicund cheerful man, suddenly stirred his spoon round in his glass, pushed the glass aside and snatched out a cigarette.

"You pedagogues are always reproaching people over methods. No one is quarrelling about that, methods are methods. But solve the basic conflict, my friends!"

"What conflict?"

"Oho! What conflict? You don't even know what it is? None of that, you solve it!"

"All right then, I will. What are you getting excited about?"

He drew appreciatively at his cigarette, his full lips ejected a small ring of smoke, then a tired smile appeared on his face.

"You won't solve anything. The conflict is one of the insoluble variety. It's no solution to say sacrifice this or sacrifice that. That's just a formal get-out! Suppose I can't sacrifice one thing or the other, what then?"

"But what's the conflict, I'm interested to know?"

My companion squinted at me through tobacco smoke; twisting his cigarette between his fingers to stress the fine shades of his sorrow, he said:

"On the one hand you have your job in society, your social duty, on the other your duty to your child, to your family. Society takes all my time: morning, afternoon and evening—the use of every moment is allotted and mapped out. And the child? It's just simple arithmetic: giving your time to your child means sitting at home, keeping out of life, becoming a philistine, in fact. You must talk to your child, you must explain a lot to him, you must bring him up, damn it all!"

He looked at me with an air of pompous impatience and stubbed out his unfinished cigarette in the ashtray.

"Have you a son?" I asked cautiously.

"Yes, in the sixth class, thirteen years old. Good fellow, learns well, but he's a young vagabond already. He treats his mother as a servant. He's rude. I never see him. And just imagine this. A friend of his came round the other day, and there they were sitting in the next room, and suddenly I hear my Kostik swearing. Not just a word or two, mind you, simply turning the air blue."

"Were you frightened?"

"What do you mean 'frightened'? At the age of thirteen there is nothing he doesn't know, no secrets exist for him. Probably knows dirty stories as well and all kinds of muck!"

"Of course he does!"

"Well, there you are! And where was I? Where was I, his father?"

"You are annoyed that other people have taught your son swear-words and dirty stories and that you had no chance to take part in it?"

"Now, you are joking!" roared my companion. "But joking does not solve the conflict!"

He paid agitatedly for the tea and ran off.

But I was not joking at all. I had asked him a question and his reply had been mere babble. He drinks tea in the club and chatters to me—he would call that social work too. And give him more time, what will he do with it? Wage a campaign against lewd stories? But how? What age was he when he himself began swearing? What is his programme? What ideas has he, besides the "basic conflict"? And where did he run off to? Perhaps to educate his son, or perhaps he was going somewhere else to discuss the "basic conflict"?

The "basic conflict"—lack of time—is the favourite excuse of unsuccessful parents. Protected from responsibility by the "basic conflict," they imagine themselves indulging in salutary talks with their children. A comforting picture: the parent talks and the child listens! But the making of speeches and sermons to one's own children is an incredibly difficult task. For such a speech to have a beneficial educative effect, a fortunate coincidence of many circumstances is required. In the first place you have to choose an interesting theme; then it is essential that you should know how to express yourself well and how to illustrate what you have to say; apart from this the child must be blessed with unusual patience.

On the other hand, suppose your speech pleases the child. At first glance it may seem that this is good, but in practice there are parents who will be furious if that happens. What kind of an edifying speech is it that aims at bringing joy to the child? Everybody knows that joyfulness can be attained by many other means; "edifying" speeches, on the contrary, aim at distressing the listener, wearing him down, reducing him to tears, to moral exhaustion.

Dear parents!

Please do not think that there is no sense at all in talking to your child. We are only warning you against hoping too much from such talks.

Just those parents who bring up their children badly and those people in general who are quite devoid of any educational ability—all of them exaggerate the value of pedagogical talks.

Educational work, they imagine, is carried on like this. The educator takes his stand at point A. Three yards away is point B defended by the child. The educator brings his vocal cords into action, the child picks up the appropriate sound waves with his hearing apparatus. The waves penetrate by means of the ear-drums to the child's soul and are distilled there into some special educational potion.

Sometimes the positions of subject and object vary a little, but the distance of three yards remains the same. As if attached to a lead, the child circles round the educator, all the while experiencing the action of the vocal cords or some other type of direct influence. Sometimes the child breaks away from the lead and in a short time is discovered in the dreadful cesspool of life. In such a case the educator, father or mother, protests in a trembling voice: "He's got quite out of hand! All day running the streets! You know what kind of boys there are in our court-yard? Young ruffians! Who knows what they get up to out there? Some of them are even juvenile delinquents, I dare say. . . ."

Both the voice and eyes of the orator beg: catch my son, save him from the street boys, put him on the pedagogical lead again, let me carry on educating him.

Such education certainly requires much spare time and, of course, it means spare time wasted. The system of tutors and governesses, permanent overseers and constant nagging, broke down long ago without ever creating in history a single vivid personality. The best, live children invariably broke loose.

A Soviet person cannot be educated by the direct influence of one personality, whatever the qualities this personality may possess. Education is a social process in the broadest sense of the term. Everything contributes to education: people, things, events, but first of all and above all—people. Of these, parents and teachers hold first place. The child enters into an infinite number of relationships with the whole complex world of surrounding reality. Each one of these relationships is irresistibly developing, overlapping with other relationships, and becoming more complicated as the physical and moral growth of the child increases.

Nothing in this "chaos" seems to yield to any calculation. Nevertheless at each given moment definite changes are created in the personality of the child. And it is the task of the educator to direct and guide this development.

Senseless and hopeless is the attempt made by some parents to shield the child from the influence of life and substitute individual domestic training for social education. It is bound to end in failure: either the child breaks out of the domestic prison or you produce a freak.

Then it is life that is responsible for the child's upbringing? But where does the family come in?

18

No, it is the family or, if you like, the parents that are responsible for the child's upbringing. But the training provided by the family collective cannot mould the child out of nothing. A limited assortment of family impressions or pedagogical lectures from father will not suffice as material for the future man. It is Soviet life in all its multiform variety that provides that material.

In the old days in well-to-do families children used to be called "angelic souls." In our day it has been said that children are "flowers of life." That is good. But rash-minded, sentimental people have not taken the trouble to think over the meaning of these beautiful words. Once children are described as "flowers," it means to such people that we should do nothing but go into raptures over them, make a fuss of them, smell them, sigh over them. Perhaps they even think we should teach the flowers themselves that they are a fragile "luxury" bouquet.

This purely aesthetic and thoughtless enthusiasm contains the seeds of its own failure. The "flowers of life" should not be imagined as a "luxury" bouquet in a Chinese vase on your table. However much you enthuse over such flowers, however much fuss you make over them, these flowers are already dying, they are already doomed and they are sterile. Tomorrow you will simply have them thrown away. At best, if you are incorrigibly sentimental, you will dry them in a bulky volume, but you can expect little joy from that: give yourself up as much as you like to memories, look at them as much as you like, you will still have nothing but hay, just hay.

No, our children are not flowers of that kind at all. Our children blossom on the living trunk of our life; they are not a bouquet, they are a wonderful apple orchard. And this orchard is ours. Here the right of property means something fine, believe me! It is hard, of course, not to admire such an orchard, hard not to rejoice over it, but it is even harder not to work in it. Be so kind as to take on this job: dig, water, get rid of the caterpillars, prune out the dead branches. Remember the words of the great gardener, Comrade Stalin:

"People should be reared with care and attention as a gardener rears his chosen fruit-tree."

Note the word: fruit. Not only fragrance, not only range of colours, but fruit, that is what should interest you especially. And for this reason do not descend upon the flowers with nothing but raptures and kisses—take up your spade, your scissors and watering-can, and fetch the ladder. And when the caterpillar appears in your garden, reach for the Paris green. Do not be afraid of it, shake it around a bit, let even the flowers feel a little uncomfortable. By the way, a good gardener never has trouble with caterpillar.

Yes, let us be gardeners. This excellent comparison will help us to explain a few things about the difficult problem of who educates the child—parents or life?

Who cultivates the tree in an orchard?

The soil and the air give it substance, the sun gives it the valuable power of combustion, the winds and storms bring it toughness in battle, its fellow-trees save it from sterility. Both in the tree and round it extremely complex chemical processes are always at work.

What can the gardener change in this laborious work of life? Should he just wait helplessly and submissively till the fruit are ripe and he can pluck them and gorge himself on them with greedy indifference?

That is exactly what savages do in the wilds of Tierra del Fuego. And that is what many parents do.

But a real gardener would never act like that.

Man learnt long ago to approach nature cautiously and tenderly. Now he has learnt to transform nature, to create new natural forms, to apply his powerful corrective to the life of nature. And we should remember that we, Soviet educationalists, are also no longer "servants of nature," but her masters.

Our education is a similar corrective. And only on these lines is education possible. To lead a child wisely and surely along the rich paths of life, amid its flowers and through its storms and tempests, is a task which every man can accomplish if he really wants to do so.

Nothing annoys me more than the disgusting panic-stricken howl:

"Street urchins!!"

"You see, everything was all right, but then Seryozha got friendly with a lot of urchins in our yard...."

This "lot of urchins" corrupt Seryozha. Seryozha roams off no one knows where. Seryozha has taken a cut of trouser-cloth from the wardrobe and sold it. Seryozha came home past midnight, smelling of vodka. Seryozha insulted his mother.

Only the most hopeless simpleton can believe that all this was brought about by "a lot of urchins," "street urchins."

Seryozha is not unique. He is a perfectly ordinary standard type, which everybody is quite tired of, and it is not "street urchins" or the "urchins in our yard," but lazy and unscrupulous parents that have made him what he is. He is not produced in a flash; the process is a persistent and patient one, beginning from the time when Seryozha was one and a half years old. A large number of thoroughly disgraceful characteristics in the family's behaviour contributed to the making of him: blank idleness, aimless day-dreaming, petty tyranny and, above all, unpardonable irresponsibility and an infinitesimal sense of duty.

Seryozha is indeed a real "street urchin," but it was the family, and only the family, that made him one. Perhaps in your yard he does meet failures like himself; together they make up the usual gang of youngsters, all of them equally demoralized and equally "street." But in that same yard you will find dozens of children for whom the family body and the family corrective have created principles and traditions which help them to overcome the influence of the street boys without avoiding them and without barricading themselves off from life, within the family walls.

The decisive factor in successful family upbringing lies in the constant, active and conscious fulfilment by parents of their civic duty towards Soviet society. In those cases where this duty is really felt by parents, where it forms the basis of their daily lives, there it necessarily guides the family's work of upbringing too, there no failures or catastrophes are possible.

But there is, unfortunately, a category of parents, a fairly numerous category, with whom this rule does not work. These people seem to be good citizens, but they suffer either from inability to think consistently, or from a weak sense of direction, or from being too little observant. And for this reason alone their sense of duty does not operate in the sphere of their family relationships, nor, consequently, does it operate in the sphere of their children's upbringing. And for this reason alone they meet with more or less serious failures, and for this reason alone they produce for society human beings of dubious quality.

Others are more honest. They say sincerely: "You have to know how to bring up a child. Perhaps I am not doing it right really. It takes knowledge to bring up children."

In other words: everybody wants to bring up their children well, but not everyone knows the secret. Some people have discovered it, some people make full use of it, but you are completely in the dark, no one has revealed the mystery to you.

This being so, the eyes of all turn towards the teachers' training colleges and institutes.

Dear parents!

Between ourselves: in their families our pedagogical brethren produce, proportionately, about the same quantity of defective goods as you do. And, on the contrary, fine children are often brought up by parents who have never seen either the front door or the back door of pedagogical science.

And pedagogical science pays little attention to family upbringing. That is why even the most learned pedagogues, although they know the why and wherefore of things very well, when bringing up their own children try to rely more on common sense and worldly wisdom. But perhaps more often than others they are guilty of a naive belief in the pedagogical "secret."

I once knew such a professor of pedagogics. He would always treat his only son as a problem to be solved with the aid of books and profound psychological analyses. Like many pedagogues he believed that there must exist somewhere in the world some kind of pedagogical trick which would bring complete and delightful satisfaction both to educator and child, satisfy all principles and bring about the reign of peace and quiet and eternal bliss! The son was rude to his mother at dinner. The professor thought for a moment and arrived at an inspired solution:

"Fedya, since you have insulted your mother, it follows that you do not appreciate our home, that you are unworthy to sit at our table. Very well, from tomorrow onwards I shall give you five rubles a day—eat your dinner where you like."

The professor was pleased. In his opinion he had reacted to his son's rudeness brilliantly. Fedya was also pleased. But the trick plan did not work. There was a period of peace and quiet, but the eternal bliss was missing.

The professor expected that in three or four days' time Fedya would come and fling his arms round his father's neck, saying: "Father, I was wrong! Don't shut me out from home!"

But it did not happen like that, or rather, not quite like that. Fedya became very fond of visiting cafés and restaurants. The only thing that disconcerted him was the small amount his father had assigned him. He made one or two amendments to the scheme; he rooted about the house and showed some initiative. Next morning, the professor's trousers were found missing from his wardrobe and in the evening the son came home drunk. In touching tones he proclaimed his love for his mama and papa, but did not raise the question of returning to the family table. The professor took off his belt and waved it in front of his son's face for some minutes.

After a month the professor put up the white flag and asked for his son to be sent to a labour colony. According to him Fedya had been spoilt by various comrades of his. "You know what children there are about!"

Some parents, if they heard of this affair, would undoubtedly say: "Very well! But all the same, how *is* one supposed to act if one's son is rude to his mother at dinner?"

Comrades! Perhaps you will ask me next how one should act if one loses a purse full of money? Think it over and you will find the answer at once: buy yourself a new purse, earn some more money and put it into the purse.

If a son insults his mother, no tricks will do any good. It means that you have brought up your son very badly and that you have been doing so for a long time. You must begin the work of bringing him up all over again, you must change a lot of things in your family, think over a lot of things, and, above all, put yourself under the microscope. And as for how you should act immediately after rudeness, that is a question to which one cannot give any general answer—it depends on each individual case. One must know what kind of a person you are and how you have acted towards your family. Perhaps you yourself were rude to your wife in the presence of your son. Incidentally, if you treated your wife badly when your son was not at home—take that into consideration too.

No, tricks in family upbringing must be firmly discarded. The care and upbringing of children is a big, a serious, and a terribly responsible task, and it is, of course, also a difficult task. No easy tricks can help you out here. Once you have a child, it means that for many years to come you must give him all your power of concentration, all your attention and all your strength of character. You must be not only father and guardian of your children, you must also be organizer of your own life, because your quality as an educator is entirely bound up with your activities as a citizen and your feelings as an individual.

Chapter Two

"But what will be added? That will be settled after a new generation has grown up: a generation of men who never in all their lives have had occasion to purchase a woman's surrender either with money or with any other means of social power, and of women who have never been obliged to surrender to any man out of any consideration other than that of real love, or to refrain from giving themselves to their beloved for fear of the economic consequences."

FREDERICK ENGELS

*O*NCE WHEN I was young I was invited to spend my holidays with a prince's family, preparing his not very bright son to retake some examinations. The family was passing the summer on its estate not far from our provincial town. I was tempted by the good wages and the opportunity of acquainting myself with the aristocratic life. At the hot empty station I found a long gleaming carriage—a four-wheeler—awaiting me. The pair of black horses and the driver's back also impressed me: I even experienced a certain reverence for the realms of the nobility, of which till then I had read only in books.

My battered little suit-case bounced up and down ill-manneredly on the floor of the carriage, and a feeling of depression came over me. What in the devil's name had brought me into this aristocratic world? Here they had their own rules, carriages, even taciturn coachmen, who themselves had a tremendously blue-blooded air—like the horses, which must have been of equally noble descent. . . .

I spent two months on the estate, and the feeling of depression born on the road there did not leave me until the last day. But on the way back to the station, in that same carriage, the same battered suit-case bounced up and down cheerfully and nothing worried me: neither the carriage, nor the coachman, nor anything else in that fabulously rich, unattainably lofty, brilliant aristocratic world.

This world did not please me. The prince himself, a Major-General of His Majesty's suite, "worked" somewhere at court and did not visit his estate once. The family passing the summer there consisted of a tall, thin, long-nosed princess, two young daughters with equally long noses, and a similarly long-nosed twelve-year-old cadet, my charge, so to speak. Apart from the family, there were about twenty people in the dining-room every day; I never quite discovered who they were. Some of them lived on the estate, others stayed as guests for two or three days. The latter were neighbours, a few of whom were highly-titled persons; until then it had never occurred to me that there was so much trash to be found in our province.

The whole company to a man astonished me with its spiritual worthlessness. Never before in my life had I met such a collection of useless individuals. Perhaps for this reason I was incapable of noticing if they had any good qualities at all.

As I looked at them I could not help remembering my father. Every day for years he had been getting up at five o'clock in the morning at the sound of the hooter. Fifteen minutes later he was already walking past the grey fences of our sandy street, carrying with him a little red bundle containing his lunch. At six o'clock in the evening he would arrive back from the factory, dusty and serious, and the first thing he would do would be to lay out on the stool in the kitchen the neatly folded red handkerchief in which he had for so long been carrying his lunch. Could any of these princes and counts, Major-Generals of His Majesty's suite, their guests and hangers-on ever have thought for a moment how much an ordinary cotton handkerchief costs, how one must look after it, how carefully one must shake it out after lunch and fold it in four, and then double again!?

Now I remember the prince's family as a monstrous caricature: it was more a criminal association than anything else, a company of idlers, united round their ringleader. I observed every detail of the princely life with disgust: the stupid empty haughtiness, which was of no use to anyone, the abundance both of dinner and supper, the cut-glass, the endless rows of knives and forks, the figures of the lackeys, whose role in life was insulting to the very nature of man.

Even now I do not know how long one can live such an inactive, satiated life without becoming as stupid as the beasts of the field. A year or two, perhaps even five, but not for centuries, surely?

But *they* lived so for centuries. Day after day they would chatter about somebody's successes, somebody else's intrigues, about weddings and funerals, about awards and disappointments, about the tastes and eccentricities of idlers similar to themselves, about the purchase and sale of estates.

My pupil was a mentally backward boy. His sisters and mother seemed to be just as mentally backward. But not even simple arithmetic, to say nothing of great mental development, was really essential to them. Wealth, title, the niche belonging to him at court, everyday moral and aesthetic canons worked out long ago and long ago obsolete, a simple domestic training—all this was quite sufficient to determine the path in life of the future prince.

And yet, in spite of all this, the real essence of their life consisted of grabbing, incessant, constant anxiety

over accumulating things, the most primitive, most unpleasant and disgusting meanness, not very successfully
concealed by pompous etiquette. It meant nothing to them
that they had a lot already! Somewhere a railway was
being built, somewhere else a pottery company was being
formed, someone had brought off a successful deal with
his shares; everything caused them concern, worried them,
agitated them; everywhere they were attracted and frightened by opportunities and dangers; they suffered from
indecision and could never part with their anxieties. The
surprising part of it all was that this family actually
grudged themselves some things. The princess spoke long
and regretfully about having to write a letter to Paris,
cancelling an order for some dresses because the money
was needed by the prince "for business purposes," and
my pupil just as regretfully recalled that last year they
had wanted to buy him a yacht and never did so.

On returning to my own working family I was deeply
convinced that I had visited an antipodal world so strange
and repulsive to me that no comparison of it with the
working-man's world was possible. My world was im-
measurably richer and more colourful. Here were the real
creators of human culture: workers, teachers, doctors,
engineers and students. Here were personalities, convictions, effort, argument—here there was struggle. My father's acquaintances, "old hands" like himself, were clev-
erer, sharper and more human than the aristocrats. Our
family godfather Khudyakov, a painter, came on Sunday
to see my father, sat down opposite me, twisted his gap-
toothed mouth into a malicious grin and said:

"Did you ask me if I want their company? For all I
care they can go to the devil! I wouldn't drink a glass
of vodka with a sponger, not even if he was sweet as pie
and made of money. When I come to see Semyon Grigo-

ryevich here, we sit down and talk about this and that; you can live all right without princes, but without us painters? Lumme! What sort of a life would it be? Pretty bare, if you ask me!"

Later on, when I grew a little wiser and had a little more experience of life, and particularly after the October Revolution, I realized that there was even something in common between aristocratic families and the families of our acquaintances.

I remember well how my godfather married off his daughter. She was a fine rosy girl, who very much wanted to spend the rest of her days with a young mechanic called Nesterenko. But old Khudyakov said to her: "What's Nesterenko? Bit of a mechanic. What's he earn? When he's got grey hair he won't be getting more than ruble fifty a day! Drop it!"

His daughter cried, but old Khudyakov said:

"Don't come to me with your grizzling. The only daughter I have and you want to lower me in my old age. Nesterenko's no husband for you!"

His daughter had another cry, but married an engine-driver's mate called Sverchkov all the same.

"No sense at all!" Khudyakov said to my father during one of his Sunday visits. "Nesterenko or no one! What a lovely moustache he's got—that's the way she thinks! Now Sverchkov, he's a passenger-driver's mate already; in a year or two they'll give him an engine—maybe only a shunter, shall we say—but he'll be an engine-driver all the same. Have I worked all these years for nothing? Is there a five-hundred-ruble dowry going here, or is there not?"

And in our world engine-drivers did not mix with every painter. When I was about seven I looked upon engine-drivers as the cream of the aristocracy. My godfather Khudyakov was a very highly qualified painter—a coach decorator—but Sverchkov's marriage to his daughter was nevertheless an obvious misalliance.

My father did not support my godfather and on this occasion showed general disapproval of his attitude towards the upper classes.

"Listen here, Vasıl," he said to him, "I don't like it, you know, the way you are always hob-nobbing with the gentry!"

"Who's hob-nobbing with who?" said my godfather confusedly and jerked his straggly goat's beard away from the hospitable herring on his plate towards the jasmine bushes outside the window.

"Yes, hob-nobbing. Who were you out fishing with last Sunday? With that . . . old pot-belly. . . the railway inspector! And your wife, where does she spend all her time? At Novak's place. Isn't that so?"

Khudyakov made a show of being insulted.

"At Novak's? My wife? Spends all her time there, does she? Now then, Semyon Grigoryevich, drop that! Never had anything to do with the gentry in my life and not going to. And as for fishing, well, that's my pleasure! I'd go fishing with a general!"

Father nods slyly at my indignant godfather:

"Aha! With a general, eh? A general wouldn't have a boat but the inspector's got a boat. And bacon in his knapsack too!"

My father was right in reproaching godfather Khudyakov, because my godfather really did hob-nob with the gentry. It was particularly unpardonable if his wife had really been calling on Novak. The railway inspector was simply a well-to-do man, but senior conductor Novak was a representative of the real gentry, higher even than the engine-drivers. No one in our settlement was equal to Novak, unless it was the stationmaster. But the stationmaster's claim to superiority lay not so much in wealth as in his sleek face, his superb uniform and the mysterious luxury of his government flat, for, of course, we had no idea how many rooms it contained.

Novak, however, was rich. His big court-yard, barricaded off from the rest of the world by high fences, was the centre of the Novaks' family life, which was also a mystery to us. Out of this yard bulged the shapeless pot-belly of a two-storied brick house. The ground-floor contained a grocer's shop, which also belonged to the Novak family. With this shop we had some acquaintance, since from early childhood our parents had sent us there to buy kerosene, sunflower-seed oil and tobacco for Father. But of the Novaks' remaining wealth the only objects visible to our gaze were the lace curtains in the windows. The word "lace" suggested to me absolutely unattainable standards of luxury.

Senior conductor Novak, a lean man with a steel-grey beard clipped severely on all sides, drove past our gate twice a week in a well-sprung carriage, and alongside his shiny boots there always stood an equally shiny brown bag, in which, according to the general opinion, the senior conductor kept the money he received from the "bilkers." When I was little I also imagined the "bilkers" as mysterious beings, as tiny gnomes bringing happiness.

Novak had tidy, good children, with whom our parents used to reproach us. They were dressed up in dazzling school-uniforms, and later they began to wear badges on their shoulders. They would walk down our street, proud and inaccessible, surrounded by the offspring of other rich families: the priest's children, the sons of the chief accountant, and those of the policeman, the building inspector and the railway inspector.

In spite of the complete aloofness and mystery of this gentry, it was actually through them that the ideals and standards of everyday life and, consequently, of up-bringing reached our working families from those exalted spheres with which I had chanced to come in contact during my holidays. From the prince's palace to the cottage of painter Khudyakov there was a ladder by which family customs—the laws of capitalist society—descended to us. Of course, there was between the one and the other not only a quantitative but also a qualitative abyss—the abyss created by class. The proletariat lived according to different moral and ethical laws, deeply human in essence. But if the long-nosed princesses were to inherit a title, an estate, jewellery and dreams of their own yacht, then Dunya Khudyakova, the daughter of a humble craftsman, also received an inheritance of sorts: a "wardrobe," a sewing-machine, a bed with nickel knobs on it and dreams of a gramophone.

The family of the old days, including the family of a craftsman or a petty official, was according to the above laws an accumulating organization. Of course, the accumulation was different and the results were different. Novak made money out of the "bilkers," the railway inspector out of the unchecked workers' pay accounts, and painter Khudyakov—out of a fifteen-hour working day. After he had finished at the factory he used to paint the floors of the rich, or gild cast-iron images of Christ for gravestones. Capital accumulation was necessary both for the children's schooling, for the daughters' dowries, for a "peaceful old age" and to enable the family to keep up appearances. Thanks to family accumulation, lucky individuals would penetrate into a social stratum which was not merely free of poverty but which offered hopes of rising into "real" society.

One of the most important steps in this direction was a successful marriage. With us, just as in aristocratic families, marriages were rarely made for love. Our marriages, of course, did not have that same Domostroi* and Zamoskvorechye** flavour as those of the aristocratic and merchant families, where young people got married without even seeing each other according to the tyrannical decisions of their fathers. Our young people met one another more or less freely, got to know one another and went out courting, but the brutal law of the struggle for existence worked almost mechanically. Material considerations in making a marriage were often decisive. A daughter's dowry of two or three hundred rubles was, on the one hand, an insurance policy for future prosperity, and on the other, it attracted respectable suitors. Only the very poorest girls had the opportunity, when getting married, of being guided by such insignificant arguments as beautiful eyes, a pleasant voice, a kind heart, and so on. But if the girl was a little richer it was already difficult for her to discern whom he was "making eyes at."

> *At the oxen,*
> *At the cows,*
> *At my white face,*
> *Or raven brows.*

And in such cases the other words of the song were a very poor consolation:

> *Oxen and cows*
> *Soon dead do lie,*
> *White face and raven brows*
> *Will never die.*

* Domostroi—a book written in the XVI century expounding the correct manner of life for a Russian family of that period—nowadays the term is synonymous with family tyranny.—*Tr.*

** Zamoskvorechye—a part of Moscow mainly inhabited by merchants until the Revolution.—*Tr.*

Suitors always seemed to know very well that in comparison with oxen and cows a "white face and raven brows" were goods which deteriorated terribly quickly.

The master of the house was the father. It was he who directed the family's material struggle, he who managed its arduous desperate scheming, he who organized capital accumulation, he who counted the kopeks, and he who determined the fate of the children.

The father! He is the central figure of history! Master, overseer, teacher, judge and sometimes executioner, it was he who led the family from one rung of the ladder to the next. He, the property-owner, the accumulator of capital, and the despot, a stranger to all constitutions except that of God, possessed terrible power, power increased by love.

But he has another aspect. It is he who has borne on his shoulders a terrible responsibility for his children, for their poverty, sickness and death, for their burdensome life and their burdensome exit from life. For century after century this responsibility was foisted on him by life's masters, the extortioners and violators, landlords and knights, financiers, generals and factory-owners; and for century after century he supported its unbearable burden, added to by the selfsame love, and groaned, suffered and cursed a heaven which was as innocent as he—but refuse this responsibility he could not.

And therefore his power became even more sacred and even more despotic. But the masters of life were pleased to have always at their service this odious figure answering for their crimes, the figure of the father weighed down by power and duty.

A Soviet family cannot be a paternal monarchy, since the old economic motive power of the family has vanished. Our marriages are not made according to material considerations, and our children do not inherit anything of fundamental material importance within the bounds of the family.

Our family is no longer an isolated group of paternal possessions. The members of our family, from the father down to the infant born yesterday, are members of a socialist society. Each one of them upholds the honour and dignity of this lofty title.

And above all: every member of the family is definitely assured of a choice of paths and opportunities—a wonderful variety of them, provided on a nation-wide scale. Now the victorious progress of every person depends more on himself than on family forces.

But our family is not a chance combination of members of society. The family is a natural collective body and, like everything natural, healthy and normal, it can only blossom forth in socialist society, freed of those very curses from which both mankind as a whole and the individual are indeed freeing themselves.

The family becomes the natural primary cell of society, the place where the delight of human life is realized, where the triumphant forces of man are refreshed, where children—the chief joy of life—live and grow.

Our parents are not without authority either, but this authority is only the reflection of social authority. The duty of a father in our country towards his children is a particular form of his duty towards society. It is as if our society says to parents:

You have joined together in goodwill and love, rejoice in your children and expect to go on rejoicing in them. That is your own personal affair and concerns your own personal happiness. But in this happy process you have given birth to new people. A time will come when these people will cease to be only a joy to you and become independent members of society. It is not at all a matter of indifference to society what kind of people they will be. In handing over to you a certain measure of social authority the Soviet state demands from you correct upbringing of future citizens. Particularly it relies on a certain circumstance arising naturally out of your union —on your parental love.

If you wish to give birth to a citizen and do without parental love, then be so kind as to warn society that you wish to play such an underhand trick. People brought up without parental love are often deformed people. And since society does possess real parental love for every one of its members, however young he may be, your responsibility for your children can always assume real forms.

Parental authority in Soviet society is authority based not only on the delegated power of society, but on the whole strength of public morality, which demands from parents that at least they should not be morally depraved.

It is with such authority and such love that the parents form particular component parts of the collective body of the family, differing from its other component parts—the children.

Our Soviet family, like its predecessor, forms an economic unit. But the Soviet family economy is necessarily the sum total of wages earned by labour. Even if they are very large, even if they exceed the normal requirements of a family, even if they accumulate, this accumulation is accumulation of an entirely different character from that of a family in capitalist society.

When the natural and technical forces mobilized by senior conductor Novak—"billkers," acquaintances, two-storied houses and the grocery trade—reached the desired proportions, he left the walk of life of a senior conductor and purchased a small estate of fifty dessiatins* not far from our town. Novak bought this estate of an impoverished gentleman Pchelintsev, who afterwards went to serve in the very same transport organization that had but lately produced the new landowner Novak. The loss of Novak from our sphere was thus duly compensated, perhaps even with excess, since now our ranks were reinforced by a person of pure descent.

Everyone was pleased on this score. The only exception was Novak's son, a dull and whining student at the Commercial Institute.

"Pater has gone in for adventuring!" he used to say. "A good life meant nothing to him, he had to go bothering himself with a crowd of peasants."

But this was the judgement of "thoughtless youth." Old Novak was of a different opinion.

"What does that booby know about it? Dresses himself up with gold epaulets and all the rest of it and thinks he's sitting pretty! But when he's through at the Institute what will he do? Go into government service? I've had enough of serving and bowing down to every blown-up nobody. And when he gets a couple of thousand dessiatins from me, with a starch factory thrown in, he will begin to understand that it is worth a bit more than those gold epaulets of his. Of course, we'll have to suffer for a time—there's a lot of money needed. But the only thing he thinks of is riding around in a coach and pair."

The economy of our family is built up under completely new conditions of social economy and, accordingly, under completely new conditions of social morality. In the prospects lying before our family there is no hopeless poverty. On the other hand, there are no starch factories

* *Dessiatin*—former Russian measure, equal to 2.70 acres.—*Tr.*

and private estates. Thus the problem of family economic policy in the Soviet state arises in entirely new forms. Most important of all is the fact that it cannot be only the father who is responsible for the well-being of the family. The family, Soviet society as a whole are called upon to answer for this well-being.

One can imagine even in our country a family which satisfies its needs with some effort, sometimes even with great effort. We have come across some such families whose example could be very instructive to many. In the next chapter we shall deal especially with one excellent family, whose life struggle, in spite of extremely difficult circumstances, was nevertheless the struggle of a Soviet collective for a better life, with never a sign of hopeless destitution.

The instincts of accumulation, which directed the old life, have been almost completely eradicated from our life. It is difficult even to imagine one of our citizens feeling, even in the secret depths of his soul, the stirring of the old regret: "Ah, what a pity I can't start up a little shop!"

The instinct of accumulation in the old society was a permanent regulator of consumption. Accumulative greed sometimes reached such heights that it negated itself. The grabbing arms became so long that they lost the ability to serve the gullet of their master and were only fit for grabbing.

In our country no one except a madman can deny himself something on the ground that he has decided to raise a little capital and put it into circulation.

This circumstance is of great political, economic and moral importance. Organized greed, which is the basic motive of all capitalist society, has been erased once and for all from our ethical catalogue. It differs from consumers' greed, which is logically admissible even with us, by a very complicated pattern of psychological and time factors, since it embraces both lust for power, ambition, arrogance, love of servility and that intricate chain of dependencies, which necessarily accompanies vast power over a multitude of people and a multitude of goods.

This organized greed has been wiped out for the first time in the history of the world by the October Revolution, and this fact is briefly recorded in Article 6 of the Stalin Constitution:

"The land, its mineral wealth, waters, forests, mills, factories, mines, rail, water and air transport, banks, communications, large state-organized agricultural enterprises (state farms, machine and tractor stations and the like), as well as municipal enterprises and the bulk of the dwelling houses in the cities and industrial localities, are state property, that is, belong to the whole people."

This article, for all its modest simplicity, is the foundation of the new morality of mankind.

But our Constitution also has a tenth article, which says:

"The personal property right of citizens in their incomes and savings from work, in their dwelling houses and subsidiary home enterprises, in articles of domestic economy and use and articles of personal use and convenience, as well as the right of citizens to inherit personal property, is protected by law."

This article guarantees the citizens' rights to consumer goods. It is these rights which form the real goal of the great struggle of humanity and which have always been violated by the exploitation of man by man.

In our country these rights are not limited by law. They are limited by the actual state of our national wealth, and, since this wealth increases every day, the individual's opportunities of consuming also increase every day. Our state sets itself the clear and acknowledged aim of attaining universal wealth; therefore every family is confronted with a wide field of material opportunities.

On the basis of Article 10 of the Constitution the Soviet family collective is the complete master of its household property, which originates exclusively from labour. This economic arena of the family collective also becomes to a considerable degree the educational arena.

Our society is marching forward openly and consciously towards communist society.

With us, moral demands on a person must be higher than the average level of human conduct. Morality requires general emulation of the most perfect conduct. Our morality must already be the morality of communist society. Our moral code should march in the van of both our economic structure and our laws, reflected in the Constitution; it should envisage even higher forms of society. In the struggle for communism we must even now foster in ourselves the qualities of a member of communist society. Only if we do this shall we maintain that high moral sense which now distinguishes our society so strongly from any other.

Many cannot as yet conceive in practice the great law of communism: "from each according to his ability, to each according to his needs." Many are not yet capable of imagining so high a principle of distribution, one which presupposes unprecedented forms of honesty, justice, scrupulousness, reason, trust and purity of man's moral character.

The profound meaning of educational work, and particularly the work of the family collective, consists in the selection and training of human needs, in bringing them to that high moral sense which is possible only in classless society and which alone can urge on man to struggle for further perfection.

A morally justified need is, in fact, the need of a collectivist, that is, a person linked with his collective by his sense of the common aim, of the common struggle, by the living and certain awareness of his duty towards society.

In our society need is the sister of duty, responsibility and ability; it is the manifestation of the interests not of a consumer of social benefits but of an active member of socialist society, of a creator of those benefits.

A young lad came to see me. He was probably about twelve years old, but may have been younger. He sat down in an armchair facing me, rubbed the edge of the table with his hand and made as if to speak, but was too overcome. His head was round and shaven, his cheeks were plump, and his big eyes filled with such a usual variety of tears. I noticed the snow-white neck-band of his undervest.

This young lad was an actor. I had seen many like him. His face wore an expression borrowed, probably, from the cinema; with the tender muscles of his forehead knitted into an irritable frown he seemed to be mimicking an old man.

"Well? Say what you want. What's your name?" asked, looking at him keenly.

The lad heaved a wonderful sigh, drew his hand along the table once more, turned his head deliberately aside, and in a deliberately sepulchral voice said:

"Kolya. But what is there to say? I've nothing to live on. Nothing to eat."

"No father?"

Kolya turned the tap on a little harder and shook his head silently.

"And mother?"

He placed his arms between his knees, bent forward a little, raised his eyes to the window and acted magnificently.

"Mother! What use is she? What can you expect if she's only working ... in the cloak-room ... at a club!"

The lad upset himself so much that he no longer bothered to change his pose, and kept on looking out of the window. The tears were still in his eyes.

"I see," I said. "Well, what do you want me to do?"

He glanced at me and shrugged his shoulders.

"Something will have to be done. Send me to the colony."

"To the colony? No, you are not suitable for the colony. It would be hard for you there."

He rested his head sadly on his hand and said pensively:

"How shall I live? What shall I eat?"

"But you are living with your mother, aren't you?"

"Can anyone live on five rubles? And you must have something to wear."

I decided that it was time to launch a counter-attack.

"Now you tell me something else—why have you given up school?"

I did not expect Kolya to withstand my sudden attack, and thought he would break down and burst into tears. Nothing of the kind. Kolya turned his face towards me and exhibited masterly surprise.

"How can I go to school if there's nothing to eat?"

"Didn't you have any breakfast today?"

Kolya rose from the armchair and bared his sword. At last he had realized that the heart-broken pose and the tearful eye would not produce the right impression on me. Against such sceptics as me one must act decisively. Kolya straightened up and said:

"What are you questioning me for? If you don't want to help, I'll go somewhere else. Breakfast! You needn't worry yourself about my breakfast."

"Ah, so that's the kind you are!" I said. "You are a fighter!"

"Of course," whispered Kolya, but lowered his eyes.

"You are an impudent fellow," I said slowly. "You are downright impudent!"

Kolya brightened up. At last good boyish tones came back into his voice. And all the tears vanished.

"You don't believe me? You don't believe me? Is that it? Well, say so then!"

"Of course I shall say so. I don't believe you and it's all lies. Nothing to eat, nothing to wear! Are you sure you are not dead yet, you poor fellow! From starvation!"

"Well, you needn't believe me if you don't want to," said Kolya airily, making for the door.

"No, wait," I stopped him. "You wasted a lot of time sitting here telling lies! Now we'll go."

"Go where?" said Kolya in a fright.

"Home, to see your mother."

"Hark at him! I'm not going anywhere! Why should I?"

"What do you mean, why? You are going home."

"There's no need for me to go home. I don't care what you want."

I got angry with the boy.

"That's enough talk! Tell me your address! You won't? All right, sit down and wait here!"

Kolya did not tell me his address, but sat down in the armchair and grew quiet. Five minutes later he got into a car and meekly told me where he lived.

Looking crushed and miserable, he led me through the spacious court-yard of a new workers' club, but now his grief was that of a child, and so his nose, his cheeks, the sleeve of his black jacket and other devices for soothing the nerves took an active part in it.

In a small clean room, with curtains and flowers and a bright Ukrainian carpet on the floor by the bed, Kolya straight away sat down on a chair, put his head on the bed and wept, mumbling something inaudible, and complaining against someone, but holding his cap firmly in his hand all the time. His mother, a young woman, with the same big eyes and plump cheeks as her son, took his cap out of his hand and hung it up on a nail, then smiled at me.

"What's he been up to there? Did you bring him back?"

Kolya stopped his sobs for a moment in order to forestall any tricks I might try to spring on him.

"No one brought me! I brought him myself! He kept on and on about coming! Well, go on, talk about me...."

Again he buried his face in the soft bed, but now cried somehow only on one side and with the other listened to what his mother and I were saying.

His mother remained quite calm.

"I don't know what to do with him. He used not to be like this, but then he went to live with my brother—my brother is director of a state farm in the Chernigov Region—and this is the result. And don't think what he says is true: he doesn't know himself what he wants. He has learnt to keep asking for things. Everywhere he goes. He's given up school, and he was in the fourth class, you know. If only he would study, but he keeps on going round to the heads, worrying them. And just ask him what he hasn't got. He has clothes to wear and shoes on his feet and a good bed. I wouldn't say we go in for much fancy cooking, but he has never gone hungry. We can get food from the club dining-room, and I cook at home on the primus as well. But of course it was better at the director's: it's country there, after all, and a state farm too—they've got plenty of live-stock."

Kolya stopped crying, but kept his head on the bed and poked about with his foot under the chair, obviously thinking to himself and protesting inwardly against the modest sentiments of his mother.

His mother amazed me with her wonderful optimism. It was clear from her story that she had a difficult life with her son, but everything was all right and she was content with everything.

"It was worse before: ninety rubles, think of that! But now I'm getting a hundred and twenty, with my mornings free. I earn a little extra on one job and another. And I'm studying too. In three months' time I will be transferred to the library and be getting a hundred and eighty."

She smiled with calm certainty in her eyes. Her manner showed no sign of strain, not a hint of feverish excitability or lack of confidence in herself. She was an optimist to the core. Compared with her bright character her son's senseless and insincere rebellion seemed very wrong to me. But his mother did not find anything out of the ordinary about it.

"Let him rage for a bit. It will do him good! That's what I told him: if you don't like it with me, find something better. If you want to give up school, give it up, please yourself. But mind what I say, I won't have any grumbling here, in this room. Find someone else who wants to listen to a little fool like you. They spoilt him at his uncle's. Free cinema every day there! But where can I find money for the cinema! Let him sit down and read a book! It doesn't matter, he'll get over it! Now he wants to go to the colony. He's got some friends there, so of course!..."

Kolya was by now sitting quietly on the chair, watching the smiling, lively gestures of his mother with warm, attentive eyes. She noticed his attention and nodded, reproaching him with affected tenderness.

"Pooh, sits there like a young lord! It's not good enough for him with his mother! No, I won't talk to you, find something better, go somewhere else and start cadging there..."

Kolya threw his head back, then looked away slyly.
"But why talk like that, ma? I'm not cadging at all.
Under Soviet rule I have the right to demand."

"Demand what?" asked his mother, smiling.

"Anything I want," he replied even more slyly.

Let us not judge who is to blame in this conflict. Judgement is a difficult business when one does not know all the facts. I liked both the son and the mother. I am a great admirer of optimism and very fond of young lads who trust Soviet rule to such an extent that they are carried away and will not even trust their own mothers. Such boys do a lot of silly things and cause us old people much disappointment, but they are always delightful! They smile pleasantly at their mothers, then show us bureaucrats a whole handful of demands, and snap out:

"Send me to the colony."

"Send me to the flying school, I want to be a pilot."

"I will work and study, honest I will!"

And yet.... And yet things had not turned out very well with Kolya and his mother. Somehow the son's needs had taken a particular line which had nothing in common either with his mother's struggle or with her successes and hopes. Who was to blame for this? Not his director uncle, of course. His stay with his uncle had only applied a spark to Kolya's amorphous, ill-educated pretensions.

Both the flying school and the colony, and even the cinema and good food are excellent things. It is natural for every lad to strive for them.

But it is quite understandable that we have no right to regard every group of freely formed desires as a need! This would mean giving full play to every individual passion, and such full play could only result in individual strife with all the consequences sadly attendant upon it. Chief among these consequences is the maiming of the personality and the ruination of its hopes. That is the old story of the world, for the caprices of need are the caprices of exploiters.

Kolya's conduct may seem at first glance to be the conduct of a Soviet boy so entranced by the movement of history that he is already bored by the progress of the family chariot. The general atmosphere of this case is so pleasant that one cannot help wanting to aid Kolya and satisfy his hazy desires. Many people do so. I have seen a lot of such favoured boys. They rarely turn out very well. Those like Kolya are young despots, more than anything else, even if only to a very small degree. They first overwhelm mother and father, then pin down the representatives of state institutions with their demands, and here they pursue their line insistently, backing it up with anything they can lay hands on: complaints, tears, acting and impudence.

Concealed behind Kolya's Soviet appearance and behind his childish pretending lies a moral vacuum, the absence of any kind of collective experience, which every child should by the age of twelve possess. Such vacuums always occur if from the children's early years the family has had no unity of life, no everyday habits, no routine of effort, no exercise in collective give-and-take. In such cases a child's needs expand in the isolated play of his imagination, bearing no connection whatsoever with the needs of other people. A morally valuable need can only grow up in the course of collective experience. Of course, at the age of twelve it will never appear in the shape of a strong desire, since its roots lie not in the sparkling visions of pure fantasy, but in the complex soil of as yet ill-defined collective experience, in the intermingling of the characters of many people more or less closely connected with the child, in awareness of human help and human need, in feelings of dependence, obligation, responsibility and much else.

That is why a rightly organized collective is so important in early childhood. Kolya did not live in such a collective—he only had the association of his mother. And however good a person his mother may have been, simple association with her alone could not give any positive results. Rather on the contrary: there is nothing more dangerous than the passive association of a good person, since this is the most favourable environment for the development of egoism. This is one of those cases where many good people throw up their hands and exclaim: "Who on earth does he take after?"

Alyosha is fourteen. He blushes and looks sulky.

"What, you've got first-class tickets? I won't go first-class!"

His mother looks at him with severe surprise.

"Why not?"

"Why did you go *de luxe* last year? And now first-class?"

"Last year we had more money...."

"What's money got to do with it?" says Alyosha contemptuously. "Money? Huh, I know what the reason is. It's just because I am going. Any old thing is good enough for me!"

"Think what you please," his mother replies coldly. "If you don't like it you need not go at all."

"There you are, there you are!" crows Alyosha. "I need not go at all! You'll all be glad! Of course! You'll even be able to sell the ticket. It's all money, isn't it!"

His mother shrugs her shoulders and walks away. She must have time to think how to deal with such dreadful questions.

But Nadya, Alyosha's elder sister, is not so easy-going and she never puts things off. Nadya remembers the alarms of the Civil War, the goods-vans during the evacuation, the chance accommodation in frontline towns; she remembers the clenched teeth and the burning passion of struggle, the harsh uncertainty of the morrow and the inspired faith in victory.

Nadya looks mockingly at her brother, and Alyosha can see by the way she bites her lip that she also condemns him. He knows that any minute now his sister will descend on him with the full weight of her unbearable girlish scorn. Alyosha gets up from his chair and even starts humming a tune—just to show how calm he is. But all in vain; the tune is interrupted by a short and deafening "burst."

"No, you just explain to me, you sissy, when you managed to get used to *de luxe*?"

Alyosha looks round and finds a boyish evasive answer.

"Did I say I was used to it? I'm simply interested. Anybody can be interested, can't he...."

"And you aren't interested in a third-class carriage by any chance?"

"Yes, I am, only ... that'll come later ... next time. What business is it of yours anyway?"

"It is my business!" says his sister seriously. "In the first place you haven't any right to be going to the seaside. No right at all! You are quite healthy and you have done nothing to deserve a holiday, absolutely nothing, you understand! Why should we pamper people like you? Why? Just tell me that."

"So that's what you are driving at, is it?" Alyosha begins sceptically. "According to you then I have no right to eat my dinner, didn't deserve that either...."

But he realizes the need for a strategic retreat. What the evening will bring no one can tell. Nadya is capable of any dirty trick, and the prospect of the seaside may recede into those distant epochs known as the "grown-up" epochs. What might it all end in? He would be lucky if he got as far as the local pioneer camp! In fifteen minutes Alyosha raises his hands jokingly.

"I give in! I'll go in the goods-van if you like!"

Alyosha's need for a *de luxe* carriage was not born in the play of his imagination—it grew out of experience, but none the less everyone realizes that this need is to some extent immoral. His mother realizes this too, but she is incapable of changing the situation.

Not all experience in our country is moral experience. Our family is not a closed-in collective body, like the bourgeois family. It is an organic part of Soviet society, and every attempt it makes to build up its own experience independently of the moral demands of society is bound to result in a disproportion, discordant as an alarm-bell.

The disproportion in Alyosha's family arises from the fact that the needs of the father and mother mechanically become the needs of their children. The father's needs result from his great, responsible and intensive labour in Soviet society, from the importance of that labour. Alyosha's needs are not justified by any collective labour experience, but are the result of his father's generosity; these needs of his are a parental donation. In principle such a family is the oldest kind of paternal monarchy, something like an enlightened absolutism.

In our country such families are exceptions. With them the verbal Soviet ideology is made to combine with experience of the old type. The children in such a family partake regularly of unjustified satisfaction. The tragic future of such children is obvious. Ahead of them lies a difficult dilemma: either they must start going through the stage of natural growth of their needs from the beginning when they are already adults, or else they must present society with such great and such highly qualified labour as to deserve society's sanction for great and complex needs. The latter course is possible only in exceptional cases.

I have discussed this subject with various comrades. Some of them get into a panic.

"What can you do about it? If I go on holiday with my family, do you think I ought to travel in one carriage and the family in another?"

Such panic affirms only one thing: unwillingness to go to the root of the problem and do the active thinking required to create a new attitude. A *de luxe* carriage is not dearer than the fate of one's children, but this is not just a matter of carriages. No tricks will right the situation if there is no proper tone in the family, no steady sound environment.

A journey with father in any class of carriage on certain occasions is not in the least harmful, if it is obvious that this is only a pleasant occasion not arising from the children's right to excessive comfort, but from their desire to be together with their father. There are many other Soviet families where the needs of the children are not connected with the services of the father; in such a family Alyosha would be guided by a different logic.

All this certainly does not mean that here some kind of special drill must be adopted for the children. The problem is solved according to the general style of the whole family. And if the father himself, as a citizen, has the right to additional comfort, then, as a member of the family, he should also restrict himself. Some standards of modesty are obligatory even for him, especially since modesty is always to be found in the biographies of our great men:

"We mount the staircase. In the windows hang white linen curtains. These are the three windows of Stalin's flat. In the tiny hallway the first thing that leaps to the eye is a long soldier's great-coat, above it hangs a soldier's cap. Three rooms and a dining-room. Furnished simply, as in a decent but modest hotel. The dining-room is oval in shape; here dinner is served—from the Kremlin kitchens or prepared at home by the cook. In a capitalist country neither the flat nor the menu would satisfy an average civil servant. There is a little boy playing here, too. The elder son Yasha sleeps in the dining-room—they make a bed for him on the divan; the younger boy sleeps in a tiny room rather like an alcove."

HENRI BARBUSSE

Moral depth and unity of family collective experience is a completely necessary condition of Soviet upbringing. This applies equally both to families with enough and to families with less than enough.

In our country he alone is a man of worth whose needs and desires are the needs and desires of a collectivist. Our family offers rich soil for the cultivation of such collectivism.

Chapter Three

J MET Stepan Denisovich Vetkin at the beginning of the
summer of 1926. Even now I remember his arrival
with some embarrassment. It was like the invasion of
a hostile army, made suddenly, without a declaration
of war.

Yet there seemed to be nothing warlike about the
event. Stepan Denisovich came peacefully and shyly into
my little study, bowed very politely, holding his cap in
front of him in both hands, and said:

"If you are very busy forgive me for bothering you—
I have the minutest request to make."

Even when using the word "minutest" Stepan Denisovich did not smile; his expression was restrainedly serious, and rather more anxious than gloomy.

He sat down in a chair facing me, and I was able to
have a better look at his face. He had a good moustache
covering his mouth, and under this moustache he would
somehow purse his lips very pleasantly as if he were
sucking something, although there was in fact nothing in
his mouth—this gesture also expressed anxiety. Stepan
Denisovich's red beard was slightly twisted to the right,
probably because he often tugged at it with his right hand.

Stepan Denisovich said:

"Well, you see, as a matter of fact I am a teacher,
not far from here, at Motovilovka...."

"That's good to hear, then we are colleagues...."

But Stepan Denisovich did not share my enthusiasm. He clutched a large section of his red beard and explained rather dryly, looking slightly aside:

"I dare say it is good. Of course, I like the job, but to be quite frank—it doesn't work out. That is, it's all right as far as the teaching goes, but organizationally it doesn't work out."

"What's wrong?"

"Not really organizationally, that is, one should say, from the point of view of everyday life. I would like you to give me a job . . . as a blacksmith."

I did not show my surprise. He darted a glance at me and continued even more dryly, with a particularly attractive seriousness that inspired great confidence in his words:

"I'm a good smith. A real smith. My father was a smith too. At a craft school. That's how I managed to become a teacher. Well, you have a little factory here and, after all, you need a good smith. And I'm a teacher as well."

"All right," I agreed. "Do you need a flat?"

"Well, how shall I put it? A room, of course, or two rooms. My family is a fair size . . . a very fair size."

Stepan Denisovich pursed his lips and shifted about on his chair.

"Being a teacher's a good job, but it won't support a family like mine. And apart from that we live in a village. Where will the kids go?"

"How many children have you?"

He looked at me and smiled for the first time. In that smile I at last saw the real Stepan Denisovich. His anxious face had nothing in common with his smile; when he smiled his teeth showed cheerily, white and gleaming. With the addition of his smile Stepan Denisovich seemed kinder and more sincere.

"That is the hardest question for me. I'm really ashamed to answer it, but very often I have to, you know."

His smile flashed out once more and melted away behind his moustache; his lips pursed again anxiously and again he turned away from me.

"Thirteen. Thirteen children!"

"Thirteen?!" I burst out in utter astonishment. "You don't say so?!"

Stepan Denisovich made no reply, only fidgeted even more anxiously on his chair. And I felt terribly sorry for this pleasant man, and an overwhelming desire to help him came over me; but at the same time I also felt animosity—the kind of animosity that always arises if someone acts in a way which seems to you obviously imprudent. All these feelings of mine resolved themselves into an exclamation that surprised me myself:

"Well I'm damned! But how... how did you manage it?"

He listened to my ill-mannered outburst with his former expression of weariness and anxiety, smiling only with the tips of his moustache.

"A family can possess from one to eighteen children. I have read that there are sometimes eighteen. Well... I happened to get thirteen."

"What do you mean 'happened to get'?"

"How else then? If some people have eighteen it means there must be thirteen somewhere. And that's what I happened to get."

I soon reached an agreement with Stepan Denisovich. We really did need a good blacksmith. Stepan Denisovich reckoned that as a smith he would earn more than as a teacher, and our organization was able to meet him half way in his reckoning.

The question of a flat was more difficult. With great effort I could squeeze out one room for him and that meant a whole series of transferences and removals. True, our workers became so interested in such an outstanding family that no one even thought of protesting. Our storeman Pilipenko had something to say on this score.

"But I consider that's pigging it. No one minds making concessions, of course, but all the same a chap ought to have a little savvy and common sense! Do what you like but keep a look-out, that's what I say. Suppose you've got three, for instance. Three, four, then you take a look and see number five's arrived! Well, watch out, says I, five means you've got to keep count—the next one'll make six. You should keep your wits about you and calculate!"

But Comrade Chub, the old instrument-maker, who had six children, explained that simple arithmetic would not solve the problem.

"So that's what you say, is it: count! Do you think I didn't count? Aha! But what can you do about it: it's poverty. Poverty, that's what does you down! A rich man's got two beds, he goes to sleep by himself and that's all there is to it. But a poor man makes do with one bed. Count as much as you like, but it'll take its toll and you won't even notice it...."

"Something you didn't count on like," chuckled the storeman.

"Miscounts take place sometimes, of course!" laughed Chub as well, who was always ready for a joke.

The fat and round accountant Pyzhov listened to their conversation patronizingly and then produced his contribution to the problem.

"In such cases a miscount is quite possible. The main factor here is the additional coefficient. If you have one child and the second is, so to speak, in the offing, then you are expecting an addition of one hundred per cent. A prudent man will think a moment: hundred per cent, that's a big coefficient. But if you have five already, well, the sixth is only twenty per cent—hardly a coefficient at all. A chap just shrugs his shoulders: let it come, I don't mind taking a risk on twenty per cent."

Everyone laughed. Chub was particularly carried away by the fantastic play of the coefficients and demanded immediate application of this theory to his own case.

"Well I'm blowed! That means that if I've number seven coming up—how'll it work out, this...."

"Number seven?" Pyzhov merely glanced skywards and answered precisely:

"In that case the coefficient will be sixteen point six per cent."

"Next to nothing!" gasped Chub delightedly. "Nothing to worry about at all!"

"That's how the chap worked up to thirteen," gurgled the storeman.

"Quite so," confirmed accountant Pyzhov. "The thirteenth has a coefficient of eight point three per cent."

"Well, that's not even worth paying attention to." Chub was simply overcome by the latest discoveries in this field.

It was in this cheerful spirit that everyone greeted Stepan Denisovich when he came back to look at the flat. Stepan Denisovich took no offence, he understood that the laws of mathematics are irresistible.

The whole company of us inspected the flat. The room was of average size, about fifteen square metres. It was situated in one of the cottages which our factory had inherited from the old regime. Stepan Denisovich kept munching and sucking anxiously while he looked over the room.

"But I have two rooms back there..." he recalled sadly, as if talking to himself. "Well, can't be helped, we'll manage somehow...."

What could I do? Quite at a loss, I asked Stepan Denisovich a stupid question:

"Have you got much furniture?"

Vetkin looked at me with barely perceptible reproach in his eyes.

"Furniture? Do you think I bother about furniture? There's nowhere to put it."

He suddenly gave a wonderful smile as if to help me out of my embarrassment.

"As a matter of fact there's not much room for inanimate objects."

Chub scratched his unshaven chin slyly and screwed up one eye.

"Under such objective conditions it's not furniture our comrade here needs, but bunks, like I have in the instrument shed. If the chief's got no objection we can put in some bunks."

He measured the height of the room with his eye.

"Three tiers. With room for an extra fourth on the floor."

"You won't get thirteen in here," said storekeeper Pilipenko sadly. "What cubic space of air will it leave for breathing? None at all. And there are two of you into the bargain."

Vetkin glanced now at one consultant, now at the other, but did not look distressed. Probably he had long ago taken account of all these circumstances and fitted them into his general plan of operations. He repeated his former decision:

"Well, I'll bring the family over on the tenth. Could you let us have some kind of a horse? There are a few odds and ends to carry, and the little ones won't manage all the way from the station on foot."

"A horse? Certainly! Two if you like!"

"Thanks. Two, of course, will be better, because, after all... it's a family moving."

On Sunday, the 10th of May, the Vetkin family made its appearance on the territory of our factory. The factory was situated not far from the town, with which it was joined by a special road made of cobble-stones. Early in the morning two factory nags dragged into the town two vehicles that might have been carriages and might equally well have been waggons or carts. By midday the road was crowded as never before. There seemed to be an exodus of family couples, pretending they were out for a Sunday walk to take a breath of the fresh air and enjoy the local landscape.

At two o'clock in the afternoon a procession appeared —there is no other word fit to describe it. A three-year-old boy sitting on the first cart held a small toy flag which added to the triumphal nature of the procession.

The two carts were leading. They were mainly full of the "odds and ends," but on the first sat the standard-bearer, and on the second two smaller children. The "odds and ends" consisted of objects small in dimensions, except for a cupboard planted right in the middle of the first cart, which gave it a certain air of fixed solemnity. It was a kitchen cupboard—one of mankind's happiest inventions—a cupboard and a table at the same time. Such articles always smell wonderful of warmth, freshly baked bread and children's happiness. Besides the cupboard I noticed a big samovar, two bundles of books and a bale of pillows. All the rest were ordinary domestic trifles: prongs, brooms, a bucket, iron pots and so on.

Beside the second cart walked a girl of about seventeen in an old faded cotton frock, barefoot and bare-headed. You could see she always went about like that, for although the summer had only just begun her hair had faded considerably and her face was covered with a deep ruddy tan that was already peeling off her cheeks. But all the same her face was very pleasant: serious, with a well-shaped mouth. Her light-blue eyes sparkled clear and calm beneath her straight clever brows.

Behind the carts came two boys of about equal age and height, carrying a boiler covered with a striped piece of cloth. These two must have been about thirteen. Behind them walked the main body of boys and girls between five and twelve years old. The two youngest—a pair of plump full-cheeked little girls—toddled along in front holding hands, taking tiny steps over the clean warm cobble-stones with their bare feet, and looking very worried: although the carts were moving slowly along the road these young walkers found it difficult to keep up such a pace.

The big boys, who made up the rest of the party, were busy. Each one was carrying something in his arms or on his shoulders, now a mirror, now a bundle of frames, and the eldest was carrying a gramophone horn.

The whole company made an unexpectedly favourable impression on me: everybody's hair had been cut with the clippers, their sunburnt faces seemed clean, even their bare feet were only specked with today's dust. No one had a belt, but the collars of their cotton shirts were neatly buttoned; there were no holes visible, only the lad carrying the horn had a bright-coloured patch on his knee. What pleased me particularly was that not one member of the procession wore a nasty or unpleasant expression: there were no sores, no scrofula, no signs of mental backwardness. They looked at us calmly and without embarrassment, but did not stare indifferently, sometimes calling across to each other, without lowering their voices, yet without making too free.

I overheard a few words of such a conversation.

"... There's a dry spot here.... That's a willow."

"You can make baskets out of them."

"Daddy's sure to do that!"

Daddy himself, the creator and leader of the entire army, followed behind, carrying the gramophone box carefully in his arms. Beside him, a bright yellow kerchief flung back from her black hair, walked a beautiful rosy-cheeked woman, smiling at us with her big liquid eyes as she stepped along. When he passed us Stepan Deniso-vich blossomed out in his wonderful smile and, raising his cap, said:

"Here we are! Do what you like about it, but we've arrived! Your fellows are gaping a bit, aren't they! This is my wife, Anna Semyonovna!"

Anna Semyonovna bowed her head ceremoniously and stretched out her hand, then shot a glance round with her black eyes.

"He needs something to worry about: gaping!" she said in a steady contralto. "They'll get used to it. I don't mind as long as they are good people, not spiteful."

At that moment there was a movement among the attendant crowd. The wife of Chub, the instrument-maker, a stout matronly woman, who had until then looked on at the procession rather disapprovingly, raised her hands and exclaimed: "Oh what a shame! Oh dear, oh dear! Such little mites and all the way from the station on foot! How did they manage it!"

She rushed over to one of the little girls and swept her up in her arms. The little girl's small, still troubled face appeared over her shoulder, and her light-blue eyes continued to stare out anxiously at the world. In a moment the other little mite had been hoisted on someone's shoulders. Our people mingled with the procession. Accountant Pyzhov came up to the Vetkins and said, stretching out his hand: "Welcome home! Don't lose heart, that's the main thing! You are doing right, you know: personnel!"

Taking advantage of the summer season, Stepan De-nisovich decided to accommodate the main body of his army in the open air. For this purpose he built something like a veranda beside his cottage. There was a lot of waste material lying about in various corners of our yard, and with my permission Stepan Denisovich made use of it, appointing the reserve forces of his army to deliver the goods, while the main forces busied themselves with the work of construction.

Even before the Vetkin family arrived I had become interested in an important educational problem: does this family possess any kind of organizational structure, or is it, so to speak, an amorphous mass? I put this question straight to Stepan Denisovich when he called to see me about something.

Vetkin was not surprised at my question and smiled approvingly.

"That's right, it is a very important question, this question of structure, as you call it. Of course there is a structure, although it's quite a problem. It's very easy to start on the wrong lines...."

"For example?"

"Well, I'll explain. You can do it according to age, then it'll be all right for the jobs, but wrong from the educational point of view, because the little ones may run wild. What it boils down to is that you have to approach the problem from different angles. For the household jobs I have a main team of four: Vanya, Vitya, Semyon and another, Little Vanya. Big Vanya is fifteen and Little Vanya is ten, but he's smart, too, and can do a lot of jobs."

"How did you come to have two Vanyas?"

"Happened like that in the muddle. Big Vanya is right, I like that name, although Igor and Oleg are all the rage nowadays. Well, and the other one was born in 'sixteen—during the war and everything. As a teacher I was exempt, but you could never be sure of them, they pulled me up before the military and kept me there for a fortnight. And the wife had just had a baby. What with the bother and shortages and excitement, and the god-fathers not knowing their job either, you know what it's like in the country. The vicar must have been in a hurry, just took a look at the calendar and saw what saint's day it was. Ivan the Martyr. So into the water with Ivan and that was that. There's nothing much wrong with it as a matter of fact. Later on, perhaps, they'll get mixed up, but now it doesn't matter: one is Vanya and the other Little Vanya, they've got used to it already. Vanya's fair but Little Vanya's dark, like his mother."

"So that's your domestic team, is it?"

"Yes, that's the domestic team. They go to school together, and at home if there's something to be done they always set about it together. They'll make good workers. And they are all boys, too. Well, there's the structure for you. Then there is another team. Vasya, eight years old, will be going to school in autumn. He's nearly fit to join the older boys' team, but he's free for the time being. And besides him there's Lyuba, who's seven, and Kolya—six. Not much use about the house yet, but they are learning how to fetch and carry, or perhaps one of them will run to the co-operative stores sometimes. They can read and their counting up to twenty is satisfactory."

"It's they who are bringing the materials now, isn't it?"

"That's them. Vasya, Lyuba and Kolya, that's their job. Well, and below them come the small fry: Marusya's only five and the others, Vera and Grisha, are younger still. And Katya and Petya are the smallest of all—twins, only came the year before last."

"Isn't the eldest a girl?"

"Yes, Oksana! Oksana is way ahead of them all. In the first place she's come of age, secondly she can do everything. I dare say she's not far behind her mother in household matters. She needs thinking about specially.

She will make a good citizen, and she wants to go to the Rabfak.* I'll be considering that in the autumn."

Big Vanya's first team was working on the building of the veranda. Stepan Denisovich himself gave them very little help because he had already started work in our forge, and only after four o'clock would he poke his dishevelled head over the finished framework of the veranda, concerning himself mainly with the question of constructing the roof. But even in the evenings it was Big Vanya who did the managing.

"Don't climb up there," I heard him tell his father once. "We'll do it ourselves in the morning. It would be better if you got hold of some nails. We are short of nails."

The team only had at its disposal the nails which Little Vanya pulled out of the old boards. All day long he would sit at this job, for which he used pincers and a claw-hammer. Little Vanya's production created a "bottleneck" in the construction work, and Big Vanya issued an order to the reserve team bringing in materials: "Don't throw the stuff down just anyhow. If there's a nail in it, take it to Little Vanya, and if there isn't, give it to me."

The chief of the reserve, eight-year-old Vasya, a serious, stocky lad with a big forehead, did not, however, allow the work of his team to suffer; he mobilized a representative of the "small fry," five-year-old Marusya—a wonderfully cheerful rosy-cheeked little body. Marusya would inspect every board curiously, finding fault with each suspicious-looking mark; then, puffing up her al-

* *Rabfak*—abbreviation for Workers' Faculty. During the first years of Soviet power, in order to lay the foundation for a new intelligentsia of the working masses as rapidly as possible, the Soviet government, while simultaneously expanding the network of ordinary schools, created so-called Workers' Faculties, which were affiliated to institutions of higher education and prepared workers and peasants especially for these institutions.—*Tr.*

ready plump cheeks, she would put a board now on one side, now on the other. As she worked she kept chanting tenderly: "With a nail.... Without a nail.... With a nail.... Three nails.... And this one... without a nail.... And this one... with a nail...."

Only occasionally would she stare in alarm at some suspicious-looking piece of wire stuck to the board and march worriedly over to Vanya or Vitya.

"Is this a nail too?" she would ask dramatically. "Or is it something else?... Wire? What is wire? Don't you want this one with a nail?"

The young Vetkins surprised people round about by the amazing serenity of their characters. Hardly a sound of crying was to be heard in this overflowing family. Even the youngest Vetkins, the twins Katya and Petya, never struck up such deafening choruses as could be heard coming sometimes from the Chub family, for instance. Besides being very quick and enterprising, Chub's children were a tough, cheerful crowd. They played a lot, organized all the youngsters in our yard, got up to many pranks and jokes, and their voices were audible here, there and everywhere. Very often these voices struck a distinctly minor key and sometimes rose to a steady, pernicious howl, full of reproach and injury, swelling suddenly to the crescendo of a murder shriek. The parent Chubs fought actively against such excesses, shouted themselves, scolded and even cursed their offspring, and in extreme cases let fly with a box-on-the-ear, or a good slap, or other direct forms of coercion. Such scenes often lent the Chub family rather the character of a classical tragedy such as *Richard III*, in which, as everyone knows, children are murdered wholesale. In reality, of course, there was nothing tragic about it at all.

The young Chubs, after shouting themselves hoarse and getting their deserts according to disciplinary custom, would wipe away their tears and soon forget all their injuries and troubles, including their own importunities, which had served as the immediate source of the conflict. Then they would set off with cheerful faces to continue their happy childish lives at the other end of the yard. The old Chubs did not harbour their grief either. On the contrary, the consciousness of having fulfilled their parental duty increased the energy they needed to deal with the other domestic tasks confronting them.

Nothing of the kind happened with the Vetkins. Even Katya and Petya in their most pessimistic moods restricted themselves to a brief whimper, mainly symbolic in character. The elder offspring of the Vetkins never even whimpered. This family's conflicts were not brought out on the social arena, and it may have been that there were no conflicts.

Our people at the factory were quick to notice this peculiarity of the Vetkins; everyone tried to explain it in some way. In doing so, no one mentioned the educational talents of the parents.

"It's in their characters," said Chub. "Nature made them so. And there's nothing good about it if you take the broad view. People ought to be able to do anything. What's the use of a man who doesn't know chalk from cheese! If there's anything wrong a man ought to shout— he ought to have a heart in him. It's quite normal for a child to cry: he's a live person, not a dummy. When I was a boy I was the biggest trouble-maker of the lot and I used to catch it hot, I can tell you. But now I don't make trouble, although if someone comes asking for it, all right then, I know how to shout too. It's natural."

Accountant Pyzhov held a different opinion.

"That isn't the point, Comrade Chub, it's not a matter of character but of the economic basis. When you have one or two and they see something—it's 'give'! All right, here you are! Give me this! Here you are! Give me that! Well, of course, you get fed up, you can't carry on like that all the time! Then the shouting begins, because you gave once and now you refuse. But Vetkin—he's got thirteen. Do what you like, there is always going to be a shortage or deficit somewhere. Here no one so much as thinks of shouting 'give'! What do you mean 'give'? Where am I going to get it? I'm surprised myself how Stepan Denisovich manages without a book-keeper. In a family like his you've got to think over everything that drops into the common fund, how many grammes to each person. And it's not just a matter of dividing it up—you've got to use the differential method, one thing for the older, another for the younger. That's why their characters are so peaceful: each one sits waiting for his portion, shouting won't help anyway."

"Now you put it in an intellectual form, Comrade Pyzhov, but it's not like that," retorted Chub. "I've also got six. No matter what method you try, all the same you can't give everything he wants. But he'll shout, you know, and there's no stopping him: give, give, give! And the result is that whoever shouts the most, gets the most. And if he doesn't get it by shouting, he'll use force. My Volodya's the one for that—impetuous-like!"

Vetkin listened to these philosophical essays with a restrained smile of superiority and replied thus: "If a person's impetuous the question is whether he should be or not. One impetuous man will go for another impetuous man and the knives'll be out in next to no time! What is needed is a good atmosphere, then anything can be done. But once you start talking about so-and-so being impetuous you don't get anywhere! And as for the children crying and yelling, that's just nerves. Do you think you're the only one with nerves? They have them too. Outwardly a boy may look all right, cheerful and everything, but in fact, you'll find, his nerves are as bad as your ladyship's.

That's why he yells. If you don't ruin his nerves from the day he's born, why should he yell?"

"My kids nervy?" exclaimed Chub in astonishment. "Oho, I like that!"

"What are you oho-ing about?" rejoined Vetkin and stroked his moustache, covering a smile with his hand. "Your own nerves are only fit for scrap, anyway."

Vetkin had difficulty in providing enough food for his family. True, we assigned a fair-sized plot of land on the allotment for his needs, and Anna Semyonovna and Oksana soon set to work on it. We also helped Vetkin in one or two other matters: a horse and plough, seeds and one very important item—potatoes. But for the time being the allotment only meant work and expense.

Stepan Denisovich did not complain, but neither did he hide his difficulties.

"I'm not losing heart. For the present the main thing is bread. If there's enough bread to go round for a start, then it's all right. But all the same, the absolute minimum is half a pood of bread, 500 grammes each, rather a small portion as a matter of fact. Half a pood every day!"

We all realized that every member of the Vetkin family must possess the wisdom of a snake. Vetkin himself put this wisdom into practice at work. He really was a good smith and his teacher's training helped him a lot too. And because of this his wages were considerably higher than the average wages of our workers.

But I was very surprised when, in answer to my proposal that he should do overtime in the evenings, Vetkin replied: "If it's needed for the factory I won't refuse—that's a different thing. But if you are just suggesting it to help me out, then it doesn't matter, because you can get into a real mess on those lines...."

He smiled awkwardly and then could not hide his smile, although he tried for all he was worth to tuck it away behind the thick curtain of his moustache. This meant he felt rather embarrassed.

"A man ought to work seven hours a day, but if he does more he wears out too quickly. Have children and die—that's not my idea of life. That's how, which insect is it . . . a butterfly lives for a day. Lays her eggs and good-bye: nothing else to do. Perhaps it's all right for a butterfly because she really hasn't anything else to do, but a man has lots to do. I want to see how Soviet rule gets on and how we are overtaking those . . . . Fords and suchlike. What with the Japanese, and the Dnieper construction work, there's such a lot to keep your eyes open for. Seven hours' work at the forge is enough for me."

"But you have only just said," I objected, "that if it's necessary for the factory. . . ."

"That's a different matter. If the factory needs it—that's that. But don't my children need me? They need a father to be a father to them and not what I've seen sometimes, not a father but a horse: dull eyes, hump-back, nerves no good for anything and about as much soul as a dead duck! What's the use of such a father, I'd like to know? Just for earning the daily bread. Why, better to bury him straight away and let the children be fed by the state—the state won't grudge them. I've seen one or two of those fathers: strains his guts out, doesn't understand anything—next day he's on the floor, dead, and the children are orphans; and if they aren't orphans they are idiots, because there ought to be joy in a family and not just grief all the time. And people go on boasting: 'I've given up everything for the children!' Well, you were fools for doing so, that's all I can say—you gave up everything and the kids got sweet nothing. Maybe our food isn't very rich, but there's a bit of life and company in our family. I'm well, Mother's a cheerful one and they've all got souls in their bodies."

I must admit that in those days such reasoning on Stepan Denisovich's part, if not actually unpleasant to me, did not fall on fertile soil. Logically it was difficult to disagree with him, but it was also difficult to conceive what limit could divide such a philosophy from egoism or sheer laziness. I had grown accustomed to thinking that the sense of duty would only be effective and morally high when it was not very closely associated with arithmetic or the chemist's shop.

I wanted to see what practical form Stepan Denisovich gave to all his theory. But I still could not find time to call on the Vetkins—particularly as their position gradually improved. Living in the other half of Vetkin's cottage were two girl weavers. These girls, on their own initiative, gave up their room to the Vetkins and moved over to live with a friend in another cottage. Stepan Denisovich busily set about reorganizing his living quarters.

It was already August when instrument-maker Chub and I found ourselves going to town one day. We were walking along a narrow twisting path through a young oak forest. Chub, as usual, was talking about people.

"Vetkin has sent his son off to take an exam—the big one, that is. He'll be living with his uncle in town. That's where he is now. Give me an uncle like that and I'd bring up not thirteen but thirty children if you like. Everyone is lucky in different ways: one has a good head, another has a nice beard, and the next one has an uncle!"

"What kind of an uncle is he?"

"Oho! He's in clover there all right! Chairman of the Town Co-operative! Four rooms, a piano, sofas, yards of cloth, food—like a tsar!"

"What, does he steal it then?"

"Steal? Oh no, he buys it. You can always buy plenty in your own shops, you know. If I had my own shops, wouldn't I do some buying too? Not half, I would. New

Economic Policy* they call it! There's NEP and NAP and SNAP too! Under SNAP there would be enough for all my nephews and nieces as well. You just ask Stepan Denisovich why he got fixed up with his uncle. Couldn't he have put his Vanya into our factory training school? Oh no, he must go to his uncle because there's NEP there!"

At that moment from behind the oak-trees on the same winding path Stepan Denisovich and Vanya appeared. Vanya was wandering along behind, whacking the young trees as he passed them with a twig. He wore that complex expression on his face which only boys wear when, out of respect and love for their elders, they submit to the latter's decisions, but at the bottom of their hearts maintain some point of principle of their own. And one can see this clearly by their barely noticeable, but nevertheless persistent and ironic smile, and by a light touch of the same irony in their sad eyes.

"Did he pass?" shouted Chub when they were still at a distance.

Stepan Denisovich did not even smile.

"He did," he grunted, looking back crossly at his son and heading past us.

But suddenly he stopped, and, looking at the ground, said:

"Have you ever heard of aristocratic pride? Because if you haven't, here's an example of it for you!"

With a somewhat histrionic gesture Vetkin pointed at Vanya. This representative of the aristocracy held his boots in one hand and in the other the twig, with which he now scratched the soil at his bare feet, examining the scratchings with the same complicated look, made up of

* *New Economic Policy* (NEP)—introduced by the Soviet government after the Civil War Allowing capitalism to exist temporarily, while key positions were held by the proletarian state. The policy was designed to achieve the gradual victory of the socialist economy, and the building of a classless society.—*Tr.*

two expressions: one sad and upset, the other artful and malicious. The latter expression did, perhaps, indeed reflect a positively aristocratic idea

Stepan Denisovich tried to wither Vanya with an angry glare, but did not succeed: Vanya turned out to be tough as boxwood. Then Stepan Denisovich appealed to us.

"Apples! He's fond enough of apples if he scrumps them out of a state-farm orchard. But if they are on somebody's table, then he won't have anything to do with them!"

Such an annoying attitude toward apples could not, of course, be expressed in words, and Stepan Denisovich again glared at Vanya.

Vanya made an undecipherable movement with his head, which consisted of twisting it in several different directions, and said:

"Was it only the apples? It's not just because of the apples, in any case ... I won't live there!"

Stepan Denisovich again turned to us to emphasize the dissolute character of Vanya's words, but Vanya went on: "What do I need their apples for? Or their sweets? Or that ... sturgeon?"

Vanya suddenly burst into a laugh and turned his blushing face away, whispering rather awkwardly: "Sturgeon. ..."

The recollection of this delicacy did not amuse Vanya for long; besides, his laugh had been rather sarcastic. The next moment Vanya showed us the serious side of this sarcasm and said with an expression of real condemnation: "We haven't anything like that at home and I don't want it! I don't want it—and that's that!"

Apparently these words contained Vanya's final opinion, for when he had spoken them he straightened up, smacked his legs sharply with the twig as if it were not a twig but a riding-whip, and looked at his father. At that moment there was really something aristocratic in Vanya's figure.

Stepan Denisovich did something in the right corner of his moustache, as if he had begun to smile, but dropped the idea, and said scornfully: "What a proud man! Just look at you!"

He turned abruptly and stalked on in the direction of the factory. Vanya shot a rapid glance at our faces as if he wanted to catch us out at some crime or other, and peacefully moved on in the wake of his father.

Chub cast a warm glance after the receding figure of the boy, coughed, and rummaged in his pocket for tobacco. For some time he smoothed out a crumpled piece of cigarette-paper, slowly sprinkled the tobacco along it, all the while looking thoughtfully in the direction where Vanya had already disappeared. Only when he had wetted the paper with his tongue, rolled the cigarette and put it between his lips, did he fumble in the deep pocket of his dirty jacket and say gruffly:

"Yes, there's a boy.... But what do you say, is he right or isn't he?"

"I think he's right."

"Is he?"

Chub began to search for matches in another pocket, then in his trousers, then somewhere under the lining, and smiled.

"The world decides everything easily. Take you, for instance. You said at once: he's right. But maybe he's wrong.... There's my matches now, you can scratch yourself all over before you find 'em sometimes.... And in this case it's life, the truth of life you are after! What do you mean he's right? All very well for you to talk, but Vetkin's got thirteen. Has that young ragamuffin the right to throw his weight about? Apples, sturgeon, I like that! And what if his dad runs out of spuds?"

"Hold on, Chub, you've only just been condemning Vetkin...."

"I did so, and why not? What's good about it? That uncle of theirs is a son-of-a-bitch, and Vetkin wants a finger in the pie too."

"Well?"

"But that's a different question. That's a point against the old man, but how does it concern the kid? He ought to understand that it's hard for his father and that his father thinks this is the best way out. ... Ah, found my matches, see where they got to!... Nowadays the kids are like that—want to do everything themselves and understand everything themselves, but it's you who've got to answer for 'em!"

Vanya had his own way and entered our factory training school. The uncle in town was thus left as a potential reserve.

The case I have described interested me from several aspects. I wanted to have a closer look at Vanya's character as a whole, and another thing needed explaining: how are such characters made? For us educationalists the second question is of such great importance that I was not ashamed to learn a few things even from such an amateurish educational organization like the Vetkin family. Besides, it could not have occurred to me that Vanya's character was a gift from nature and not the result of good educational work.

Among our so-called "broad public" it is widely known that Lombrozo's theory is incorrect, that good upbringing can mould an interesting and healthy character out of any raw material.

This is a correct and pleasant conviction, but unfortunately in our country it does not always lead to practical results. This happens because a considerable number of our educationalists profess their scorn for Lombrozo only in theoretical discussions, in reports and speeches, at debates and conferences. On these occasions they speak out firmly against Lombrozo, but on the job, in the everyday practical sphere, these opponents of Lombrozo do not know how to work accurately and expediently on the moulding of character, and have always a tendency in difficult cases to slip away quietly and leave the natural raw material in its original form.

This practice formed the basis of many extravagant writings and theories. Hence paedology, hence also, in the form of subtle passive resistance, came the theory of informal education, and hence, even more naturally, came the usual worldly-wise habit of giving things up as a bad job, which was always accompanied by the usual gestures and the usual phrases:

"A terrible boy!"

"A hopeless fellow!"

"We are quite helpless!"

"He's incorrigible!"

"We can't do anything with him!"

"A special regime is needed!"

The destruction of paedology and the nation-wide collapse of "informal education" have taken place before our eyes. But, because of this, things have become even more difficult for unsuccessful teachers, since now they have no theory to hide their practical helplessness, or rather, to be quite frank, their invincible idleness.

Lombrozo can be crushed to the ground by only one means—great practical work on the education of character. And this work is not at all easy; it requires effort, patience and persistence. Many of our educators think quite sincerely that it is enough to do a little dance over the refuted Lombrozo, pronouncing a few anathemas against him, and their duty is over.

All this "practical" trouble arises, however, not simply out of idleness. In the majority of cases there is present a real, sincere and secret conviction that, as a matter of fact, if a man was born a bandit, he will die a bandit, that only

76

the grave cures the hunch-back, and that no apple falls far from an apple-tree.

I profess infinite, reckless and unhesitating belief in the unlimited power of educational work, particularly under the social conditions pertaining in the Soviet Union. I do not know a single case where a genuinely valuable character was formed without a healthy educational background or, on the contrary, where a perverted character came about in spite of correct educational work. And therefore I had no doubt about where to look for the natural source of the nobility of Vanya's nature—in wise and understanding family upbringing.

And I had a talk with Big Vanya at the first convenient opportunity, which happened to occur in that very same wood, only right in the depths of it, well away from those twisting paths into the town. It was a day-off and I was just wandering about there, tempted by the chance of being alone and thinking over various problems of life. Vanya was gathering mushrooms. Some time ago Stepan Denisovich had said to me:

"Mushrooms are a fine idea. When a man's short of money he can go out and gather up a few mushrooms. It's a good relish and free too! Berries are the same. And there are stinging-nettles as well, only they must be young."

Vanya was walking about the forest with a big bag, gathering mushrooms. A moist, appetizing heap of them was already peeping out of the bag, and Vanya had made a kind of additional bag out of the tail of his shirt, where he was putting his latest finds. He greeted me and said:

"Dad's terrifically fond of mushrooms. Fried and salted. Only here there aren't any 'whites,' and he likes 'whites' best of all."

I sat down on a tree stump and lit a cigarette. Vanya took up his position opposite me on the grass, propping the bag against a tree. I put my question straight to him.

"Vanya, I am interested in a certain question. You refused to live with your uncle out of pride. . . . Was your father right about that?"

"Not out of pride," answered Vanya and looked steadily at me with his clear blue eyes. "Why out of pride? I simply don't want to, what do I need that uncle for?"

"But, after all, it's better at your uncle's. And it would be a help to your family."

I said that and at once felt a pang of conscience; I even smiled guiltily, but the blue of Vanya's eyes was still as clear as before.

"It's true it is hard for Dad, only . . . why should we break away from each other? It would be even harder then."

Very likely my face wore a particularly stupid expression at that moment, because Vanya burst out laughing merrily, even his bare feet danced mockingly up and down on the grass.

"What do you think? What do you think Dad sent me to Uncle for? Do you think it was so that there would be not so many of us? No fear! Our dad, he's a sly one . . . a real . . . a real old fox, he is! He wanted it to be better for me! You see what kind he is!"

"It would be easier for you and easier for him too," I insisted.

"No, it's not that," Vanya continued as cheerfully as before. "What difference does one person make to him? He's all right. And now I am knocking up twenty-eight rubles at the factory training school. He just wanted to help me."

"But you refused a better offer?"

"Why, what's better about it?" said Vanya, serious now. "Do you call it good, leaving Dad in the lurch? Is that good? And there is nothing better there, it's all worse. They eat well there, that's the only thing. But it's far better at home. You sit down at table and it's real

78

fun. Our dad's a card and so is mother! Of course, we don't eat sturgeon. But do you think sturgeon is nice?"

"I think so."

"Pooh, I don't like it at all. It's rotten! But what about taters and mushrooms, eh? A whole saucepan of them! And Dad throwing in a joke here and there. And my brothers and sisters are good too. I won't miss much by not going there."

So nothing came of that conversation. Vanya would not admit to being proud and assured me that it was better at home. When we parted he said to me affectionately but with a challenge in his voice:

"You come and have supper with us today. Taters and mushrooms. Think there's not enough to go round? Oho, you come and see!"

"Well, I'll come then!"

"Honestly, come to supper! Seven o'clock. All right?"

At seven o'clock I set off to the Vetkins. At a table on the veranda sat Stepan Denisovich, reading the paper. Anna Semyonovna and Oksana were busy in the open-air kitchen nearby. Oksana glanced at me without raising her hands from the frying-pan, and, smiling warmly, said something to her mother. Anna Semyonovna looked round, gathered up her apron, wiped her hands and came forward to meet me.

"How nice to see you! Vanya said you would be coming. Stepan, come on, look after your guest, you've had enough time studying politics."

Stepan Denisovich removed his glasses and put them down on the newspaper. Then he plucked his beard and started pursing his lips, but this was hospitable anxiety, with a little touch of irony about it. At the door of the cottage stood Big Vanya, holding the top of the door with both hands and smiling. Vasya slipped under one of his arms into the cottage; and peeping out from under the other, crouched rosy-cheeked Marusya with her hands on her knees, screwing up her eyes at me.

Five minutes later we were sitting on the benches round the big table. There was no table-cloth, but the natural wood of the table was clean and gleaming. As I sat down I could not help passing my hand lovingly over its pleasant white surface. Stepan Denisovich noticed this gesture.

"You like it? I like a plain table too. It's the real thing, no pretending about it. But with a table-cloth, you know, there are some people who will buy a dark one on purpose, so as not to show the dirt. Here you've got real cleanliness, and no nonsense."

At home Stepan Denisovich was a new man, more confident and cheerful, the muscles of his face worked more freely and he hardly ever sucked that mysterious fruit-drop he seemed to keep hidden in his mouth. Near the stove, which was draped with a white curtain, stood Big Vanya, Vitya, Semyon and Little Vanya—the whole main team—smiling and listening to their father.

Suddenly into the room flew seven-year-old Lyuba, the darkest of the Vetkins—her face was almost the colour of an olive. Unlike the others she wore a necklace of red cornel berries, which in our parts are called "glodi."

"Oh," cried Lyuba, "I'm late, I'm late! Come on, Vanya!"

Stern, brown-eyed Little Vanya bent down to the bottom shelf of the cupboard and methodically began to pass Lyuba first a basket of sliced bread, then some deep plates, then several knives, two salt-cellars and some aluminium spoons. His sister responded to Little Vanya's lofty calm with feverish activity round the table, which caused a kind of warm, friendly breeze through the room.

While Lyuba and Little Vanya were laying the table, Big Vanya and Vitya pulled out from under one of the bunks two little trestles and placed a broad board on them, just as clean as the table. Thus, next to the bunk, a long camp-table was set up, which was immediately laid with the plates brought by the whirling figure of olive-skinned Lyuba. I had scarcely looked round before a company gathered at this table: Marusya, Vera, Grisha, Katya and Petya—all the "small fry" of the family. Each one of them brought along a piece of furniture. Marusya rolled out a round block of wood from under the bunk. The twins, Katya and Petya, must have come from the other room. They walked in, serious and even a little worried, both of them pressing tiny wooden stools to their sittumdowns. They were fully equipped. Still holding fast to their stools, they squeezed their way up to the improvised table and, as soon as they sat down, fell silent in serious expectation.

Four-year-old Vera, on the other hand, was an unusually merry character. She was very like Marusya, just as red-cheeked and lively, only Marusya had already grown plaits, while Vera's hair was clipped short. As soon as she sat down at the table she clutched her aluminium spoon and began to make faces, not at anybody in particular, simply looking at the bright sunlit window and banging the table with her spoon. Little Vanya glanced round at her from the cupboard and frowned angrily at the spoon. Then Vera started making faces at him, drawing in her cheeks slyly and raising her spoon, threatening to bring it down with a crash on the plate. She was just about to burst into loud, uproarious laughter, when Big Vanya caught her hand with the spoon in it. Vera raised her lovely big eyes and smiled tenderly and appealingly at him. Vanya, without releasing her hand, bent down and whispered something to which Vera listened attentively, looking sideways. Then she whispered in that loud, booming whisper, which only four-year-olds command: "Aha ... aha ... I won't ... I won't."

I was lost in admiration of this play and missed the most triumphant moment: both on our table and the "small fry's" camp-table appeared iron pots of potatoes, big ones for us, and smaller ones for the "small fry"; and Anna Semyonovna had already changed her dark kitchen apron for a fresh pink one. Oksana and Semyon brought in two deep bowls of fried mushrooms and placed them on the table. The family calmly took their places. To my surprise Big Vanya sat down not at our table but at the camp-table, at the narrow end, beside Marusya. Frowning cheerfully, he raised the lid of the pot and a dense fragrant cloud of steam poured forth. Marusya puffed out her cheeks and peeped into the pot, delighting in the heat of its fiery breath. Looking round at the whole company, she suddenly began singing loudly and clapping her hands.

"Taties in their jackets! Taties in their jackets!"

Our table looked round sympathetically at the little ones, but they paid no attention to us. Vera also started clapping and singing, although she had not even seen the potatoes. Katya and Petya remained as serious and aloof from all worldly temptations as ever, and did not even look at the iron pot.

"Vera will be a contralto," said Stepan Denisovich. "Hear how she follows? Just a bit sharp, though, a bit sharp."

Big Vanya was already putting potatoes on Vera's plate and threatening her jokingly.

"Vera, why do you sing sharp?"

Vera stopped singing and got mixed up between the potatoes on the plate and her brother's question.

"What?"

"Why are you sharp?"

"Sharp?" Vera asked again, but by this time the potatoes had already won her attention completely and she forgot about her brother.

Anna Semyonovna served my plate, her husband's and her own, then handed the reins to Oksana. Everyone set about skinning their potatoes. But all of a sudden Big Vanya leapt up from the camp-table with a shout of panic.

"We've forgotten the herring!"

Everyone laughed loudly. Only Stepan Denisovich looked reproachfully at Vanya.

"You're a great one! You might have done us out of our herring."

Vanya ran out of the cottage and returned hot and excited, carrying deep plates in both hands, full of sliced salted herring mixed with onion.

"The herring is his idea," said Stepan Denisovich. "Ah, you funny fellow, nearly forgot it!"

I also smiled at Vanya's forgetfulness. And I felt like smiling all the time in this pleasant company. I have been out visiting on several other occasions, but I do not remember ever being received by such a united family. Usually the children would be ushered off into some family nook and the feasting reserved only for the grown ups. Many other details of the supper called my attention. For example, I very much liked the way in which the children could at any moment combine interest in me, as a guest, with their interest in food and with remembering their duties, while at the same time not forgetting their own little concerns. Their eyes shone gladly as they dealt busily with the affairs of the table, but in the intervals they could find time to remember "outside" subjects, which were a mystery to me, for I caught snatches of their conversation: "Where? On the river?" Or, "Not Dynamo, Metallist...." Or, "Volodya's telling whoppers, he didn't see...."

The Volodya in question was, of course, Chub's. Volodya had a habit of "telling whoppers" to the neighbouring tribes.

All these circumstances interested and gladdened me, but at the same time I felt a very real and wolfish appetite. I suddenly longed for potatoes and mushrooms. And here there was salted herring as well. It was not laid out in parade order on a special narrow dish, and the ringlets of onion did not surround it in a gentle escort of honour; there was nothing pretentious about it at all. Here the herring was piled in delicious haphazard abundance to the very edge of the deep red and white plate. And the white segments of onion were mixed in with it in friendly unity, soaked in sunflower-seed oil.

Over supper the talk was of the new and the old life.

"The wife and I weren't afraid of anything even in the old days," said Stepan Denisovich, "but as a matter of fact there were a good many things to be afraid of: first, the poverty, second, the policeman, and third, life was a bore. I hate a boring life more than anything else."

"Do you have more fun these days?" I asked.

"Depends what you mean by fun," smiled Stepan Denisovich, glancing into the potato pot. "There's Oksana here, she's just starting at the Rabfak. Look at it how you like, but in eight years' time she will be a constructional engineer, you know! If you counted them all, my dad must have dreamed about twenty thousand dreams in his sixty years. Well, what did he dream of? All sorts of nonsense, I'll be bound. But I guarantee he never dreamed his daughter was a constructional engineer! Couldn't have done, even if he was drunk."

"And did you dream it?" asked Anna Semyonovna, shooting a glance at him.

"What do you think? Why, only yesterday night I dreamed that Oksana had come home and was giving me a present of a fur coat, but in the dream I couldn't make out what fur it was. And I said to her: What do I need a fur coat like that for; I'll feel uncomfortable wearing a fur coat like that in the forge. It's not for the forge, she says, come on, let's go to the construction works, I'm building a radio station on Severnaya Zemlya. And she's wearing a great big fur coat too, like a boyar."

Oksana, who was sitting beside me, contracted her neat clever brows and blushed, not so much because of what her father said as from the universal attention—everybody found it pleasant to look at the future builder of a radio station on Severnaya Zemlya.

"Oksana! I'll come and visit you with Dad too. You bring me some felt boots," said Vasya.

There was laughter at table and many similar practical proposals were put forward.

"You didn't dream of me, Dad, by any chance, did you?" asked Big Vanya, without hiding a smile. "It means a lot to me!"

"Yes, I did," Stepan Denisovich nodded, waving his beard over his plate with humorous conviction. "Of course I did, only it wasn't a good dream. It seems that you had gone to see your uncle and then some people came running to me, shouting: quick, quick, your Vanya's got the belly-ache, he ate one of his uncle's apples. He's poisoned himself with an apple!"

Everyone roared with laughter, and Vitya even shouted right across the table: "And with the sturgeon! It was their sturgeon did it!"

Now everyone was looking with happy, merry eyes at Vanya, who stood at his camp-table, laughing without embarrassment and looking at his father. Then he asked, loud and cheerfully: "Well, did I die ... of poisoning?"

"No," replied Vetkin. "You didn't die. They ran for the ambulance and saved your life."

When the potatoes and all their array were eaten, Stepan Denisovich himself brought in a great big polished samovar, and we started drinking tea. The tea was simple and original. Two Ukrainian cakes, each no less than half a metre in diameter, were carried in on big wicker-work platters. I had met these cakes before and always been struck by their magnificence. Very probably they touched the tender national cords of my Ukrainian soul. These were the famous "korzhi z salom"* of which an old proverb says: "Trouble makes you eat fat cakes."

The inside of a korzh is thinly scattered with small cubes of bacon fat round each of which the pastry becomes very tasty, moist and rather salty. To strike such a spot and bite through it is the real essence of gastronomic delight. The upper surface of the korzh is like a boundless plain, white in some parts, pink in others, and here and there the plain undulates with soft little mounds made of thin dry crust. "Korzh z salom" cannot for some reason be cut with a knife but must be broken, and its hot flaky lumps are also something one never forgets.

The Vetkin family greeted the korzhi with shouts of delight. At the "small fry's" table a real ovation took place; even the twins, Katya and Petya, abandoned their stoic calm and let forth tender streams of shy, uncertain laughter.

At our table Semyon and Vitya, who had apparently not been forewarned of the appearance of the korzh, stared at it in surprise and then shouted in one voice: "O-oh! Ko-orzh!"

Stepan Denisovich's ruddy face beamed in welcome at the korzh.

"That's a real achievement, I must say," he said, rubbing his hands. "As a matter of fact, this is really kulak culture, but in this case it's not only permissible, it's good for you."

That supper marked the beginning of my close acquaintance with the Vetkin family. And to this day I have remained a friend of this family, although I must admit

* *Korzhi z salom*—Ukrainian for "cakes made with bacon fat."—*Tr.*

my friendship was not without its utilitarian aspects: there was a lot to be learnt from the Vetkins and, above all, they gave you a lot to think about.

Stepan Denisovich's way of bringing up his family is not perhaps remarkable for its technical perfection, but it touches the most sensitive cords of Soviet educational thought; it possesses a good, healthy collective spirit and plenty of good creative optimism, and there is also that sensitive consideration of details and trifles without which real educational work is utterly impossible. Such consideration of details is no easy matter. It requires not only attention, but also constant and patient thought. Trifles hardly make themselves heard, there are many such trifles and their voices merge together in a confusing clamour of sound. And not only has one to understand all this confusion, one has to plan out of it important future events, which go far beyond the bounds of the family.

Yes, Stepan Denisovich welded his family into a collective body with home-made implements, but he did so persistently and patiently. Of course, there were short-comings in his family and he made mistakes. His young-sters were, perhaps, too orderly and calm—even the "small fry" had a kind of sedateness about them. Among the child society of our yard the Vetkin children were always advocates of peace. They were cheerful, lively, active and inventive, but they firmly avoided quarrels and conflicts.

One day on the volley-ball court Volodya Chub, a fiery, strong-featured lad of about fourteen, refused to give up serving at the proper time. His team did not protest, since Volodya really was good at serving. The captain of the opposing team was Semyon Vetkin. It was a scratch game without a referee. Semyon kept the ball in his hands.

"That's not right," he said.

"It's none of your business," shouted Volodya. "Have someone serving all the time in your team too!"

Any other boy in a situation like this would undoubtedly have made a scene or given up the game, for no Themis can weigh questions of justice so precisely as young boys. But Semyon just smiled and put the ball in play.

"All right then! It's only their weakness! They've got to win somehow."

And yet Volodya's team lost. Whereupon a heated and irritable Volodya assailed Semyon with demands for satisfaction.

"Take your words back! What do you mean we're weak!"

Volodya had his hands in his pockets and one shoulder thrust forward—a sure sign of aggression. And Semyon, still smiling, gave Volodya complete satisfaction.

"I take my words back! You have a very strong team. Just like that!"

To illustrate his meaning Semyon even lifted his arm skywards. Proud of his moral victory, Volodya said: "I should think so! Let's have another game. Then you'll see."

Semyon agreed and lost this time, but left the court with the same peaceful smile on his face. Only when they parted did he say to Volodya: "But I don't advise you to do that always. Ours was a friendly match, that's different. But in a serious match the ref' would send you off the court!"

But Volodya was now rejoicing in his victory and took Semyon's statement without offence.

"Well, let him, anyhow we won!"

On this occasion, as on many others, a fairly confused conflict of educational principles came to the surface. In part I was even pleased by Volodya's heated "unjust" impetuosity and his desire for victory, while Semyon's tractability seasoned with humour could seem dubious. I mentioned this outright to Stepan Denisovich and was very surprised to hear from him a definite, precise answer, which proved that this problem, too, had not only interested him, but had been given a thorough solution.

"I think it's right," said Stepan Denisovich. "My Semyon's a clever lad—he acted quite rightly."

"How can it be right? Volodya was insolent and got his own way. A struggle shouldn't end like that!"

"He didn't get anything at all. An odd serve means nothing. As a matter of fact, Volodya showed weakness. and Semyon strength. And great strength at that, don't you think so? It depends what the conflict is about. Here there are two conflicts, not one. One is for the ball, the other is more important—for agreement between people. Why, you said yourself—they didn't fight, didn't quarrel, even played an extra game. It's very good."

"But I doubt it, Stepan Denisovich, such conciliation, you know. . . ."

"Depends when," said Vetkin thoughtfully. "I consider it's time now to get out of the habit of squabbling about various things. Before, people really did live like beasts. Get hold of a man's throat and you're all right, but don't let go or he'll get his teeth in yours. That won't do for us. We must be comrades. After all, if a comrade throws his weight about, he can be warned, we have the organization for that. Here there was no referee—bad organization. But what of it? That's nothing to go at each other's throats for."

"And if Semyon happens to meet a real enemy?"

"That's another matter. If that happens and it's a real enemy, don't worry about Semyon. If need be, and I think it must come to that, don't worry: he'll get him by the throat . . . and he won't let him go!"

I thought over what Stepan Denisovich had said, recalled Semyon's face and realized clearly that Stepan

Denisovich was right in that: Semyon would certainly not let a real enemy go.

Since then many years have passed. I saw the Vetkins live, develop and grow richer. The firm ties between them never disappeared, and their faces never wore any harassed expressions, nor any expressions of need, although need was always knocking at their door.

But need, too, gradually decreased. The children grew up and began to help their father. At first they contributed their Rabfak and factory training school grants to the family funds, then they began to bring in their wages too. Oksana did become a constructional engineer and the other Vetkins also turned out good Soviet people.

We at the factory liked the Vetkins and were proud of them. Stepan Denisovich had a profoundly social nature, could respond to every task and every problem, and everywhere contributed his thoughtfulness and calm, smiling confidence. Our Party organization admitted him to its ranks with real ceremony in 1930.

The Vetkin family's style of upbringing has been the subject of my close attention and study till this day, but others have also learnt from them. Thanks considerably to the influence of the Vetkins, Chub's family improved too. And in itself it was not a bad family. In the Chub household there was more disorder, more accidents, more go-as-you-please, and much that was left unfinished. But they had a lot of good Soviet passion and a kind of artistic creativeness. Chub himself very rarely acted as the father-despot in his family. He was a good warm-hearted civic character and for this reason his family grew up an exuberant, healthy collective body.

The Chubs were rather envious of the Vetkins' imposing numerical superiority. When a seventh child, a son, was born to the Chubs, Chub himself fairly leapt for joy and threw a stupendous celebration for everyone, during which in the presence of his guests and offspring he made speeches of this kind:

"The seventh son is a special occasion. I was my father's seventh too. And the women said to me: the seventh son is the lucky one. If the seventh son takes a hen's last egg and puts it under his armpit and carries it there for forty days and forty nights, he is sure to hatch out a devil, just a little one for your own household purposes. He'll do whatever you tell him. The number of eggs I spoiled! My dad even warmed my pants for it, but I never hatched a devil: you might carry it till the evening but in the evening you'd either crush it or drop it. That's a difficult business, that is—hatching out your own devil."

"How many thousands of years people have been bothering with these devils," said Pyzhov, the accountant. "They used to say everybody had one attached to him, but taking it all round it's had very little effect on the balance of life, and the productivity of these devils has really been rather low."

Stepan Denisovich stroked his moustache and smiled.

"You have some little devils breeding at your place even now, Chub. If you look under the bed—you'll probably find one sitting there."

"Oh no," laughed Chub, "no, there aren't. Under Soviet rule we don't need 'em. Well! Drink up, you people! Here's to catching up and passing the Vetkins!"

We clinked glasses cheerily, for this was not such a bad toast.

Chapter Four

ONEY! Of all human inventions this invention came nearest to the devil. In nothing else was there such scope for the practice of baseness and deception, and so no other sphere provided such favourable soil for the growth of hypocrisy.

It would seem that in Soviet life there were no place for hypocrisy. And yet its bacteria do crop up here and there and we have no right to forget about them, just as we must not forget about the bacteria of influenza, malaria, typhus and other similar ills.

What is the formula for hypocrisy? Egoism, plus cynicism, plus a wishy-washy background of idealistic foolishness, plus the wretched aestheticism of affected humility. Not one of these elements can endure in Soviet life. It is a different matter where both God and the devil intervene in human affairs and claim the right of leadership. The hypocrite has one pocket for money, another for the prayer-book, the hypocrite serves both God and the devil and fools them both.

In the old world the man who accumulated money could not help being a hypocrite to a greater or less extent. For this it was not at all necessary to play the Tartuffe all the time. In the end, decent forms were found even for hypocrisy, forms rid of primitive pose and comic simplicity. The most inveterate exploiters learned how to shake workers' hands, how to chat with the proletariat about various things, to slap shoulders and crack jokes and to accompany the practice of patronage and philanthropy with worthy modesty and slight blushes. The result was an extremely agreeable and attractive picture. Not only were they in no hurry to glorify the Lord, they even pretended they had nothing to do with Him and that in general there was no need for gratitude either on earth or in heaven. That was a splendidly wise policy. A Tartuffe laid himself out to please the Lord; his fawning was active, determined and unrestrainable, but just for this reason that kind of Tartuffe reeked ten miles away of the devil, who, by the by, did not even bother to hide himself but took up his quarters right on the spot in his old armchair, smoked his tobacco and leisurely awaited his turn to appear in public.

That was the crudest form of hypocrisy, reminiscent in its technical aspect of Stephenson's locomotive. Modern Western hypocrites have everything arranged with enviable thoroughness—no God, no saints, but at least it does not smell of the devil, in fact it does not smell of anything, except scent. We recommend people interested in this subject to acquaint themselves with a classical example of hypocrisy—André Gide's *Voyage au Congo*.

But all this purity is only aesthetic technique, nothing more. As soon as the crowd disperses, as soon as mama and papa are left in the intimate family circle, as soon as they are faced with the problems of educating their children, then our two friends at once appear on the scene: both the tidy, clean-shaven, affably beaming God and the disreputable, rotten-toothed, insolently grinning devil. The former supplies the "ideals," the latter has a pocket jingling with money—no less pleasant a commodity than the "ideals."

Here in the family, where there was no need for any "social" tactics, where omnipotent zoological instincts and unrest held sway, where live irrefutable progeny swarmed about in the open, here it was that the unjust, blood-thirsty and shameless system, whose repulsive face it was impossible to disguise under any make-up, revealed itself with almost ruffianly lack of ceremony. And its moral contradictions, its practical business-like cynicism seemed insulting to the essential purity of a child.

And therefore it was here, in the bourgeois family, that a persistent attempt was made to drive the devil into some far-off corner, together with his money and the rest of his devilish tricks.

That was why the bourgeois family strove to keep the sources of family wealth secret. It was bourgeois society that initiated vain attempts to separate childhood from money, here it was that stupid and futile efforts were made to bring up the exploiter with a "lofty moral charac-ter." Such attempts, with their plans of idealistic altruism, a mythical "kindness" and unacquisitiveness, were, in fact, nothing but a school of the same refined hypocrisy.

Nikolai Nikolayevich Babich seemed to be a cheerful man. He very often sprinkled a business talk with strange unnecessary ejaculations designed to show his lively, cheerful character, such as: "Oh help!" or "Holy Mother of God!" When the occasion offered, he liked to recall an anecdote, which he would recount very loudly and at great length. His face was round but in this roundness there was no good nature, no gentleness of feature; its lines had little flexibility and were frozen into an expressionless mask. His forehead was large and bulging, lined with too regular folds of wrinkles which, if they moved, did so all at once, as by a word of command.

At our factory Nikolai Nikolayevich was head of the office.

We lived together in the same bungalow, which had been built on the edge of the town during the period when bungalows were all the fashion with us. Our bungalow contained four flats; they all belonged to our factory. In the other flats lived Nikita Konstantinovich Lysenko, the chief engineer, and Ivan Prokofievich Pyzhov, the chief accountant—both of them old colleagues of mine, who had been with me ever since the days when we got to know Vetkin.

This bungalow was the scene of our family affairs, which were common knowledge to all of us. Here I finally clarified for myself the problem of money in the family collective. In their approach to this problem my neighbours differed greatly from each other.

From the first days of our acquaintance Nikolai Niko-layevich Babich amazed me by the solid gloominess of his household. Everything in his flat rested on flat, cumbersome legs; the table, the chairs and even the beds—everything was coated with a film of seriousness and inhospitality. And even at those moments when the host blossomed out in a smile the walls and furnishings of his flat seemed to frown even harder and treat the master of the house himself with disapproval. So Nikolai Nikolayevich's smile never awakened any response in his guests; but that did not worry him.

As soon as he had to address his son or daughter his smile vanished with extraordinary suddenness, just as if it had never existed, and in its place appeared a curious expression, the wearied expression of the habitual benefactor.

His children were nearly the same age, between thirteen and fifteen. Their faces were beginning to show the same round and immobile woodenness as their father's.

It was not often that I called on the Babiches, but when I did I nearly always witnessed this kind of conversation:

"Daddy, give me twenty kopeks."

"What for?"

"I've got to buy a note-book."

"What kind of a note-book?"

"An arithmetic one."

"What, already filled up your last?"

"There's room for one more lesson."

"I'll buy you two note-books tomorrow."

Or a conversation of this kind:

"Daddy, Nadya and I are going to the cinema."

"Very well."

"But what about money?"

"How much are the tickets?"

"Eighty-five kopeks each."

"Eighty, I think."

"No, eighty-five."

Nikolai Nikolayevich goes over to the cupboard, takes some keys out of his pocket, unlocks a drawer, sorts out something, locks the drawer and lays out on the table exactly one ruble and seventy kopeks.

His son counts the money, grasps it in his fist, says "thank you" and goes away. The whole of this operation lasts about three minutes, and during this time the boy's face grows gradually redder, until by the end of the operation even the tips of his ears are glowing. I noticed that the degree of redness was in inverse proportion to the size of the required sum and achieved its deepest hue when the son asked:

"Daddy, give me ten kopeks."

"For the tram?"

"Yes."

The same ritual takes place at the cupboard drawer, and two five-kopek pieces are placed on the table. The son, blushing, grasps them in his fist, says "thank you" and goes away.

Once the son asked not for ten kopeks but for twenty, and explained that the other ten kopeks were needed for Nadya's tramfare.

Nikolai Nikolayevich had gone up to the cupboard

96

and put his hand into his pocket for the keys, but suddenly he stopped and turned to his son.

"I don't like to see you asking for your sister. She has a tongue, has she not?"

This time Tolya's blushes reached their maximum before the end of the operation.

"She's doing her home-work."

"No, Tolya, that won't do. If she needs money she can ask. Or it makes you a kind of cashier. Is that proper? Perhaps we should buy a purse for you to keep money in? That won't do at all. It will be a different matter when you start earning yourself. Here are ten kopeks, and Nadya can come and ask herself."

In five minutes Nadya appeared at the door and her ears were already glowing like fire. She did not launch her petition at once but first made a rather unsuccessful attempt at a smile. Nikolai Nikolayevich looked at her reproachfully and the smile immediately gave place to further confusion: even Nadya's eyelids went red.

"Daddy, give me some money for the tram."

Nikolai Nikolayevich asked no questions. I expected him to take from his pocket the ten kopeks he had ready and give it to Nadya. But no, he again advanced towards the cupboard, again took out his keys, and so forth. Nadya picked up the ten kopeks from the table, whispered "thank you" and left the room.

Nikolai Nikolayevich followed her with dull virtuous eyes, waited until the door had closed and then brightened up.

"Tolya has already been spoiled somewhere, drat the boy! Only to be expected, of course, with all those comrades of his. And the neighbours! You know how they live at the Lysenkos'. Holy Mother of God! Their children are so corrupted, bless my soul! And with Pyzhov you just throw up your hands! Thinks he's clever, does Ivan Prokofievich! Why, it's impossible to bring up the children—

the examples they get here, oh help! But my daughter, she's modesty itself, did you see? You bet your life, she is! Oh yes, pure as they make 'em! Of course, she'll grow up, you can't do anything about that, but purity must be drummed in from childhood. Or else, what with the goings-on around here: boys about on every street, their pockets jingling with money. I don't know what their parents are thinking of!"

The chief engineer, Nikita Konstantinovich Lysenko, had a good-natured face. He was tall and rather dry-boned, but his features were ruled by an organized dictatorship of good nature, which had grown so accustomed to dominating his face that even at moments of near catastrophe at our factory it did not quit its well-warmed seat and merely observed how all the remaining forces of Nikita Konstantinovich's soul strove to deal with a dangerous fire or some other threatening disaster.

Nikita Konstantinovich's system was diametrically opposed to Babich's. At first I thought it had been instituted by his personal good nature, without the participation of his will and without any attempts at theoretical creative work, but later I realized my mistake. True, good nature also took some part in it, incidentally, not so much an active part as a passive one—in the form of a certain silent approval and perhaps even mild delight.

But the chief authority on upbringing in the Lysenko family was the mother. Yevdokia Ivanovna was a determined and well-read woman. Very rarely did one see Yevdokia Ivanovna without a book in her hand, and although her whole life was sacrificed to reading, it was by no means a fruitless passion. Unfortunately she always read old books with yellowed pages, bound in shabby spotted covers; her favourite author was Sheller-Mikhailov. Had she read new books she might have become a good Soviet woman. But now she was just a "thinking lady," rather slovenly, with a whole assortment of ideals generated exclusively from different varieties of "Good."

It must be confessed that the Soviet citizen has become rather unused to this kind of thing, and our young people have probably never even heard of it.

In the days of our youth the priests summoned us to do good, the philosophers wrote about it, Vladimir Solovyov devoted a thick volume to Good. In spite of all the attention that was lavished on this theme, however, Good never succeeded in becoming an ordinary, everyday object, and as a matter of fact it was only an obstacle to good work and good temper. Where Good hovered over the world on its downy wings, smiles died away, energy petered out, struggle ceased, everyone began to feel queer in the pit of his stomach, and their faces took on a sour bored expression. Disorder reigned in the world.

The same disorder existed in the Lysenko family. Yevdokia Ivanovna did not notice it, since by a strange misunderstanding neither order nor disorder was to be found either in the nomenclature of Good or in the nomenclature of Evil.

Yevdokia Ivanovna strictly observed the official list of virtues and took an interest in other questions too.

"Mitya, it is not good to lie! You ought always to tell the truth. A man who lies holds nothing sacred in his soul. Truth is dearer than anything else on earth, and you told the Pyzhovs that our tea-pot is silver when it's not silver at all, but nickel-plated."

Mitya, a freckled lad with no eyebrows and big pink ears, blows on the tea in his saucer and does not hurry to respond to his mother's reproof. Only when he has emptied his saucer does he say: "You always exaggerate, Mother. As a matter of fact, I didn't say it was silver, I said it was silver in colour. And Pavlusha Pyzhov said there aren't any silver-coloured tea-pots. So I said: what colour are they then? And he said: just nickel-plate colour.

He doesn't know anything: nickel-plate colour! The tea-pot is nickel-plated but the colour is silver."

His mother listens to Mitya wearily. In the play of silver and nickel-plate colours she detects no signs of the moral problem. In any case Mitya is a strange boy: you can't tell where the principle of Good or where the principle of Evil lies in him. Only yesterday evening she said to her husband: "Children nowadays seem to grow up amoral somehow!"

Now she examines the children. The eldest, Konstantin, is in the tenth class and looks very decent in appearance. He wears a grey jacket and tie; he is tidy, silent and respectable. Konstantin never takes part in the family conversation; he has his own affairs and his own opinions but does not find it necessary to tell other people about them.

Mitya is twelve. Of all the members of the Lysenko family he seems to be the most unprincipled, perhaps because he is a chatterbox and when chattering really does exhibit an amoral freedom. Not long ago Yevdokia Ivanovna thought she would inspire her son to do a good deed: to go and see his sick uncle, her brother. But Mitya said smiling: "Mum, just think, what's the sense of it? Uncle is fifty and he's got cancer. Even a doctor can't do anything about such illnesses, and I'm not a doctor. He'll die anyway and there's no need to interfere."

Lena is still small, it will be a year before she goes to school. She resembles her father in the abundance of lazy indifference amply visible on her face. This leads her mother to expect that in the future Lena will be a more active representative of the idea of Good than the boys.

Lena leaves the table and wanders round the room. Her mother watches her with a loving glance and returns to her book.

The Lysenkos' room is filled to overflowing with dusty furniture and littered with old newspapers, books, withered flowers, useless, broken, dust-covered odds and ends: big jugs and little jugs, marble and china dogs, monkeys, shepherds, ash-trays and plates.

Lena stops by the sideboard and, rising on her toes, peeps into the open drawer.

"Where's the money gone?" she cooes, brightening up and turning to her mother.

Mitya shoves his chair back noisily and dashes over to the drawer. He rummages about in the muddle of its contents with one hand, then plunges his other hand in, looks Lena over angrily, and also turns to his mother.

"Have you spent all the money already? You have, have you? And what if I need some for the excursion?"

His mother is deep in the adventures of Anton-Goremyka. She cannot immediately grasp what they want of her.

"For the excursion? Well, take some, what are you shouting for?"

"But there isn't any!" roars Mitya, pointing at the drawer.

"Mitya, it isn't good to shout like that...."

"But what about the excursion?!"

Yevdokia Ivanovna looks dully at Mitya's excited face and at last grasps the situation.

"No money? Impossible! Surely Annushka can't have spent it all! Go and ask Annushka."

Mitya rushes into the kitchen. Lena stands at the open drawer and dreams about something. Her mother turns over the page of her book. Mitya runs in from the kitchen and howls in panic: "She says there was thirty rubles left! But there's nothing!"

Yevdokia Ivanovna, sitting at the uncleared breakfast table, is still living in the last half of the nineteenth century. She does not want to interrupt the pleasant tale of sufferings and jump half a century forward, she does not want to switch over to the question of the thirty rubles. And today she is lucky. Serious, unapproachable Konstantin says coldly:

"What are you kicking up such a row for? I took the thirty rubles. I need it."

"And you didn't leave anything. Do you think that's right?!" Mitya pushes his heated face towards him.

Konstantin makes no reply. He goes over to his table and occupies himself with his own affairs. However indignant Mitya may be, he cannot help admiring the confident dignity of his elder brother. Mitya knows that his brother has a big wallet made of brown leather, and in this wallet things happen which mystify and interest Mitya; in the wallet there is money and little notes and tickets to the theatre. Konstantin never speaks of the grown-up secrets of this wallet, but Mitya occasionally observes his brother putting it in order.

Mitya tears himself away from these tempting thoughts and remembers sadly: "But what about my excursion?"

No one answers him. Lena at the end of the bed has opened Mother's hand-bag. At the bottom of the hand-bag lie two rubles and some change. Lena does not need much: there is nothing to buy at the kindergarten but at the corner of the street ice-creams are sold; they cost exactly fifty kopeks. Biting her lower lip Lena picks up the change. Her financial crisis is completely solved, now she has nothing more to say to the grown ups and has already forgotten the recent disturbance. In her palm lie three twenty-kopek pieces. But suddenly even this tiny fortune vanishes. Mitya's impudent hand snatches the silver instantaneously from Lena. Lena looks up, stretches out her empty hand to Mitya and says serenely: "There's some more left there. That is for an ice-cream."

Mitya glances into the bag and empties the change out on the bed. Lena unhurriedly gathers up the money from the orange coverlet and walks past her mother to the hallway. Mitya does not mention his success to his mother either, and does not even bother to shut the bag. All is well again, and the room relapses into the silence of its dusty disorder. Flies continue to make their breakfast on the uncleared table. Konstantin is the last to leave after carefully fastening the lock of his drawer. Yevdokia Ivanovna, without raising her eyes from the page, transfers herself to the cushion-littered sofa.

Later in the evening Nikita Konstantinovich also looks into the sideboard drawer, meditates over it for a moment, glances round and says: "Yevdokia, is all the money gone? But it's five days to pay-day! How's that?..."

"The children took the money!... They needed it."

Nikita Konstantinovich again meditates over the drawer, then feels in his side pocket, pulls out a shabby wallet, looks into it and turns to his reading wife.

"All the same, Yevdokia, we must introduce some ... some sort of account system or something.... Why, it's five days ... to pay-day."

Yevdokia Ivanovna looks up at her husband through her old-fashioned gold pince-nez

"I don't understand.... What account?"

"Well ... some account ... after all, money...."

"Ah, Nikita, you say 'money' in such a tone, as if it were the main principle. Suppose there is no money. That does not mean we must revise our principles."

Nikita Konstantinovich takes off his jacket and closes the door into the room where the children sleep. His wife watches him with a wary eye, prepared for battle. But Nikita Konstantinovich does not intend to argue. He has for long professed faith in his wife's principles and it is not principles that are worrying him now. He is concerned with the problem of where to get money before pay-day.

Yevdokia Ivanovna, nevertheless, thinks it necessary to reinforce her husband's moral character.

"There is no need for the children to be taught about all kinds of money problems at this early age. It's bad enough for grown ups to be always counting: money, money, money! Our children should be brought up well away from such principles. Money! And it's very good that our children are not keen on money, they are extremely honest and take only what they need. What a fearful thing, you know: at twelve years old to be reckoning and counting up all the time. That mercenary spirit has poisoned our civilization enough already, don't you think so?"

Nikita Konstantinovich is not very interested in the fate of civilization. He thinks that his duty consists in managing a Soviet factory well. As for civilization, Nikita Konstantinovich is prepared to remain quite indifferent to its premature ruin as a result of poisoning by a mercenary spirit. But he is very fond of his children, and in his wife's words there is something comforting and pleasant. As a matter of fact, she is right: why should children be mercenary? And so Nikita Konstantinovich dropped off to sleep blissfully in the atmosphere of virtue created by his wife's words. As he dozed off he decided to ask chief accountant Pyzhov tomorrow for a loan of fifty rubles.

Sleep had already touched Nikita Konstantinovich when his consciousness was stirred for the last time by a glimpse of the joyful figure of Pyzhov, and somewhere far away, among the last shreds of reality, flashed the thought that Pyzhov was a mercenary man and everything of his was counted and reckoned up: money, children ... and joy of life itself ... smiles too ... profit and loss of smiles....

But that was the beginning of a dream.

In the morning Nikita Konstantinovich left for work as usual, without breakfast. And an hour later Yevdokia Ivanovna entered the children's room and said:

"Kostya, have you any money?"

Kostya turned his puffy face towards her and asked in a business-like fashion:

"Do you need much?"

"No ... about twenty rubles...."

"And when will you return it?"

"On pay-day ... in five days' time...."

Kostya raised himself on his elbow, pulled the new brown leather wallet out of his trousers and silently handed his mother two ten-ruble notes.

His mother took the money and only at the door did she heave a sigh: she had a feeling her son was beginning to show signs of the mercenary spirit.

Ivan Prokofievich Pyzhov was a man of remarkable corpulence. Indeed, I have never met a fatter man in my life. Probably he suffered from chronic obesity, but he never complained of it, looked a picture of health and was active and tireless as a young man. He rarely laughed, but his gentle features expressed so much joy and good restrained humour that he did not need to laugh. Instead of laughter, joyful tremors kept darting across his face; they told other people far more than Ivan Prokofievich's tongue, although his tongue was quite expressive too.

Pyzhov had a complicated family. Besides himself and his wife—a slim woman with big eyes—it consisted of two sons aged nine and fourteen, a niece, a pretty girl who was tall and buxom and seemed far older than her sixteen years, and an adopted daughter, ten-year-old Varyusha, whom Ivan Prokofievich had "inherited" from a friend.

There was also a grandmother, a rather dilapidated old soul, who was, however, a wonderfully jolly and active character and full of humorous turns of speech.

At the Pyzhovs' there was always plenty of fun. During the twelve years of my acquaintance with them I do not remember a day when there was not a laugh or a joke in the family. They all liked to pull each other's leg, knew how to work up to a joke and search for it, and often they all looked as if they were lying in ambush, each waiting slyly for some misfortune to overtake his neighbour so as to have a good laugh at his expense. Such a habit ought by rights to have led to general ill-humour and annoyance, but there was no trace of such a thing. On the contrary, this "treachery" seemed to have been invented on purpose to destroy in embryo the various unpleasantnesses and woes of life. Perhaps that was why the family never suffered from sorrow and tears, quarrels and conflicts, bad humour and pessimistic moods. In this respect they strongly resembled the Vetkin family, but the latter had less outward joy, laughter and practical jokes.

The Pyzhovs were hardly ever ill. I remember only one occasion when Ivan Prokofievich himself went down with a bout of flu. I was informed of this by the elder boy Pavlusha. He burst into my office, excited and beaming, directed an ironic smile at me and cocked a knowing eye at a group of machine parts on my table.

"Our dad's slipped up today! Flu! They've called the doctor! He's in bed drinking brandy! And he can't come to work. I'm to tell you.... See what happened? And he used to say: I'm never ill. Well, he went a bit too far this time!"

"Did the doctor say he had flu?"

"Yes, he did. Flu's not dangerous, is it? Yes, he's slipped up this time all right! Will you be coming round?"

Ivan Prokofievich was lying in bed, and beside him, on a small table, stood a bottle of brandy and several glasses. Crouching against the door-post in the bedroom were Seva, the youngest in the family, and Varyusha, casting wicked glances at their father. It was obvious that Ivan Prokofievich had only just repelled an attack by this pair, for little tremors of triumph were darting across his face and his lips were compressed in a satisfied grin.

When he noticed me, Seva started jumping up and down and laughing loudly.

"He says brandy's medicine. And the doctor drank and drank and then said: You've got me drunk, damn you! 'Tisn't medicine, is it?"

Varyusha, swinging on one half of the white door, added with quiet malice:

"He said the first person to get ill would be a sissy. And now he's got ill himself. . . .".

Ivan Prokofievich frowned scornfully at Varyusha.

"Shameless girl! Who got ill first? Was it me?"

"Who then?"

"The sissy happened to be Varyusha Pyzhova. . . ."

Pyzhov made a plaintive face and began singing to a tune from *Prince Igor*: "Oh, Daddy, oh, Mummy!"

Varyusha looked at him in surprise.

"When? When? When did I sing like that?"

"What about the time when you had tummy-ache?"

Pyzhov clutched his stomach and wagged his head from side to side. Varyusha gave a shriek of laughter and threw herself on the sofa. Pyzhov smiled, content with his victory, picked up the bottle and appealed to me.

"Take this wretched boy away, will you? He's got a habit of drinking castor oil and is trying to make me do the same."

Seva even gasped at the unexpectedness of the blow; he opened his mouth, without finding anything to say. Pyzhov's face broke into a smile: "Aha!"

"Have a drink?" he said to me.

I was surprised.

"Are you ill? Or is it a joke? Why drink?"

"But why not! Just think: never been ill for eight years. It's as good as if you had just finished balancing the year's accounts. You can drink brandy and read books, you are in bed, everything's brought to you, people come and see you. It's a holiday! Have a glass?"

107

The grandmother toddled in from somewhere and busied herself round the patient.

"Whoever heard such a thing, ill in summer!" she fussed. "The summer sun for a beggar will run, but a winter's night a tsar can't light. Flu they call it. Why weren't there any such illnesses in our day? Autumn we might catch cold, and get fever and the rheumatics. We used to cure them all with vodka. My father never saw any other medicine. Down it goes and warms your toes, however you feel it'll make you reel."

Seva and Varyusha were now sitting together on the sofa, watching their cheerful grandmother with quizzical good humour. Beautiful Fenya, the niece, came in from the kitchen. Putting her hands behind her back, she shook her fair head and smiled with her clear grey eyes.

"Is this medicine good for healthy people as well?"

The gold-gleaming glasses in our hands were raised to her in silent assent. Ivan Prokofievich cocked his head to one side.

"Fenya, you clever thing, say something else as witty as that!"

Fenya blushed, tried to keep the smile on her face, but did not manage it and had to retire to the kitchen. The spectators on the sofa shouted and waved their arms.

When they had vented their triumph, Seva said to me excitedly:

"Today he's beating everyone because he's ill. But when he's well—oh no, then no one will let him off!"

Seva cut short his smile and showed his teeth at his father, interested to see what effect he had produced.

His father screwed up one eye and scratched his neck.

"Go on! What do you think of that, now? He calls this letting a sick man off. Of course I'm sick or I'd have caught him by the leg...."

In this cheerful family there was, nevertheless, the strictest discipline. The Pyzhovs had mastered the rare

108

art of making discipline both a pleasant and joyful affair, without taking its responsibilities any less seriously. In the lively faces of the children I always read both keen readiness for action and sharp awareness of their surroundings, without which no discipline is possible.

What especially attracted me was the financial organization of the Pyzhov family. It seemed to be a perfect system, long tested by experience and embellished with old and familiar traditions.

Ivan Prokofievich declined the honour of being the originator of this system.

"I didn't invent anything!" he would say. "A family is an economic unit, of course. Money is received and spent, I didn't invent that. And once there's money, there must be order. You can only spend money in a disorderly fashion if you've stolen it. But once there is debit and credit, there must be order. What is there to invent! And besides, think of the children. When are you going to teach them? Now is just the time for that."

What surprised me most was that Ivan Prokofievich did not keep any accounts at home. He never noted anything down and did not teach his children to do so. According to him, this was unnecessary in the family.

"Accounts are needed for control. But there are seven of us, and we are control enough for ourselves. But once you start making them note things down, they'll grow up bureaucrats—that's also a danger. We accountants, you know, give the world more bureaucrats than anyone else. It's the work that does it!"

The merry eye of Ivan Prokofievich could discern all the details of his family's financial operations without resorting to accounts.

He used to distribute pocket-money at the week-end in quite a ceremonial fashion. After dinner that evening nobody would leave the table. Fenya would clear the plates away and sit down next to Ivan Prokofievich. He would lay out his wallet on the table and ask: "Well, Seva, did you have enough money for the week?"

Seva holds in both hands a grimy purse made of paper. The purse contains a large number of compartments and, when turned inside out, looks like a series of dippers on an excavator. Seva shakes these dippers over the table and they let fall one twenty-kopek piece and one five-kopek piece.

"There you are, even some left," says Seva, "twenty-five kopeks."

Varyusha keeps her purse, which is just as cunningly constructed as Seva's, in a sweet-tin. Hers is clean and spotless. Its suspicious fullness attracts an ironic glance from Seva.

"Varyusha's been hoarding money again."

"Hoarding again?" Ivan Prokofievich's eyes widen. "Terrible! What will be the end of it? How much money have you got?"

"Money?" Varyusha seriously examines the interior of her purse. "Here's a ruble, here's another one ... and this is another."

She looks innocently at Ivan Prokofievich and lays out beside the purse some change and two new rubles.

"Oo-o-oh," Seva sits up in his chair.

Their elders watch the accounting with friendly sympathy, do not take out their purses and do not show their money.

"Varyusha's saving up for going to the seaside," smiles Pavlusha.

"Not for the seaside, for something else! For a tea-set and a little table and a lamp for the doll."

"Very good, very good," says Ivan Prokofievich.

I always used to wonder that Ivan Prokofievich never asked his children how they had spent their money or what they were going to spend it on. Then I realized there was no need to ask because there were no secrets in this family.

Ivan Prokofievich takes the silver out of his wallet and gives it to the youngsters.

"Here's a ruble for you, and a ruble for you. If you lose it, I'm not responsible. Check your money before leaving the counter."

Seva and Varyusha check the money carefully. Varyusha moves the ten-kopek pieces backwards and forwards, her eyes twinkle slyly at Ivan Prokofievich and she laughs.

"Come on, give me one more!"

"Surely not. There are ten there."

"Look: one, two, three...."

But Ivan Prokofievich draws the money towards him and starts counting very quickly.

"One, two, three, four, five, seven, eight, nine, ten. Well?"

Confused, Varyusha climbs higher on her chair and again begins pushing the money about with one finger. But Seva gives a roar of laughter.

"Ah! But how did he count it. He didn't count it right. Five, then seven, but what about six?"

"Well, let's see you check it," Ivan Prokofievich says seriously.

Putting their heads together, everyone begins counting the coins again. It turns out that there really are ten of them. Ivan Prokofievich's massive frame shakes with laughter. Only Fenya covers her mouth with her hand, her eyes shining at her uncle: she has seen him slip out an extra ten-kopek piece from under his wallet.

The youngsters begin to put the money away in their complicated purses.

The elder children's turn has come. Pavlusha receives three rubles every six days, Fenya five rubles.

"Is that enough?" asks Ivan Prokofievich as he gives them the money.

They nod: yes, it's enough.

"Make it do. We're not expecting any change in salaries till the first of January. If they put wages up, then we'll see, won't we?"

Not only Ivan Prokofievich but Fenya and Pavlusha are also expecting a rise. Pavlusha is studying at the factory training school, Fenya is at a technical school. They contribute all of their grants to the family funds; that is an unbreakable rule, the rightness of which no one doubts. After the paying-out Ivan Prokofievich sometimes says in the family council: "Income: my wages 475, Pavlusha's 40, Fenya's 65, total 580. Now then: Mother for the housekeeping 270, your pocket-money 50, right? That makes 320 and 260 left over. Well?"

"I know what they're after," comes Grandma's wheezy voice from the corner, "a radio, that's what they're after, some kind of four-valve or other. Last month they wouldn't stop talking about it. Two hundred rubles, they say. As if it were the last thing on earth!"

"Of course," laughs Pavlusha. "A radio, that's culture for you, isn't it?"

"I don't call that culture—paying money for a lot of shouting and whistling! If you know what's good for you, you'll buy yourself a good pair of shoes and look a picture. That's culture too. And what about Fenya's shoes?"

"I'll wait," says Fenya, "let's buy a radio."

"There's enough for shoes as well," puts in Ivan Prokofievich.

"That's it," shouts Seva, "a radio and shoes, see, Granny? There's a real picture for you."

Such budget conversations do not take place often at the Pyzhovs'. Similar problems are dealt with as they arise and are solved almost without anyone noticing it. Ivan Prokofievich considers general discussion the best way.

"One says one thing, the other another, somebody is bound to get it right! They understand everything, these accountant's children."

A good quality of the Pyzhovs' was that they did not hesitate to express even the most distant desires and dreams, which were quite beyond realization at the time. The four-valve receiver was the first thing to appear in this form. A sledge for Seva and other purchases were suggested in the same way. About more prosaic things there was no need to dream. One day, when she came in from the technical school, Fenya simply said to Pavlusha:

"These are my last stockings. I've darned them and darned them, but they won't go any further. I must have some new ones, you know."

And in the evening she spoke to Ivan Prokofievich just as simply.

"Give me some money for stockings."

"Can you wait till pay-day?"

"No."

"Here you are."

Stockings did not come out of pocket-money. Such funds were for buying soap, tooth-paste and other toilet goods, for the cinema, sweets, ice-cream, and for pens, note-books and pencils.

I always rejoiced at this cheerful family with its strict rules about money. Here money smelt neither of an affable God nor of a cunning devil. It was simply one of the normal conveniences of life, requiring no moral strain. The Pyzhovs looked upon money as a useful everyday accessory. That was why their money was not left lying about in drawers nor hoarded up with miserly fear and trembling. Ivan Prokofievich looked after it with simple and convincing seriousness, like any other necessary object.

Chapter Five

*J*N FAIRY-TALES and legends, in wonderful ballads and poems the tale is often told of happy kings and queens to whom God sent an only son or an only daughter. These princes and princesses, tsareviches and tsarevnas, always bring with them enchanting beauty and happiness. In these stories even the most hazardous adventures, involving the intervention of evil spirits, foretold by some evil fairy, only take place in order to emphasize the inevitable success of the hero. Even death—seemingly a figure of the blackest gloom and complete invincibility—even he is balked on encountering such a prince, who can always be sure of the help of kind magicians and obliging suppliers of life-giving elixirs and death potions, and no less kind and obliging composers of opera and ballet librettos.

For readers and audiences these lucky heroes possess a kind of optimistic charm. What is this charm? Neither action, nor brain, nor talent, nor even cunning, account for it. It is predetermined in the very theme itself: the prince is the king's only son. This theme requires no other logic than the logic of luck and youth. The prince has always been destined to enjoy greatness, wealth, splendour, beauty and universal love. Before him lie both the irrefutable certainty of the future and the right to happiness, a right unchallenged by any rivals or obstacles.

The radiant theme of the prince is not at all as immaterial as it may seem at first, and not at all remote from our life. Such princes are not merely the fruit of the imagination. Many parents among readers and audiences possess at home in their modest families just such princes and princesses, just such fortunate sole pretenders to success, and believe just as implicitly that they were born especially to enjoy such success.

A Soviet family should never be anything but a collective body. In losing its character as a collective, the family loses much of its significance as an organization of education and happiness. There are various ways of losing the character of a collective. One of the most wide-spread is the so-called "only-child system."

Even in the best and most fortunate cases, even in the hands of talented and attentive parents, the upbringing of an only child presents an extremely difficult task.

Pyotr Alexandrovich Ketov works in one of the central departments of the People's Commissariat of Agriculture. Fate has endowed him with a happy lot, and this was by no means an act of favour. Pyotr Alexandrovich is a powerful man, he could do much for fate itself, if fate fell into his hands.

Pyotr Alexandrovich has a good brain; he is a great master of analysis, but he never flounders or wallows in it. He always keeps the future in mind. Gazing into its splendid vistas, he can at the same time always rejoice, laugh and dream like a boy, maintain his freshness, the calm alertness in his clever eyes and his thoughtful, convincing way of speaking. He sees many people and has a flair for understanding everyone he meets. When mixing with the world he uses the same precise analysis, makes way for some people, gladly accompanies others, marches sternly forward beside a third, a fourth he takes firmly by the collar and demands explanations.

His home attracts one by its wholesome and orderly comfort, several rows of well-thumbed books, the clean, slightly worn carpet on the floor, the bust of Beethoven on the piano.

And Pyotr Alexandrovich has arranged his family life reasonably and happily. In the days of his youth, with a warm perceptive eye, he appraised the charms of beautiful women, subjected them to his accurate, cheerful analysis and chose Nina Vasilyevna, a girl with grey eyes and a quiet, slightly disdainful soul. He gave conscious leave to his feelings and fell in love deeply and lastingly, adorning his love with friendship and the subtle, gallant superiority of a man. Nina Vasilyevna with the same sweet disdainfulness acknowledged this superiority and trustingly fell in love with Pyotr Alexandrovich's courageous strength and his cheerful wisdom.

When Victor was born Pyotr Alexandrovich said to his wife: "Thank you. He is still only raw material, but we will make a great citizen out of him."

And with a happy affectionate smile Nina Vasilyevna replied: "How could your son be anything else, dear?"

But Pyotr Alexandrovich was not inclined to exaggerate the virtues of his ancestors and the guarantee of heredity; he believed devoutly in the power of education. He was convinced that, as a whole, people were brought up carelessly, that people did not know how to undertake the work of education in a proper fashion: deeply, logically and persistently. Ahead of him he visualized great parental creative work.

Victor was two years old when Nina Vasilyevna asked affectionately: "Well, your citizen is already walking and talking. Are you pleased with your son?"

Pyotr Alexandrovich did not deny himself the pleasure of admiring Victor occasionally—Victor was a big rosy happy boy—and he replied: "I am very pleased with my son. You have reared him splendidly. We may consider the first stage of our work completed. And now we shall start on you!"

He drew Victor towards him, placed him between his knees and once more threatened him with paternal affection: "We shall, shan't we!"

"We s'all," said Victor, "and how will you 'tart?"

Victor breathed the happiness and peace of a secure and cloudless life. Everything about this future citizen was so healthy and pure, he had such a serene, clear glance, such a promising forehead like his father's, and his mother's light disdain in his grey eyes, that his parents could afford to be proud and to expect a wonderful future for him.

Nina Vasilyevna could see a great success ripening every day before her eyes: her son was becoming more and more handsome, affectionate and charming, his speech developed quickly and elegantly, he walked and ran with confident childish grace, his jokes, laughter and questions could win anyone's heart. This boy was such a real, living delight to her that even the future citizen faded into the background a little.

The present was so wonderful for Nina Vasilyevna that she did not want to think of the future. She just wanted to live side by side with the life she had created, admiring it and taking pride in her great maternal success. She would meet many strange children and examine them carefully, and it was pleasant for her to feel a rare human freedom: she was envious of nobody.

And suddenly she had a great desire to create yet another, equally wonderful young life. She imagined side by side with Victor a little girl, with fair hair, a clever forehead and laughing grey eyes, a girl whom she would call... Lida. She would bear a striking resemblance to Victor and at the same time possess something of her own, something that had never before existed in the world, something so difficult to imagine because there had never been anything like it before; and that something could only be created by the motherly happiness of Nina Vasilyevna.

"Pyotr! I want a girl."

"What girl?" Pyotr Alexandrovich was surprised.

"I want to have a daughter."

"You mean you have the urge to bear another child?"

"No, I want to see her grow. A daughter, you understand? My future daughter."

"But, Nina, how do you know that it is certain to be a daughter? Suppose it's a son?"

Nina Vasilyevna thought for a brief moment. A second son? But that would certainly be no less wonderful than a daughter. And anyhow . . . she might have a third child, a daughter. What a charming company!

She overwhelmed her husband in a flood of joy and shy womanish emotion.

"Listen, Pyotr, what a bureaucrat you are, it's terrible! A son like Victor, you understand? And at the same time not quite like him, different, you see . . . dear to you . . . special! And a daughter can come later! What a family it will be! Just think, what a family!"

Pyotr Alexandrovich kissed his wife's hand and smiled with that same superiority which had been allowed from the very start.

"Nina, this is a serious question, let's talk it over."

"All right, let's then."

Nina Vasilyevna was sure that the picture of a beautiful family, so clear in her own imagination, would tempt him too, and that he would abandon his cold air of superiority. But when she began to speak she felt that instead of something alive and splendid she could produce nothing but a string of ordinary words, exclamations, helpless waves of the hand, nothing but pale woman's chatter. Her husband looked at her with affectionate condescension, and with almost a moan she fell silent.

"Nina, one cannot give rein to such a primitive instinct!"

"What instinct? I'm talking to you about people, about future people...."

"It seems so to you, but it is really instinct...."

"Pyotr!"

"Wait, darling, wait! There's nothing to be ashamed of in it. It's a fine instinct, I understand you, I feel the same. The beautiful family you speak of could attract me, but there is an aim even more noble, even more beautiful. Listen."

Docilely she placed her head on his shoulder, and he stroked her hand and talked, looking at the glass door of the bookcase as if behind its shiny transparence he really could perceive the noble vistas of which he spoke.

He talked of how in a big family it was possible to bring up only an average personality; the mass of ordinary people were brought up thus, and that was why one so rarely came across great human personalities, fortunate exceptions in the grey, colourless crowd. He was convinced that the average type of man could be far higher. But it was only possible to educate a great man if one devoted to him all the love, all the reasoning power, all the ability of a father and mother. One must cast aside the usual gregarious idea of a family as a mere herd of children to be provided with irregular care and the prime necessities of feeding, clothing and some kind of education. No, what was needed was profound work on your son, the filigree work of education. Such work could not be spread over many children. One must answer for the quality. And quality was possible only if one's creative powers were concentrated.

"Imagine it, Nina, we shall produce only one man, but he won't be a standard type, he'll be really brilliant, an ornament to life...."

With eyes closed Nina Vasilyevna listened to her husband, felt the slight movement of his shoulder when he raised his arm, saw the tip of his soft tender moustache, and the picture of the beautiful company of children faded away in a mist, and in its stead rose a picture of a brilliant youth, courageous, wonderful, finely educated, a great public figure and a great man of the future. This image was somehow fleshless and bloodless, like the image in a remote fairy-tale, like a drawing on a cinema screen. Her dreams of yesterday had been more alive and lovable, but her husband's fairy-tale and his voice and the train of his thought, the strength and boldness of which were still new to her, and a woman's age-long habit of believing in male strength—all this made so consistent a whole that Nina Vasilyevna did not want to resist. With deeply hidden sadness she bade farewell to her motherly dream.

"All right, my dear, all right. You see further. Let it be as you think. But... this means... we shall never have any more children?"

"Nina! There must not be. Never."

From that day a change came over Nina Vasilyevna's life. Everything round her grew more serious, life itself became more intelligent and responsible, as if only now she had at last put aside her dolls and for ever parted with her virgin placidity. Strange though it may seem, having renounced the creative task of a mother, only now did she feel all the weight of a mother's toil.

And now Victor would give her a different kind of joy. Even before, he had been the apple of her eye and she could not bear the thought of losing him, but formerly his living charm created all the charm of life, as if his being provided some wonderful life-giving rays. Now there was only he, just as dear and beautiful as before, but apart from him there seemed to be nothing, no dream, no life. This made Victor even dearer and more attractive, but, beside love, alarm entered and took possession of her soul. At first Nina Vasilyevna did not even try to think what kind of alarm this was or whether it was reasonable and necessary. It was simply that whenever she happened to look into her son's face, she would discover there, now a suspicious paleness, now a flabbiness, now dullness in his eyes. She jealously watched his moods, his appetite, and in every trifle she began to imagine the precursors of disaster.

At first the sensation was sharp. Then it passed. Victor grew up and developed, and her fear changed. It no longer awakened suddenly, chilling her heart and making her feel faint. It turned into a fear that was a habitual part of her everyday life.

Pyotr Alexandrovich did not notice anything wrong in the life of his wife. Her sweet disdainfulness vanished, the calm soft lines of her face were transformed into a severely beautiful framework, her grey eyes lost their liquid sparkle and became more clear and limpid. He thought of this and arrived at an explanation: life goes on and youth fades and with it fade beauty and tenderness of line. But everything is wonderful, life has fresh riches in store, who knows, perhaps more perfect than the riches of youth. He noticed the awakening of new anxiety in his wife, but concluded that this, too, was a blessing—perhaps anxiety is the real substance of a mother's happiness.

As for himself, he felt no trace of fear. He divided his time strictly between his work and his son; in both departments much real human effort was expended. Every day Victor revealed new brilliant possibilities. Pyotr Alexandrovich felt as if he were discovering a new country overflowing with natural gifts and unexpected beauty. He would show his wife all this abundance, and she would agree with him.

"Look how much we are doing with the boy," he would say to her.

And his wife would smile at him, and in her severe limpid eyes he could see a smile of joy, all the more beautiful because of the rarity with which it appeared.

Victor made rapid progress. At five he spoke Russian and German correctly, at ten he made the acquaintance of the classics, at twelve he was reading Schiller in the original and was carried away by him. Pyotr Alexandrovich strode along beside his son and was himself amazed at his rapid pace. His son dazzled him by the tireless brilliance of his mental energy, the profound depth of his talents and the ease with which he mastered the most difficult and most subtle turns of thought and combinations of words.

The further Victor developed the more definite his character became. His eyes quickly lost the sparkle of youthful spontaneity; more and more often they expressed reasoned restraint and appreciation. Pyotr Alexandrovich joyfully observed in this traces of his own great talent for analysis. Victor never misbehaved, was affectionate and accommodating with people, but in the movements of his mouth there soon appeared a knowing sneer "just to himself," something akin to his mother's smile in her youth, but colder and more detached.

This knowing sneer was not only for the world at large but for his parents as well. Their painstaking self-sacrificing work, their parental joy and triumph were fully appreciated by Victor for what they were. He well knew that his parents were preparing an exceptional career for him and he felt capable of being exceptional. He saw and understood his mother's fear on his account, saw how wretchedly unfounded it was, and smiled the same comprehending smile. The sole object of his parents' love, care and faith, Victor could not be mistaken: he was the centre of the family, its sole principle, its religion. With the same early awakened power of analysis, with the already cultivated reason of an adult, he acknowledged the logic of events: his parents revolved around him like helpless satellites. This developed into a convenient habit and an agreeable aesthetic. It afforded the parents pleasure; the son with delicate restraint was prepared not to oppose them.

At school he made excellent progress and outpaced everybody. His comrades were weaker than he not only in ability, but in their attitude to life. They were ordinary children, talkative, easily excited, finding joy in primitive games, in mock battles on the playground. Victor passed through school with ease, wasted no energy on minor encounters and did not dissipate his strength in chance enthusiasms.

The Ketovs' family life proceeded happily. Nina Vasilyevna acknowledged the truth of her husband's judgement: their son was growing up to be a wonderful man. She did not regret her former dreams. That deep tenderness which had once painted in her imagination a picture of a large happy family had now turned into concern for Victor. Blinded by her concern, she did not perceive the beginnings of her son's cold restraint, which she took for a sign of strength. She did not notice that in their family warmth of feeling had been ousted by ordered rationalization and wordiness. Neither she nor her husband could see that an opposite process had begun: the son was beginning to form the personalities of the parents. He did this unconsciously, without theory or aim, guided by his current everyday desires.

At the suggestion of his teachers, Victor "skipped" the ninth class and proceeded triumphantly to the university. His parents held their breath and craned forward to see the victorious finish. At this time Nina Vasilyevna began to serve her son like a slave-woman. The regrouping of forces in the Ketov family was now completed with amazing speed, and the filigree work of educating the son stopped by itself, without further ado. The father still permitted himself sometimes to talk about various problems with his son, but he lacked his former confident superiority; besides he was not confronted by a person who needed education.

Victor automatically ceased to be a member of the Komsomol. Pyotr Alexandrovich learned of this in a chance conversation and permitted himself to be surprised.

"Have you left the Komsomol? I don't understand, Victor...."

Victor looked past his father and on his slightly puffy face the smile, which he always wore now, like a uniform, did not change—a smile expressing polite animation and indifference.

"I did not leave, I just automatically ceased to be a member," he said quietly, "quite a normal operation."

"But you are not in the Komsomol now?"

"That is an extraordinarily correct conclusion, Father. If you automatically cease to be a member, you are no longer in the Komsomol."

"But why?"

"You know what, Dad? I realize you may be horrified at this important event. For your generation it was all very important...."

"And isn't it for yours?"

"We go our own way."

Still smiling, Victor began thinking of something else and seemed to forget about his father. Pyotr Alexandrovich coughed and began to turn over the pages of an office file lying before him. As he did so he examined his feelings and discovered nei'her panic nor extreme surprise. He thought for a second of the office, of his assistant's son who had never joined the Komsomol, then a similar thought occurred to him about dialectics. Every new generation differs from its predecessor. Quite possibly the Komsomol did not satisfy Victor, especially if one took into account the fact that just now, he was showing remarkable ability for mathematics.

At seventeen, by special request, Victor was admitted to the mathematical faculty and soon began to astound the professors by his erudition, his brilliance and his powerful thrusts into the very depths of mathematical science. Almost without noticing it, Pyotr Alexandrovich gave up his study to him, which was then transformed into a sacred altar visited by a higher being, Victor Ketov—the future luminary of mathematics, the representative of a new generation which would undoubtedly effect lightning advances in the history of humanity. In secret meditation Pyotr Alexandrovich foresaw that the deeds and progress of this generation would indeed be astounding; he and others like him had done well to clear the path for it, and he in particular by his wise decision about the concentration of quality had determined the path of such a genius as Victor. New paternal pride awakened in the soul of Pyotr Alexandrovich, but his outward conduct was somewhat marred by signs of dependence. He began to pronounce the word "Victor" in almost mystic tones of respect. Now when he returns from work he no longer throws cheerful glances around him, no longer jokes and smiles. He nods silently to his wife and looking at the closed door of his son's room asks in a whisper:

"Is Victor at home?"

"He's studying," answers Nina Vasilyevna quietly.

Pyotr Alexandrovich has learned somewhere to walk on tiptoe. Balancing with his arms he softly approaches the door and pushes it cautiously ajar.

"May I come in?" he asks, poking only his head into the room.

He leaves his son, feeling elevated and triumphant, and says in hushed tones: "Victor's doing well. Excellently. They have already put him down to prepare for a professorship."

Nina Vasilyevna smiles submissively.

"How interesting! But I'm worried, you know. He seems a little too fat. He works so much, I am afraid for his heart."

Pyotr Alexandrovich looks frightenedly at his wife.

"Do you think it's a disease?"

"I don't know, I'm simply afraid. . . ."

This is the beginning of new worries and new fear. For several days the parents examine their son's face and experience mixed feelings of delight, devotion and alarm. Then come fresh raptures and fresh misgivings; they fill life, overflow its shores like the waves at high tide, and hide from view the trivial events of life. Hidden is the fact that their son has long ago ceased to be affectionate, that he never uses words of welcome, that he has two new suits while his father has only one worn outfit, that his mother prepares his bath for him and clears up after him and her son never says "thank you" to her. Hidden is the approaching old age of the parents and the really alarming signs of serious illness.

Victor did not attend the funeral of a fellow-student and sat at home reading a book. Pyotr Alexandrovich noticed this with surprise.

"Weren't you at the funeral?"

"No, I wasn't," replied Victor without taking his eyes from the book.

Pyotr Alexandrovich looked sharply at his son and even shook his head—he felt so cold and ill at ease. But this impression, too, passed off and was forgotten as a bad day is forgotten among the palmy days of summer.

The parents also missed the startling appearance of a new theme: however brilliantly Victor studied he did not deny himself pleasures. He often went out, and sometimes he returned smelling of wine and woman's scent; memories hovered in his constant smile, but never did he breathe a word to his father and mother about this new side of his life.

By the time his son was entering his fourth year Pyotr Alexandrovich contracted a stomach ulcer. He grew pale and lost weight. The doctors demanded a surgical operation and assured him that it would effect a complete cure, but Nina Vasilyevna fainted at the mere idea of a piece being cut out of her husband's stomach. Victor as usual lived his own remote life and kept to his room or left the house altogether.

No decision could be reached over the operation. An old friend of Pyotr Alexandrovich, a well-known surgeon, sat in the armchair beside the sick man and lost his temper. Nina Vasilyevna did not know where to turn in the midst of this misfortune.

Victor came in dressed up to the nines and smelling of scent. Without changing his smile or his expression in any way he shook the surgeon's hand and said: "Still at the couch of the invalid? What news?"

Pyotr Alexandrovich looked up at his son delightedly.

"We are thinking of an operation. He keeps on trying to persuade me. . . ."

With his usual smile Victor interrupted his father.

"Dad, you don't happen to have five rubles? I've a ticket for *The Sleeping Beauty*. . . . Just in case. I'm bankrupt."

"All right," responded Pyotr Alexandrovich. "You have some, haven't you, Nina? He keeps on saying it ought to be done, but Nina's afraid. And I don't know what to do myself. . . ."

"What is there to be afraid of? Have you found it?" said Victor, taking the five rubles from his mother. "A bit awkward, you know, being without money in the theatre. . . ."

"Who are you going with?" asked Pyotr Alexandrovich, forgetting about his ulcer.

"Oh, someone," replied his son evasively, also forgetting about his father's ulcer. "I'll take the key, Mother. I may be late."

Bowing attentively to the surgeon and smiling his usual smile he departed.

And his parents looked as if nothing out of the ordinary had happened.

A few days later Pyotr Alexandrovich had a severe attack. His surgeon friend found him in bed and raised an uproar.

"What are you? Cultured people or savages?"

He rolled up his sleeves, looked, listened, coughed and cursed. Nina Vasilyevna ran to the chemist's and ordered some medicine. When she came back she was pale with fear.

"Well, how is he?" she kept asking. And all the time she kept looking at the clock, waiting for the hand to show eight—at eight the medicine would be ready. Now and then she would rush out to bring ice from the kitchen.

Victor appeared from his room, making for the front door. His mother ran into him as she came from the kitchen, and began in a tired, trembling voice: "Vitya, perhaps you would call at the chemist's. The medicine is ready now and ... it's paid for. He must have it."

Turning his dishevelled head on the pillow, Pyotr Alexandrovich looked at his son and forced a smile. It was pleasant to look at one's grown-up talented son even when one had a stomach ulcer. Victor looked at his mother and also smiled: "No, I can't. I'm in a hurry. I'll take the key."

The surgeon jumped up and rushed towards them. It was not clear what he was going to do, but his face was pale. However, he just said very warmly and simply:

"Why give him the bother? Surely I can fetch the medicine. It's such a trifle!"

He snatched the prescription out of Nina Vasilyevna's hand. At the door Victor was waiting for him.

"You are probably going in the other direction, aren't you?" he said. "I'm heading for the centre."

"Of course," answered the doctor dashing downstairs.

When he returned with the medicine, Pyotr Alexandrovich still lay in the same position, his dishevelled head on the pillow, his bright feverish eyes staring at the door of Victor's room. He forgot to thank his friend and in general did not say much all the evening. And only when his friend was leaving did he say decisively: "Do the operation.... I don't care."

Nina Vasilyevna dropped into the armchair: in her life it had become so hard to distinguish where joy ended and sorrow began. Joy and sorrow seemed suddenly and unexpectedly alike.

Incidentally the operation was successful.

I have told just one of the sad stories about an only son-tsarevich. There are many such stories. Parents with only children need not be up in arms against me, for I have no desire to frighten them. I am only recounting what I have myself seen happen.

One does come across fortunate cases in such families. Some parents do possess supernormal sensibility, which enables them to create the right family spirit and to organize comradeship for their son, which to a certain extent can make up for the lack of brothers and sisters. Very often in our country I have come across fine characters among the only children of unmarried mothers or widowed fathers. In this case the great loss or the undoubted hardship of loneliness provide a great stimulus to the children's love and care for their parents, and put a brake on the development of egoism. But these cases arise in an atmosphere of grief, they are unhealthy in themselves and by no means solve the problem of the only child. The concentration of parental love on one child is a terrible error.

Millions of examples—yes, millions—can be brought forward to confirm the huge successes of children from big families. And on the contrary, the successes of only children are extremely rare. As far as I have been concerned personally, my encounters with the most unbridled egoism, which destroys not only parental happiness but also the successes of the children themselves, have almost always been with only sons and daughters.

In the bourgeois family the only child does not present such a social danger as in ours, because the very character of society does not contradict the qualities cultivated in single offspring. Cold harshness of character, covered by a formal politeness, weak emotions of sympathy, the habit of individual egoism, deliberate careerism and moral evasiveness, indifference to humanity as a whole—all this is natural in a bourgeois society, while it is pathological and harmful in Soviet society.

In the Soviet family an only child becomes a centre of attention which he should not become. Even if they want to, the parents cannot rid themselves of harmful centripetal servility. In such cases only unnaturally weak parental "love" can in some degree lessen the danger. But if this love is only of normal capacity the situation is already dangerous: on this one child rest all the prospects of the parents' happiness, to lose him is to lose everything.

In a large family the death of a child causes deep grief, but it is never a catastrophe, since the remaining children still demand both care and love as before. They, as it were, insure the family collective from ruin. And, of course, there is nothing sadder than the spectacle of a father and mother left completely alone in empty rooms, which remind them at every step of their lost child. Thus the fact that the child is the only one leads to a concentration of worry, blind love, fear and panic.

And at the same time in such a family there is nothing that can naturally counterbalance this. There are no brothers and sisters—older or younger—and so there is no experience of being considerate, no experience of play, love and help, no imitation, no respect, finally, there is no experience of sharing, no common joy and common effort —there is simply nothing, not even ordinary companionship.

In very rare cases the school collective manages to restore natural brakes on the development of individualism. For the school collective this is a very difficult task, since family traditions continue to work in the former direction. This problem falls more within the scope of a closed children's institution such as the Dzerzhinsky Commune, and usually the Commune managed the task very easily. But, naturally, it is better to provide such brakes in the family itself.

The danger of bringing up an only child in a Soviet family really amounts to the fact that the family loses the qualities of a collective body. Under the "only-child" system, loss of collectivity comes about as a matter of course: the family simply does not possess enough physical elements to make up a collective; both in quantity and variety of type, father, mother and son are likely to form such a slender structure that it collapses at the first sign of disproportion, and such disproportion always arises out of the central position of the child.

A family collective can be subject to other blows of a similar "mechanical" nature. The death of one of the parents may be advanced as the most likely example of such a "mechanical" blow. In the overwhelming majority of cases even such a terrible blow does not lead to catastrophe and the breaking-up of the collective; usually the remaining members of the family are able to maintain its wholeness. However, the blows which we conditionally call "mechanical" are not the most destructive.

It is much harder for the family collective to endure the destructive influences connected with lengthy processes of decomposition. These processes may, equally conditionally, be called "chemical" processes. I have already pointed out that the "mechanical" loss of collectivity, caused by having an only child, must lead to failure because of the very fact that it is bound to call forth a "chemical" reaction in the form of the hypertrophy of parental love. "Chemical" reactions in the family are the most terrible. One could name several forms of such reaction, but I want to deal particularly with one, the worst and most harmful of all.

Russian and foreign writers have seen deep into the dark recesses of human psychology. As everyone knows, literature has elaborated the theme of the criminal character or the generally unsound character better than that of the normal, ordinary or positive, moral personality. We are familiar with the psychology of the murderer, the thief, the traitor, the swindler, the petty scoundrel in many literary forms. The most revolting backwaters of the human soul now present no mystery to us. All that was naturally decaying in the old society attracted the attention of such masters as Dostoyevsky, Maupassant, Saltykov, Zola, not to mention Shakespeare.

To do justice to the great masters of literature: they were never cruel towards their fallen heroes; these writers always spoke as representatives of historical humanism, which is undoubtedly one of the achievements and ornaments of mankind. Of all types of crime it would seem that treachery alone never earned the indulgence of literature, with the exception of Leonid Andreyev's *Judas Iscariot*, but even this defence is exceedingly weak and strained. In all other cases there was always to be found in the dark soul of the criminal or the petty scoundrel a bright corner, an oasis, thanks to which even the worst of men still remained a man.

Very often this corner was love for children, one's own or somebody else's. Children are an organic part of the humanitarian idea, children seem to mark a boundary below which a man cannot fall. The crime against children lies below this boundary of humanity, and love of children is some justification for the most wretched creature. The children's gingerbread in Marmeladov's pocket when he is run over in the street (Dostoyevsky's *Crime and Punishment*) is accepted by us as a plea for indulgence.

But there is also cause to complain of literature. There is a crime which it has not worked upon, and this crime happens to be the very one in which children are wronged. I cannot recall now a single work which portrays the psychology of a father or mother renouncing their parental responsibility towards little children and leaving them at the mercy of fate to fend for themselves. It is true, there is Dostoyevsky's old Karamazov, but his children were all provided for. One does meet in literature abandoned illegitimate children, but in such cases even the most humane writers saw a social problem rather than a parental problem. As a matter of fact they gave a correct picture of history. The landowner who left a peasant girl with a child certainly did not consider himself a father; for him not only this girl and her child, but all the millions of other peasants were "cattle" to whom he was not bound by any moral responsibility. He was not conscious of any paternal or conjugal relations simply because the "lower classes" were beyond the pale of any kind of relations. Leo Tolstoy's agitation for the transference of upper-class "morality" to cover the "lower classes" as well, proved fruitless because class society was organically incapable of such "enlightenment."

A father deserting his children (in some cases even without the means of livelihood) could also be treated by us as a mechanical phenomenon, and that would make us feel more optimistic about the position of a family which has suffered so great a loss. Once he has deserted them, he has deserted them, and you can do nothing about it— the figure of the father has disappeared from the family, the situation is clear: the family collective must exist without a father, trying as best it can to mobilize its forces for further struggle. If this were so, the family drama would in no way differ from the orphaning of a family as a result of the father's death.

However, in the overwhelming majority of cases the position of abandoned children is more complicated and more dangerous than that of orphans.

Until not long ago life for Yevgenia Alexeyevna was good. She still had lively and serene memories of the love that had rioted past in her youth. It had left its peaceful mark in the shape of a big task in life, a family, which gave her a wholesome feeling that her life was being lived honestly, wisely and beautifully, as it should be. What if spring had passed, let the same stern law of nature usher in the quiet warm summer. Ahead there was still plenty of warmth, sunshine and joy.

Yevgenia Alexeyevna shared the responsibility of the family with her husband, Zhukov. Not so long ago she and Zhukov had been in love. Between them there still remained tenderness, a warm feeling of comradely gratitude and friendly simplicity. Zhukov had a long face and a nose rather like a saddle. At every turn life offered a choice of shorter faces and more handsome noses, but they held no memories of love, no travelled paths of happiness, no future joys, and Yevgenia Alexeyevna was not tempted by the offer. Zhukov was a good, attentive husband, a loving father and a gentleman.

Suddenly and ruthlessly her life was ruined. One evening Zhukov did not return from work, and in the morning Yevgenia Alexeyevna received a short note.

"Yevgenia! I don't want to deceive you any longer. You will understand—I want to be honest to the last. I love Anna Nikolayevna and am now living with her. I will send two hundred rubles a month for the children. Forgive me. Thanks for everything. N."

When she read the note Yevgenia Alexeyevna realized only that something terrible had happened, but what it was she could not imagine. She read the note a second time, then a third. Gradually every line revealed its secret, and every secret was so unlike the written line.

Yevgenia Alexeyevna looked about her helplessly, pressed her fingers to her temples and again returned to the note, as if it contained something she had not yet read. And then she did indeed notice something new: "I want to be honest to the last." A faint shadow of hope gleamed for a moment, and then again, with the same fear, she sensed the catastrophe which had taken place.

And at once her mind was invaded by a host of petty unbidden thoughts: two hundred rubles, the expensive flat, the faces of friends, books, men's suits. Yevgenia Alexeyevna shook her head, frowned and suddenly saw the most terrible, the most real disgrace: she was a deserted wife! Surely it could not be?! But what of the children?! She looked round in horror: everything was there as usual, in the bedroom five-year-old Olya was rustling something, a faint knocking came from the adjoining flat. Yevgenia Alexeyevna suddenly had an unbearable sensation—it was as though somebody had carelessly wrapped her up with Igor and Olya in an old newspaper and thrown them away into the dust-bin.

Some days passed like a dream. They were interspersed with moments of sober reason when Yevgenia Alexeyevna would sit in the chair at the writing-table, support her head on clenched fists, placed one on top of the other, and think. At first her thoughts would run in an orderly fashion—the pain and the grief and the difficulties ahead and a few remnants of love for Zhukov arrayed themselves meekly before her as if wanting her to examine them attentively and unravel everything.

But, without her noticing it, one fist opens, and now her hand is already covering her eyes and tears are trickling down, and there is no longer any order to her thoughts, only shivers of anguish and an unbearable feeling of loneliness.

Her children went on living, playing and laughing around her. Yevgenia Alexeyevna would glance at them in fright, quickly pull herself together, smile and say something sensible. Only the expression of fear in her eyes she could not hide from them, and the children were already beginning to look at her with surprise. On the first day she felt stricken at heart when she remembered that she would have to explain Father's absence to her children, and she said the first thing that came into her head.

"Daddy has gone away and won't be back for some time. He's been sent on a job. Far away, very far away!"

But the words "some time" and "far away" did not mean much to five-year-old Olya. She would run to the door at every ring, then come back sadly to her mother.

"When will he be back?"

Immersed in this awful dream, Yevgenia Alexeyevna did not notice the beginnings of recovery: now, when she woke in the morning, she no longer experienced a feeling of horror, she began to think of something practical, decided upon a few things that must be sold, cried less frequently.

Eight days later Zhukov sent a strange woman with a curt note.

"Please give the bearer my linen and suits, and also my razor-set and the albums presented to me at work, and my winter coat and the bundles of letters lying in the centre drawer of the desk—at the back. N."

Yevgenia Alexeyevna took the three suits off their hangers and spread out several sheets of newspaper on the sofa to wrap them up. Then she remembered that he needed his underclothes, razor and letters, and paused to think. Beside her stood ten-year-old Igor, attentively watching his mother. Noticing her confusion he plucked up courage and cried: "Shall I wrap them up, Mummy? Shall I wrap them up?"

"Oh God!" Yevgenia Alexeyevna sat down on the sofa and nearly burst into tears, but noticing the silent figure of the strange woman said irritably: "What were you thinking of to come like this ... empty-handed! How do you expect me to pack all this up?"

The woman looked with understanding sympathy at the newspapers spread out on the sofa, and smiled.

"They told me you'd find something, a basket or suit-case...."

Igor jumped up and shouted: "A basket? Mummy, there is a basket! The basket ... you know where it is? Behind the cupboard! Behind the cupboard! Shall I bring it?"

"What basket?" Yevgenia Alexeyevna asked vaguely.

"It's behind the cupboard! You know, the cupboard in the hall! Shall I bring it?"

Yevgenia Alexeyevna looked into Igor's eyes. They expressed only a cheerful desire to bring the basket. Soothed by it, Yevgenia Alexeyevna smiled.

"How can you bring it, dear! You're no bigger than the basket yourself, my darling!"

Yevgenia Alexeyevna drew her son towards her and kissed his head But Igor was too full of the basket.

"It's light!" he shouted, trying to tear himself away. "It's light as anything, Mummy! You don't know how light it is!"

Attracted by the noise, Olya came in from the bedroom and stopped at the door, her Teddy-bear in her arms. Igor dashed into the hall, whence came a sound of scratching and creaking.

"Oh dear, oh dear!" said Yevgenia Alexeyevna, and turning to the woman: "Help me bring the basket in, please."

Together they carried the basket in and set it down in the middle of the room. Yevgenia Alexeyevna started packing the suits. She would have been ashamed if she had packed them badly, so she carefully arranged the folds and lapels of the jackets, smoothing out the trouser-pockets and the ties. Igor and Olya took a business-like interest in this operation and twisted their lips when their mother had difficulty in packing. Then Yevgenia Alexeyevna put the linen into the basket.

"How you've piled in the shirts," said Igor. "The suits will get all rumpled."

"Yes, that's so..." Yevgenia Alexeyevna assented. But suddenly she felt a flood of resentment.

"Oh drat the things! Let them iron them. What's it to do with me?"

Igor looked up at her in surprise. Angrily she threw the three packets of letters and the shaving-set into the basket. The red case opened and scattered the linen with razor blades wrapped in blue paper.

"Oh, look what you've done!" cried Igor discontentedly and began to gather up the blades.

"Don't poke your nose in where you're not wanted!" shouted Yevgenia Alexeyevna, pulling Igor's hand away and slamming down the lid of the basket. "Take it!" she told the woman.

"Any message?"

"What message?! What message! Go!"

The woman delicately refrained from further questions, hoisted the basket on her shoulder and went out, man-oeuvring it carefully through the door.

Yevgenia Alexeyevna looked after her dully, sat down on the sofa, leaned on the cushion and wept. The children stared at her in surprise. Igor wrinkled his nose and be-gan pushing his finger into a hole in the baize of the writ-ing-desk, which Zhukov had burnt with his cigarette a long time ago. Olya leaned against the door, frowning sternly, and threw her Teddy down on the floor. When her mother recovered, Olya went up to her and asked crossly:

"And why did she take the basket away? Why did she? Who was that lady?"

Olya endured her mother's silence just as sternly and again rumbled:

"Daddy's shirts and jackets were in there ... why did she take them away?"

Yevgenia Alexeyevna listened to her deep little voice and suddenly remembered that the children still did not know anything.

The dispatch of the suits was a suspicious event even for Olya. As for Igor, probably he knew everything al-ready, he could have been told by someone in the court-yard. Zhukov's disappearance had naturally made an im-pression on everybody.

Yevgenia Alexeyevna looked hard at Igor. In his pose and his strained expression of concentration on the hole there was something puzzling. Igor glanced at his mother, then lowered his eyes again towards the hole. Ignoring Olya, who was still waiting patiently for an answer, she took hold of Igor's hand. He came and stood docilely be-fore her.

"You know something?" asked Yevgenia Alexeyevna anxiously.

Igor blinked and smiled.

"Huh! I don't understand what you mean! What should I know?"

"Do you know about Father?"

Igor became serious.

"About Father?"

Looking out of the window he shook his head. Olya tugged at her mother's sleeve and her small angry voice emphasized Igor's silent evasiveness.

"What has she taken his shirts to him for? Tell me, Mummy!"

Yevgenia Alexeyevna stood up decisively and walked across the room.

Again she looked at them. Now they were glancing at each other, and Olya was already winking playfully at her brother, not expecting anything unpleasant in life and oblivious of the fact that they had been deserted by their father. Yevgenia Alexeyevna suddenly remembered Anna Nikolayevna, her rival, with her attractive youthful fulness clad in black silk, her short hair and the slightly insolent sparkle in her grey eyes. She pictured tall Zhukov beside this beauty: what did he feel for her except lust?

"When will Father come back?" asked Igor unexpectedly, in the same simple trusting voice he had spoken the day before.

Both he and Olya looked at their mother. Yevgenia Alexeyevna made up her mind.

"He won't come back any more. . . ."

Igor went pale and his face quivered. Olya listened to the silence, seeming not to understand, then asked: "But when will he come back, Mummy?"

Yevgenia Alexeyevna now spoke sternly and coldly.

"He will never come back! Never! You have no father No father at all, you understand?"

"So he's dead?" said Igor, turning a white stricken face towards his mother.

Olya looked at her brother and repeated like an echo: ". . . dead?"

Yevgenia Alexeyevna drew the children to her and spoke very tenderly and gently, which caused a flood of tears in her eyes; and in her voice tenderness mingled with grief.

"Father has left us, understand? Left us. He does not want to live with us any more. He is living with another woman now, and we shall live without him. We three shall live together: Igor and Olya and I, and no one else."

"He's got married then?" asked Igor, musing gloomily.

"Yes, he's married."

"And will you get married too?" Igor looked at his mother with the cold glance of a little boy who is honestly trying to understand the puzzling foibles of grown ups.

"I won't leave you, my darlings," sobbed Yevgenia Alexeyevna. "Don't be afraid. Everything will be all right."

She took a grip on herself.

"Go and play. Olya, there's your Teddy. . . ."

Olya swung silently to and fro against her mother's knees, pinching her upper lip in her fingers. Finally, pushing herself away, she wandered into the bedroom. At the door she knelt down beside her bear, picked him up by one leg and dragged him carelessly away to her corner by the bed. Throwing her Teddy into a heap of toys, Olya sat down on a little painted stool and thought. She understood that her mother was unhappy, that her mother wanted to cry, so she must not go to her again and ask the question which must nevertheless be answered at all costs.

"But when will he be back?"

Her first feeling had been one of resentment more than anything else.

She was hurt to think that her life, the life of a young, beautiful and cultured woman, and the life of her children, such good, clever children, the life of the whole family, all the meaning and joy of it, could be so easily dismissed in a few words as a mere trifle, deserving neither care, nor consideration, nor pity. Why? Because Zhukov liked variety in women?

But soon the feeling of resentment was overshadowed by need, although at first she still felt resentment more.

During the twelve years of the family's existence all household expenses had been the affair of Yevgenia Alexeyevna. Although she did not even know how much her husband earned, he had always put at her disposal a large enough sum. Yevgenia Alexeyevna had always felt that she and the children had a right to this money, that for Zhukov the family was not merely an amusement but also a duty. Now it turned out that this was not so: he had been paying Yevgenia Alexeyevna this money in return for her love, for sharing her bed. As soon as he had tired of her he had gone to share the bed of another woman, and the rights of Yevgenia Alexeyevna and her children were dismissed as empty words, a mere addition to the lover's bill. Now all the duty and responsibility rested on the mother alone, she must pay this debt with her life, youth and happiness.

The sop of two hundred rubles now seemed particularly insulting. In sleepless meditation at night Yevgenia Alexeyevna would blush when she remembered the words: "I will send two hundred rubles a month for the children." He had named his own price for his children. Only two hundred rubles! Not endless years of care and worry and fear, not the anxious feeling of responsibility, not love, not a living heart, not life, just a wad of notes in an envelope!

Every night Yevgenia Alexeyevna remembered how she had stifled her shame when she first accepted this money from the messenger, how she had meticulously signed the envelope as he requested, how, when he had left, she had run to the shop and later that evening, with what shameless joy, treated the children to fancy cakes. She had looked at them and laughed, while her woman's pride and human dignity had hidden themselves away somewhere deep down inside, finding only strength enough to stop her eating any of the cake herself.

With every day that passed she became more and more used to the idea of the two hundred rubles. An obliging new conscience suggested a reasonable excuse: why indeed should Zhukov enjoy untroubled happiness, let the payment of this money month by month give him a little worry, let him pay, let that beauty of his suffer a bit!

Her conception of Zhukov grew dim, but perhaps she had no time to clarify it. Liking for him had vanished long ago, he never appeared in her imagination as a man and a husband, That Zhukov was a scoundrel, a mean and narrow-minded male, a man without feeling or honour—that was certain, but even this condemnation roused in Yevgenia Alexeyevna no passion or desire for action. Sometimes she thought that there was nothing attractive about the man which was worth regretting, perhaps it was for the better that her life with this scoundrel had ended!

And when Yevgenia Alexeyevna was given the post of secretary in a large trust, when she began to work and earn her own salary, the image of Zhukov faded away definitely into the past, wrapped in the mist of the grief she had suffered—she stopped thinking about him. Even the two hundred rubles had little to do with him, it was just money, her legal and accustomed income.

Weeks passed and turned into months. They lost the distinction of grief and became like one another, just ordinary; and against their monotonous background the woman in her awakened, youth stirred.

Yevgenia Alexeyevna was only thirty-three. This "classic" age is beset with many difficulties. The first freshness of youth is gone. The eyes are still beautiful and in a photograph they may seem "divine," but in real life they are nevertheless thirty-three years old. The lower lid can still be lifted to give the eye a provoking sparkle of promise, but at the same time it also exposes a treacherous line of wrinkles, and the challenge is no longer bold, it bears the stamp of technique. At this age a beautiful dress, a fresh new collar, a skilful touch by a dress-maker, a faint rustle of silk improve one's outlook on life.

And Yevgenia Alexeyevna returned to this woman's world, to care of herself, to the mirror. After all she was still young and good-looking, and her eyes shone and there was much promise in her smile.

...Yevgenia Alexeyevna had just received a note, the third in number.

"Y. A. I find it very difficult to pay two hundred rubles a month. The holidays are coming on now. I suggest that you should send Igor and Olga to spend the summer at my father's in Uman. They can live there till September—it will be a holiday for them and make them fit. Father and Mother will be very glad, I have already written to them. If you agree, let me know and I will arrange everything. N."

After reading the note Yevgenia Alexeyevna threw it disdainfully on the table and was about to tell the messenger that there would be no reply. But then she remembered something important. It flashed through her mind not very clearly, but seemed to suggest that a holiday in Uman would really be very good for the children. But in a few minutes "it" had already cast off its childish disguise and was insistently demanding attention. Yevgenia Alexeyevna stopped at the door, glanced sideways at herself in the mirror, and smiled. In the luminous mist of the mirror a slim dark-eyed woman answered her with a dazzling smile. Yevgenia Alexeyevna went out to the messenger and asked him to say that she would think it over and send an answer on the following day.

She sat on the sofa, walked about the room, looked at the children and thought. The children did indeed lack fun and amusement. A stay in a new place in the heart of the country, life in the garden, freedom from scenes and emotion—it was a very good idea. Zhukov had been considerate in offering them such a trip.

Lately Yevgenia Alexeyevna had not thought much about her children. Igor went to school. He had friends in the court-yard, with whom he quarrelled frequently, but after all that was usual. He never mentioned his father. Zhukov's presents, books and toys, were tidily arranged on the lower shelf of the cupboard, but Igor did not touch them. With his mother he was affectionate and straightforward but tried to avoid heart-to-heart talks; he liked chattering about various trivial subjects, about the happenings in the court-yard and school events. At the same time it was quite obvious that he was watching his mother, examining her mood, listening to her telephone conversations, and he always wanted to know with whom she had been talking. When his mother came home late he would take offence and meet her with a swollen flushed face, but, if she asked what the matter was, he would wave her aside and say with ill-feigned surprise: "What's the matter with me? Nothing's the matter with me!"

Olya was growing up a silent girl. She played good-naturedly, wandered about the rooms attending to her own affairs, went to the kindergarten and returned home as composed as ever, not inclined to talk or smile.

Yevgenia Alexeyevna could not complain of the children, but their conduct bore signs of some other secret life; and she, their mother, did not know this secret life. But she decided that in any case the situation was clear: a change of surroundings would do them good.

But Yevgenia Alexeyevna was thinking not only of the children. Involuntarily her thoughts took a side-track, and with quiet resentment she remembered that for the last six months she had had no life of her own. Work, the canteen, the children, cooking, mending, darning and ...nothing else. The telephone in her flat rang less and less frequently—she could hardly remember when she heard it last. All the winter she had not been to the theatre once. She had attended one party, to which she had set out late, after putting the children to bed and asking her neighbour to "listen in."

At the party she had been courted by a cheerful, round-faced, fair-haired guest from Saratov, the director of some publishing house or other. He made her drink two glasses of wine, after which he no longer talked of the paper shortage, but about how, in time, Soviet society would no doubt "adorn all beautiful women with every precious stone in the Urals. If not, there'll be nowhere to put them anyway."

Yevgenia Alexeyevna was not a plaster saint and liked to have a joke at dinner.

"Nonsense!" she replied. "We don't need jewels! Jewels are for the rich to deck themselves out with, our women are beautiful enough as they are. Don't you think so?"

The guest gave a subtle smile.

"N-no, I wouldn't say that. It's no use relying on jewels to make ugliness beautiful. Dress a freak up how you like, she will become even uglier. A beautiful woman will make the jewels themselves even richer and more charming and her beauty becomes really ... really magnificent. Topaz would suit you, for instance, wonderfully."

"Ah, indeed, as if I only need topaz!" laughed Yevgenia Alexeyevna.

The guest from Saratov looked admiringly at her over the rim of his glass.

"As a matter of fact, that's all talk. You are beautiful enough as it is!"

"Aha!"

"Well, I'm being honest—like every old man.... If you want me to stop, tell me what life's like here."

Yevgenia Alexeyevna told him about Moscow, about the theatre, about fashions, about people, she felt gay and interested, but suddenly she remembered that it was nearly twelve o'clock. The children were all alone in the flat. She had to hurry home before the party was over. Her hosts were indignant, the fair-haired guest took offence, but no one offered to escort her home, and she ran back along the deserted streets, anxious for her children and fleeing from the annoying embarrassment of her hasty departure.

Think of the fair-haired guest! It was the end of that encounter, and how many other similar encounters would end in the same way?

She found herself asking bitterly: surely it is not all over, surely life is not finished? Is there only mending and cleaning to come ... and old age?

In the morning Yevgenia Alexeyevna sent Zhukov a note by post, agreeing to send the children to their grandfather's. At dinner she told the children of her decision. Olya greeted the news indifferently, looking at her dolls, but Igor had some practical questions to ask: "How shall we go? By train? Can you fish there? Are there any steamboats? Are there aeroplanes?"

Yevgenia Alexeyevna answered only the first question confidently. Igor stared at his mother in astonishment.

"But what is there, there?" he asked.

"There's Grandpa and Grandma."

Olya responded glumly, still staring at the dolls.

"And why are Grandma and Grandpa there?"

Yevgenia Alexeyevna said that Grandpa and Grandma were very good people and lived there. This explanation did not satisfy Olya. She did not listen to it all and went off to play with her dolls.

After dinner Igor came up to his mother, leaned against her shoulder and asked quietly: "You know what, Mummy? Is that Daddy's Grandpa? The one with the whiskers?"

"Yes."

"You know what? I don't want to go to Grandpa's."

"Why?"

"Because he smells. He doesn't half smell!"

Igor fanned the air.

"Nonsense," said Yevgenia Alexeyevna. "He doesn't smell at all. You are making it up...."

"Yes, he does," repeated Igor stubbornly. He went away into the bedroom, and she heard him say loudly, with obstinate tears in his voice: "You know what? I won't go to Grandpa's."

Yevgenia Alexeyevna remembered her father-in-law— he had come on a visit to his son last summer. He really did have a big, old-fashioned walrus moustache. He was already over sixty, but he put up with it very well, held himself straight, downed vodka by the tumblerful and kept reminiscing about the old days when he worked as a barman in a wineshop. Round Grandpa's person hovered the pungent, unpleasant smell peculiar to slovenly, long-unwashed old men, but Yevgenia Alexeyevna had been mainly repelled by her relation's irrestrainable desire to crack jokes, accompanying his sallies of a certain kind with snorts and chuckles. He was called Kuzma Petrovich, and when leaving the table, he would always say: "Thank the Lord and all of you, said Kuzma and Demyan too."

Having said this he would wink for a long time and rock with silent laughter.

Yevgenia Alexeyevna thought that it would be "pretty bad" for the children at their grandfather's. After all, what had the old people got to live on? Their pension?

But the cottage was their own. They had a garden of sorts. Perhaps their son sent them something. What did it matter anyhow? Let Zhukov worry about that.

Something like alarm and sadness stirred within Yevgenia Alexeyevna; Zhukov's complaint about paying two hundred rubles was suspicious too; but she still cherished hopes of some change or other, some fresh smile of fortune.

A few days later Zhukov sent a note in which he described in detail when and how the children were to travel to their grandfather's. He was providing someone to accompany them as far as Uman; it was this guide who brought the note. He was a young man about twenty, fresh and pleasant, with a good smile. Yevgenia Alexeyevna felt rather relieved, but there still remained an unpleasant impression from one part of the letter which read:

"I shall pay for the guide's return ticket. Will you please give him about sixty rubles for the children's fare, Olya only needs a quarter fare—I am finding things very difficult these days."

But Yevgenia Alexeyevna let everything slide. She was feeling more and more excited at the thought that at last she would be left to herself for two or three months, completely alone, in an empty flat. She would sleep, read, go out, walk in the park, visit her friends. Apart from all this there ought to be something big enough to change her life and her future—of this she dared not even dream, but it was this that made her feel free and glad at heart.

The children did not cloud her joy. Igor seemed to have forgotten his recent protest. They were carried away by the prospects of the journey and the new places they would see. Cheerfully they made the acquaintance of their guide.

"Has the train got windows?" Olya questioned him. "Can you see everything? Fields? What are the fields like?"

The guide did not see anything of much consequence in her questions and just smiled in reply, but Igor attached great importance to them and told Olya excitedly: "The windows there are so ... well, not like in a room, they move up and down too. When you look out there is a terrific wind and everything goes rushing past."

"And what are the fields like?"

"They go for miles and miles and there are grass and trees and those ... cottages, or what you call them. And there are cows walking about and sheep. Crowds of 'em!"

Igor had a great fund of knowledge about such subjects for he had travelled several times in his life. This talk took his mind off Grandpa's smell. But when the day came to leave, Igor started snivelling first thing in the morning and sat in a corner repeating: "Mind what I say, I won't stay there. You see if I do. What are we going for, anyway? And why don't you go? What holiday? You'll be fed up without us anyhow. You see if you aren't."

Olya sat all day on her painted stool, deep in thought. When it was time to go to the station she had a real cry, kicked away her new shoes and kept stretching her arms out to her mother. Only this gesture, which she had retained since she was a baby, meant anything definite, for no words were audible through her tears.

The guide had already arrived and was cheerfully trying to persuade Olya.

"What, such a good girl crying! How can that be?"

Olya waved him aside with a tear-stained hand and howled even louder: "Ma-mm," and you could make out nothing more.

With great difficulty, by reminding them of the carriage windows and the cows in the fields, telling them about Grandpa's magic gardens and the wonderful river with white steamers and fishing boats with billowing sails, Yevgenia Alexeyevna succeeded in consoling the children. Then right until the moment of the train's departure she kept thinking what a dreadful venture she had embarked on in her desperation.

"Come on, children, let's go to the station. Don't be sad, everything will be lovely. And at the station you'll see Daddy! Daddy will come and see you off. . . ."

On hearing this Olya squealed joyfully and her little tearful face beamed with happiness. Igor wrinkled his nose with some distrust but said cheerfully: "Oh, good! We'll see what Daddy's like now! Perhaps he's different now!"

In the street Zhukov's office car was waiting for them. At the wheel sat the same old driver, Nikifor Ivanovich, as unshaven and stern as ever. Igor went wild with delight.

"Mummy! Look: Nikifor Ivanovich!"

Nikifor Ivanovich turned round in his seat, beamed as never before and shook everybody's hand.

"How are you getting on, Igor?" he asked.

"But you aren't grumpy any more, Nikifor Ivanovich! I'm getting on. . ." Igor suddenly blushed and hurried on to another question: "How many thousand kilometres have you clocked up now? Twenty-seven! Phew!. . ."

At the station Zhukov was waiting for them in the buffet. He bowed with affected politeness to Yevgenia Alexeyevna, and at once Olya's outstretched arms took possession of him. He kissed her and sat her on his knee. Olya was too confused to say anything, she just laughed silently and stroked the lapels of her father's grey suit. At last she said tenderly, cocking her head on one side:

"Is this a new jacket? Is it new? Where do you live now?"

Zhukov smiled with the expression grown ups always wear when they are delighted at a child's cleverness.

Igor faced his father awkwardly, looked at him, his head lowered, and fidgeted on one foot. Zhukov offered him his hand and asked him, just as Nikifor Ivanovich had done: "Well, how are you getting on, Igor?"

Igor did not succeed in producing an answer, he coughed rather strangely, swallowed, blushed scarlet and turned his face away. As if from nowhere tears appeared in his eyes. Standing thus, his face turned away, Igor stared through his tears at the sparkling cutlery and white cloths on the tables, the big flowers and the golden ball on the buffet counter.

Zhukov grew ruffled, carefully raised Olya and put her down on the floor. Her little hand slid for the last time over the grey lapel of the new jacket and dropped to her side. Her smile also dropped down somewhere and only a few ragged traces of it still graced her cheeks.

Zhukov pulled out his wallet and handed the guide his ticket.

"Mind you don't lose it—it's a return. And here's the letter. You will be met at the station and even if you aren't it's not far."

"Well, good-bye, youngsters," he said, addressing the children jovially, "you're off on holiday but my work's waiting for me. This work's the limit, isn't it, Igor?"

When she returned from the station Yevgenia Alexe-yevna felt overwhelmed by disorder. There was disorder in the room—the usual mess left after departure; and there was disorder in her soul. Zhukov had promised to send the car back to the station to take her home. She had sat there more than half an hour waiting for the car, given it up and queued for the bus. But to hell with him, anyhow, that Zhukov. The ticket he gave the guide was probably a free one.

Yevgenia Alexeyevna busied herself clearing up, then heated the water and had a bath. As her surroundings took on a more normal appearance, her equanimity returned. The unaccustomed solitude in the flat, the stillness and cleanliness seemed almost like a holiday. As if for the first time, she noticed the freshness of the air flowing through the open window, the ticking of the clock and the cosy softness of the carpet on the floor.

Yevgenia Alexeyevna did her hair, dug out a long-forgotten silk dressing-gown from the bottom of a drawer, spent a long time in front of the mirror, examining the intimate charm of the lace and the blue ribbons on her underwear, her shapely legs and the fine curve of her thighs.

"He's a fool, that Zhukov! You are still a beautiful woman, Yevgenia!" she said with cheerful conviction.

She twirled round once more in front of the mirror, then tripped lightly over to the bookcase and chose a volume of O. Henry. Propping her legs up on the sofa she read one story, had a good stretch, lay down and gave herself up to dreams.

But the next day passed, then another, then a third, and she realized that her dreams were running round in circles, that life had no wish to dream with her but was soberly proceeding on its usual course. At work there were the same forms and calls to the manager's office, the same queue of visitors, the same trivial, everyday news. Through the office, as usual, rolled waves of business matters. Business-like people went about their usual affairs and at four o'clock lifted their pasty faces, slammed the drawers of their desks and hurried home. What were their homes like and where were they hurrying off to? As if their wives were so attractive! They must be running for their dinner, they just felt hungry. Anyhow, Yevgenia Alexeyevna went home alone—nobody was going her way. At home, as usual, she lighted the primus stove and cooked something for herself. The noise of the primus now seemed deafening and monotonous. The dinner was equally monotonous.

At the office there were nearly thirty men round her. They were not at all bad fellows and almost all of them were slightly in love with their secretary. But they were all family men; it would be a very low trick to take them from their wives and children.

But it was uncomfortable without a man in the house, especially when her imagination had been fired by her unexpected and unusual freedom. Yevgenia Alexeyevna had already caught herself several times using a venture-some playful tone when talking to some of her office companions. She herself sensed unpleasantly how matter-of-fact and coldly deliberate this playfulness was. Her conduct had not the necessary freedom and simplicity. It was as if she were leading a bored woman about on a chain and wondering—where can I fix her up?

In the evening Yevgenia Alexeyevna would lie down and think: Heavens, I can't go on like this! What is happening? Must I fall in love or something! But how? At eighteen, love lies before one, inevitable and near, there is no need to seek and organize it. Ahead is love, a family, children, ahead is life. But now, at thirty-three, love must be made, one must hurry, one must not be late. And ahead lies not life but a kind of patching-up of the old life; what kind of mixture is one to make out of the old and the new?

Little by little Yevgenia Alexeyevna lost confidence in herself. No more than two weeks had passed, yet the confusion and unsightliness of the future was already blocking the horizon and behind it again loomed the crooked figure of old age. Looking in the mirror Yevgenia Alexeyevna no longer rejoiced at her array of lace and ribbons, but sought, and found, new wrinkles.

It was just then that the angel of love flew over Yevgenia Alexeyevna and cast upon her the rosy shadow of his wings.

This happened, as it always does, by chance. That same fair-haired guest from Saratov, who liked precious stones, arrived in Moscow on business. He came in, noisy and jovial, did the round of the offices, made demands, hauled people over the coals and was rude to them. Yevgenia Alexeyevna delighted in watching his cheerful energy, and with equal energy tried to repel his attacks. He would twist his face into a pitiful expression and, raising his voice to a squeak, say: "Beautiful one! Even you have turned into a bureaucrat! It's terrible! Soon there won't be a single unspoiled person in the place!"

"But there is no other way, Dmitri Dmitrievich, rules are rules. What do you mean you will 'just' write it out?"

"That's just what I will do. Give me paper."

He grabbed the first scrap of paper he came across and with sweeping strokes of his pencil scribbled a few lines. Yevgenia Alexeyevna read them and felt pleasantly horrified. On the paper was written: To the Trust Management. Give three tons of paper. Vasilyev."

"No good?" asked Dmitri Dmitrievich scornfully. "Tell me why it's no good. What's wrong with it?"

"Whoever writes like that? 'Give'! What are you, a child?"

"Well, how then? How are you supposed to write it? How?" went on Dmitri Dmitrievich with really childish insistence. "I suppose you want me to write: with reference to the following I request leave ... on the basis ... in view of ... and likewise taking into account. Like that, eh?"

Yevgenia Alexeyevna smiled with an air of superiority and for a minute even forgot that she was a woman.

"Well, Dmitri Dmitrievich, what do you mean 'give'? One must state one's reasons, mustn't one?"

"Monsters! Beasts! Blood-suckers!" wailed Dmitri Dmitrievich, standing in the middle of the room and waving his fist. "This is the third time I've made this journey! We've used up four tons of paper, writing, explaining, giving reasons! You know everything already, everything, by heart! No! I've had enough!"

He grabbed his terrible paper and bolted into the office of the manager Anton Petrovich Voschenko. Five minutes later he reappeared with an expression of exaggerated grief on his plump face.

"He wouldn't give any. 'Send us a planner,' he says, 'we'll check it up.' In novels such people are called murderers."

Yevgenia Alexeyevna laughed. He sat down in the corner and seemed to bury himself in gloom, but a little while later he came up to her desk and placed a sheet torn from his pocket-book in front of her. On it was written:

> *Even for the capital*
> *The people here aren't bad at all,*
> *But the man that spoils the tone*
> *Is that Voschenko Anton!!*

Yevgenia Alexeyevna felt more cheerful than she had done for a long time, and he stood in front of her, smiling. Then, glancing round, he propped his elbows on a heap of files and whispered: "You know what? Let's give this bureaucratic system the go-by...."

"And then what?" she asked with a secret thrill of alarm.

"And go and have lunch in the park. It's lovely there: green trees, fifty square metres of sky and even—you know what I saw yesterday, you'll never guess—a sparrow! A real lively, energetic little fellow, you know. Probably one of ours—from Saratov!"

At lunch Vasilyev kept on joking away and then asked a question: "Tell me, beautiful, you are a deserted wife, aren't you?"

Yevgenia Alexeyevna blushed, but with the skill of a juggler he saved her from feeling hurt.

"Now don't be offended, as a matter of fact, I," he poked himself in the chest, "I am a deserted husband."

Yevgenia Alexeyevna smiled in spite of herself; he supported her smile too.

"You and I are friends in need. And, after all, we didn't deserve it, did we? You're beautiful and I'm handsome; what, the hell, they're after, I don't know. What a finicky lot people are, it's enough to drive a man to suicide."

Afterwards they wandered through the park, ate ice-cream in a café, and in the evening found themselves at a football match. They watched and cheered.

"Marvellous thing, this football," bawled Dmitri Dmitrievich. "Specially for mental development! Well, I see they are going to spend all their time chasing that ball round.... What about seeking some other thrilling sensations? How about the cinema?"

And a minute later he made a decisive proposal:

"No, let's forget about the cinema. It's hot there and it's made me want some tea. Let's go to your place and drink tea."

Thus their love began. Yevgenia Alexeyevna did not resist love because love is a good thing, and with Vasilyev everything was gay and simple, as if it could not be otherwise.

But three days later Vasilyev was due to leave. When they said good-bye he held her shoulders and said: "You're a lovely woman, Yevgenia Alexeyevna, you're wonderful, but I won't marry you...."

"Oh, no...."

"I'm afraid to marry. You have two children, a family, and probably even without the children I wouldn't make much of a husband. I'm scared, just scared. It's very sad, you know, when your wife deserts you. Surprisingly unpleasant! Brr! And ever since then I have been afraid. Scared out of my life. I want to be on my own, it's not half so dangerous. But if you need any help one of these

157

days, to sock someone on the jaw or something like that—I'm at your service."

He left, and when Yevgenia Alexeyevna had recovered from this unexpected tornado of love, she felt sadly that she had really come to a dead end in life.

The days passed. The figure of Dmitri Dmitrievich made a place for itself in her soul and stayed there. No, it had not been an accidental flippant transgression. Dmitri Dmitrievich was a dear, attractive person, and that was why she felt so much regret, for she understood that Dmitri Dmitrievich had been frightened by the two children and the complications of a new family. She wanted to say to him tenderly: "There's no need to be afraid of my children, dear, they are wonderful, kind little creatures—they will generously return your fatherly affection."

She now remembered her children in an anguish of tenderness. In the future only they would be by her side, and the capricious charm of Dmitri Dmitrievich might be only a figment of her imagination. What was he? A chance fancy, a momentary beam of winter sunlight? The children ... why, they were the future. They alone!

She received a letter from Igor. The neat lines in schoolboy handwriting brought anxiety. Igor wrote:

"Mummy, we are living here with Grandad and Grandma. We miss you very much. It's better at home. Grandad keeps on talking to us and Grandma doesn't talk much. There is no river here and no steamers. There aren't any apples either, only cherries. We aren't allowed to climb the trees, and Grandma gives us some cherries and sells the rest at the market. I also went to the market, only not to sell cherries but to look at the people, to see what they were like. Yesterday Daddy came and went away again. Thousands of kisses.

"Your loving son,
"Igor Zhukov."

Yevgenia Alexeyevna thought over the letter. Only one line spoke plainly: "It's better at home." Grandma was probably not very affectionate with the children. She grudged them cherries. And why had their father been there? What did he want?

Yevgenia Alexeyevna's anxiety had not been thoroughly aroused before a second letter arrived.

"Mummy, dearest. We can't bear it any longer. Take us away from here. There are still no apples and they give us only a few cherries, they're very mean. Mummy, come and fetch us soon, come at once, we can't bear it any longer.

"Your loving son,
"Igor Zhukov."

At first Yevgenia Alexeyevna lost her head. What should she do? Tell Zhukov? Go herself? Send someone? Whom should she send? Aha, yes, that guide.

She ran to the telephone. For the first time since their break she heard her husband's voice on the wire. The voice was homely and familiar. But now it seemed complacent, self-satisfied. The conversation ran like this:

"Nonsense! I was down there on a job. Everything's wonderful."

"But the children don't like living there!"

"What about it? Children never know what they want!"

"I don't want to argue. Can you send that young man?"

"No, I can't."

"What?"

"I can't send anybody. And I don't want to."

"You don't want to?"

"No, I don't want to."

"All right, I'll go myself. But you must help with the money."

"No, thank you, I want no part in your ridiculous hysterics. And I warn you that I shall not send you money until September in any case."

Yevgenia Alexeyevna was about to say something more but the receiver clicked.

Never before in her life had anyone kindled such hatred in her. The dispatch of the children to Uman had been merely an advantageous deal for Zhukov. How could this wretched fellow have deceived her? Why had she been so weak-minded as to fall for his proposal? How could she? But of course she herself had acted like a greedy beast, hindered by the children. Dmitri Dmitrievich? Well, what about him? He, too, was afraid of these poor children. They were in everyone's way, everyone wanted to get rid of them, hide them somewhere.

Yevgenia Alexeyevna now acted with her anger at white heat. She managed to get three days' leave. Then she sold a pair of velvet curtains and an old gold watch and sent a telegram to Igor. But what was most important, looking with angry eyes at the telephone on the table, she said to herself:

"So you won't pay. We shall see about that!"

The next morning she handed in an application to the court. Official voices pronounced the word: "alimony."

That evening she left for Uman, strong emotions crowding upon her—sad, troubled love for her children, resentful tenderness towards Dmitri Dmitrievich and implacable hatred for Zhukov.

She spent only the time between trains at the old Zhukovs', finding there such an incandescent atmosphere of hostility and such open warfare that she could not stay an extra hour, the more so that her arrival considerably strengthened the children's side. After the first overwhelming embraces and tears the children left their mother and turned on the enemy.

Olya's little face assumed an angry frown expressing only one thing: no mercy. She came into the room with a big stick and tried hard to smash everything with it—tables, chairs, window-sills; only the windows for some reason escaped her attention. The old people tried to take the stick away from her and hide it. When she lost her weapon Olya waved her little fist at her grandfather and, biting her lips, went in search of another stick, the same relentless expression on her face. Grandpa watched her with the wary eye of a reconnaissance scout.

"A nice pair of children you've brought up, madam," he said. "Do you call that a child? She's a plague wind!"

Igor looked at his grandfather with genuine scorn.

"Plague wind yourself. What right have you got to give us the strap?"

"Don't climb the trees then!"

"Misers!" continued Igor in disgust. "Money-grubbers! Spongers! He's Kashchei and she's Baba-Yaga!"*

"Igor! How can you!" interposed his mother.

"Oho! He's called me worse things than that. Tell your mother what you said!"

"What did I say? Just listen to the yarn they told Father!" Igor began to mimic: " 'Your little dears are in Christ's bosom here.' Christ's bosom! So he's like Christ, is he? Ten cherries for dinner! In his bosom! And what did he say about you: 'Your mother cried for your father!' 'Cried,' mind you!"

Finding room somehow for the children and their luggage in the crowded third-class carriage, Yevgenia Alexeyevna glanced back desperately as if she had just escaped from a house on fire. Even in the carriage Olya's face still wore the same relentless expression, and now she took no interest in the windows or the cows. Igor

* *Kashchei* and *Baba-Yaga*—traditional figures of evil in Russian folklore.—*Tr.*

could not stop recounting various things that had been said and done. Yevgenia Alexeyevna looked at the children and wanted to cry, not knowing whether it was from love or grief.

Once again Yevgenia Alexeyevna's heart was weighed down with care and loneliness. The loneliness she now experienced was of a new kind and did not depend on people and affairs. It dwelt deep down in her inner self, nourished by anger and love. But anger left little room for love. Without reason or proof she convinced herself that Zhukov was a criminal, a menace to people and society, the lowest creature under the sun. To annoy, insult, kill or torment him could become the dream of her life.

Thus it was with harsh gloating that she listened to Zhukov's voice on the telephone after the court's decree ordering him to pay alimony of two hundred and fifty rubles a month.

"I might have expected anything from you but I never expected such a low trick. . . ."

"Oho!"

"What? You're nothing but a grasping female without the slightest conception of anything noble."

"What did you say? Noble?"

"Yes, noble. I left you a whole flat full of goods, a library, pictures, furniture. . . ."

"You did that out of cowardice, because you're a rotter and a worm. . . ."

"And now you are rubbing my name and family in the dirt. . . ."

Yevgenia Alexeyevna's strength betrayed her. With all her might she seized the telephone receiver as if it were Zhukov's throat, shook it and shouted hoarsely:

"How can a man like you have a family, you low beast!"

The imprecations she would shout failed to satisfy her, but she could not think of any others, more insulting. Even for herself this lone hatred became unbearable. She must talk to somebody about it, laying it on thick, kindle in other people the same hatred, make others call Zhukov a worm and a scoundrel. She wanted people to despise Zhukov and to express their contempt with the same force as she. But she had no one to share her anger with, and she wondered in surprise: why can't people see how low Zhukov is, why do they talk to him, work, joke, shake hands with him?

But people did not seem to notice Zhukov's revolting character and did not treat him as Yevgenia Alexeyevna wished. Only the children felt the full measure of her grief and vexation, and she had long since ceased to stand on ceremony with them. Very often she would mention her husband in their presence, expressing herself contemptuously and making free with insulting words. And it was with particular triumph that she told them of the court's decree.

"Your precious father imagines I need his charity—two hundred rubles! He forgot he's living under Soviet rule. Let him pay what the court says, and if he does not pay, he can go to jail!"

The children would listen to such tirades in silence. Olya would frown and become angrily thoughtful. Igor's face wore an ironic sneer.

The children's characters had changed since the trip to their grandfather's. Yevgenia Alexeyevna noticed this, but her mind was not free enough to consider it. No sooner had she fixed her attention on one or another aspect of the children's characters than she would be assailed by new worries and fits of anger.

Even the expression of Igor's face had changed. Before, it had always been a picture of clear and simple trustfulness, enhanced by the calm, cheerful sagacity of his hazel eyes. Now this face more and more frequently wore an expression of sly distrust and sneering condemnation. He had learnt to look sideways and narrow his eyes, and his lips could now curl almost imperceptibly and seemed to be permanently loaded with contempt.

Their neighbours held a party—the usual kind of family celebration anyone might hold. That evening sounds of the gramophone and dancing feet floated up from their flat. Igor was already in bed. Making his usual supercilious face he said: "They've stolen government money and now they're dancing!"

His mother was surprised.

"How do you know they stole it?"

"Of course, they did," said Igor with contemptuous certainty, "it's easy enough for them, isn't it? You know where Korotkov works? He's manager of a shop. Just dipped into the till for it."

"You ought to be ashamed, Igor, making up such tales. Thoroughly ashamed of yourself!"

"They aren't ashamed of stealing, why should I be ashamed?" said Igor just as confidently, looking at his mother as if he knew she had also stolen something, only he did not want to mention it.

Late in the autumn Yevgenia Alexeyevna's sister Nadezhda Alexeyevna Sokolova, who was visiting Moscow for a few days, came to stay with her. She was a lot older than Yevgenia and more heavily built. She breathed that pleasant reassuring peacefulness which is characteristic of happy mothers with large families. Yevgenia Alexeyevna was glad to see her and ardently initiated her into all the details of her prolonged misfortune. They talked mostly alone in the bedroom, but sometimes, at dinner, Yevgenia Alexeyevna could not restrain herself.

In reply to her lamentations Nadezhda once said: "Give up complaining, do! What do you keep moaning for? Get married again! You look at them? At Igor? Why, Igor needs a man more than you do. What will he grow up like, surrounded by women? Stop making faces, Igor. Look what a little tyrant your son is! He thinks his mother's got nothing better to do than follow him around. Get married. Men treat strange children better than we. They're more broad-minded...."

Igor said nothing to this, he only stared unblinkingly at his aunt. But when Nadezhda left, Igor did not spare her.

"Anyone who likes comes here.... She lived with us for five days, all free—of course it suited her nicely. At somebody else's expense ... I should say so!"

"Igor, the way you talk is beginning to annoy me!"

"Of course it annoys you! She's been feeding you up all the time about men: 'Get married, get married'! And you're just itching, aren't you!"

"Igor, stop it!"

Yevgenia Alexeyevna shouted this loudly and angrily, but Igor did not turn a hair. The same faint sneer appeared on his lips, and his eyes had a knowing unkind look in them.

Bad rumours about Igor's character were also forthcoming from school. Then the director invited Yevgenia Alexeyevna to pay him a visit.

"Tell me, how does your boy come by such moods? I don't imagine for a moment that it is your influence."

"What's wrong?"

"Quite a lot, a great deal, in fact. He does nothing but censure the teachers. He told one teacher to her face: 'You're so beastly because you're paid to be like that!' And generally in the class he's a centre ... well ... a centre of resistance."

While Yevgenia Alexeyevna was there the director called Igor in and said to him: "Igor, your mother's here. In her presence give me your word that you will mend your conduct."

Igor looked quickly at his mother and curled his lip insolently. Shifting from one foot to the other, he turned aside with a bored expression.

"Well, why don't you say something?"

Igor lowered his eyes and again turned away.

"Won't you say anything?"

Igor choked with laughter—it welled up in him so suddenly but, checking his laughter at once, he said vaguely:

"I won't say anything."

The director looked at Igor for another second or two and dismissed him.

"Well, you may go."

Yevgenia Alexeyevna returned home in dismay. She felt utterly defeated by this boyish embitteredness. Everything in her soul had for long been in disorder, as in an unkempt bedroom. But Igor was beginning to develop a complete character of his own, and Yevgenia Alexeyevna could neither understand nor even conceive its nature.

Her life was sinking further and further into irritating trivialities. At the office there were several incidents for which her nervous state was largely to blame. The alimony from Zhukov came in irregularly and she had to make complaints against him. Zhukov no longer telephoned, but rumours reached her about his life and affairs. His new wife had had a child, and Zhukov was putting forward a plea for a reduction in the amount of alimony.

In the spring he met Igor in the street, put him in his car, took him for a drive down the Leningrad Highway, and as a farewell present gave him his penknife with eleven gadgets on it. Igor returned from the outing in an elated frame of mind and kept waving his hands and talking excitedly about the new places he had seen, the jokes Daddy made, and about Daddy's car. He fastened the penknife on a string to his trouser-pocket, spent the whole day opening and shutting it, and in the evening found a twig somewhere, which he went on whittling until he had made a mess in all the rooms and finally cut his finger, but told no one about this and washed his finger for half an hour in the wash-basin. Yevgenia Alexeyevna noticed the blood and exclaimed: "Good heavens, Igor, what are you doing? Throw that beastly knife of yours away!"

Igor turned on her fiercely.

"What right have you to call it a beastly knife? How dare you! You didn't give it me! And now it's a 'beastly knife'! Because Daddy gave it to me! Is that why you don't like it?"

Yevgenia Alexeyevna wept alone because even at home there was no one from whom she could expect sympathy. Olya did not declare war on her mother and was not rude to her, but she stopped obeying her and she could do this beautifully, without fear or caution. She would absent herself for days on end either in the court-yard or at the neighbours', return home in a filthy state, never say a word about anything and take no interest in domestic matters. Sometimes she would stop in front of her mother, biting her lower lip, look at her with strange severity and, just as aimlessly, turn and go away. She never heard out her mother's admonitions to the end—no one had any authority over her. Even when her mother was changing her clothes for her, Olya would look aside, wrapped up in her own affairs.

The days passed sadly, full of confusion and despair. Not even a flicker of the happiness which not so long ago had been hers remained in her memory, and anyway what was the use of a memory that could not do without Zhukov?

In the spring Yevgenia Alexeyevna began to think about death. She still had no clear idea of what might happen, but death had already ceased to seem terrible.

Letters occasionally arrived from Dmitri Dmitrievich, tender and at the same time evasive. In April he again came to Moscow on business. He took her hand in his and his eyes seemed either to be asking for forgiveness or speaking of love. They left the office together. She quickened her step, as if hoping that he would not keep up with her. He grasped her elbow and said in a stern serious voice:

"Yevgenia Alexeyevna, you shouldn't be like this."

"How then?" She stopped and looked into his grey eyes. He answered her with a deep glance but said nothing. Raising his hat, he turned away down a side-street.

May was an eventful month.

In one of the adjoining flats a man beat his wife badly.... The man was a journalist of some reputation and a recognized authority on certain specialized subjects. Everyone believed Gorokhov to be a good and talented man. His maltreated wife spent one night with the Korotkovs. Both the Korotkovs and the Zhukovs and others knew that Gorokhov treated his wife badly and that she was unable even to think of protesting. Everyone had grown used to the idea that this was the Gorokhovs' affair, their style of family life, everyone told anecdotes about them and laughed, but on encountering Gorokhov never expressed any doubt about his being a good and talented man.

When she learnt of this fresh scandal Yevgenia Alexeyevna paced about her room for a long time, silently admired the pattern of the table-cloth, then discovered a forgotten bottle of vinegar on the dining-room table and began a prolonged examination of the decorative white letters on the dark-blue background of the label. The edges of the label were yellow and covered with various words; she was fascinated by one: *Mosregfoodinun.* Something like a spark of irony flickered in her eyes; it was not so easy to translate the abbreviation into normal speech: Moscow regional food-industrial union? But perhaps that was not it, "food-industrial" did not sound quite right somehow. Her glance rested on the modest label, and she wondered at its simplicity.

Carefully placing the bottle on the table, she went out on to the landing and down the stairs and rang at the Korotkovs' door. There she listened to the pitiful apathetic moaning of Gorokhov's maltreated wife, looked at her with dry inflamed eyes and went away, feeling neither dead nor alive.

Mounting the staircase she inadvertently pushed on Gorokhov's door. No one came to meet her. In the first room, on the bare dirty floor, sat a girl about four years old, toying with some tobacco boxes. In the second room, at a writing-table she caught sight of Gorokhov. He was a little fellow with a thin nose. He looked up at Yevgenia Alexeyevna in surprise and from habit smiled a welcome, but noticing something queer in her blazing eyes, he half raised himself from his seat. Yevgenia Alexeyevna leaned against the door and said wildly:

"Listen to me, listen, you scoundrel: I'm going to write to the newspaper about you!"

He looked at her, angry and confused, then he put his pen down on the desk and moved back the armchair with one hand.

She rushed up to him.

"I'll write everything, you'll see, you swine!" she shouted.

It seemed to her that he was about to strike her. She dashed out of the room, but there was no fear in her, she was filled with anger and longing for revenge. In her own room she immediately opened the drawer of the desk and took out some paper. Igor was seated on the carpet, sorting out some sticks and measuring their length. On seeing his mother he abandoned his task and went up to her.

"Mummy, have you had the money?"

"What money?" she asked.

"From Father. Have you got Father's money?"

Yevgenia Alexeyevna threw a surprised glance at her son. His lip was trembling. But Yevgenia Alexeyevna was still thinking of Gorokhov.

"I have. What do you want?"

"I've got to buy a 'Constructor' set. It's a game. I need it. It costs thirty rubles."

"All right.... But what has Father's money to do with it? All money's the same."

"No, it's not. Some's your money, and some's mine!"

Yevgenia Alexeyevna looked at her son astounded. She could find nothing to say.

"What are you looking at me for?" Igor scowled. "Daddy gives you the money for us. It's ours and I need to buy a 'Constructor' set.... Hand over!"

Igor's face was a ghastly combination of insolence, stupidity and shamelessness. Yevgenia Alexeyevna went pale and fell back in her chair, but noticing the sheet of paper lying in readiness ... understood everything. Deep within her she suddenly felt calm. Without wasting a single movement, her pale face expressing nothing, she took a packet of ten-ruble notes out of the desk and placed them on the glass top. Then she said to Igor, instilling in every word the thunder that had just passed through her soul: "Here's the money, see it? Tell me, do you see it?"

"I see it," whispered Igor in fright, standing stock-still as though his feet were glued to the floor.

"Look!"

On the sheet of paper lying before her Yevgenia Alexeyevna wrote a few lines.

"Listen to what I have written:

" 'To Citizen Zhukov.

" 'I return the money received from you. Do not bother to send more. Better to starve than to accept money from such as you. Y.' "

Without taking her eyes off her son, she sealed up the money and the note in an envelope. Igor's face still wore its former scared expression, but in his eyes sparks of lively interest had already awakened.

"You will take this packet to the person who abandoned you and has now bribed you with an old penknife. Take it to him at his office. Understand?"

Igor nodded.

"Take it and hand it to the porter. No talking to Fa . . . to Zhukov."

Igor nodded again. The colour was already rising visibly in his cheeks, and he watched his mother as if a miracle were being performed.

Yevgenia Alexeyevna remembered that there was something else to be done. . . .

"Ah yes! The editorial office is next door. . . . But perhaps I'll send that by post."

"Why the newspaper? Also about . . . that . . . Zhuk. . . ."

"About Gorokhov. I am going to write about Gorokhov!"

"Oh, Mummy! He kicked her, and beat her with a ruler! Will you write that?"

She looked at Igor distrustfully. Yevgenia Alexeyevna did not want to believe his sympathy. But Igor was looking seriously and ardently at her, straight in the eyes.

"Well, go along," she said with restraint.

He ran out of the room without putting his cap on. Yevgenia Alexeyevna went over to the window and saw how quickly he ran across the street, how in his hand gleamed the envelope in which she was casting off for ever the humiliation of her life. She opened the window. The sky was alive with movement: thunder clouds were gathering on the horizon. Their main forces loomed threateningly, but in front billowed cheerful white scouts; thunder rumbled, still far away; the room was growing cooler. Yevgenia Alexeyevna sighed deeply and sat down to write a letter to the newspaper. She no longer felt any anger, only a cold, hard assurance.

Igor returned half an hour later. He came in brisk and cheerful, stood in the doorway and called out:

"I've done everything, Mummy!"

With a new unaccustomed joy, his mother took him by the shoulders. He was about to lower his eyes but instead looked her in the face with a clear hazel gleam in his glance and said: "You know what? I gave back the penknife too."

Yevgenia Alexeyevna's letter to the newspaper had great publicity and she suddenly became the centre of popular attention. People came to see her. The telephone rang all day. She was not fully aware of what had happened—she only realized that it was something important and decisive. Of this she was convinced when she spoke to Zhukov on the telephone.

"Look here, how am I to take your note?"

Yevgenia Alexeyevna smiled into the receiver.

"Take it as a slap on the face!"

Zhukov spluttered into the telephone, but she rang off.

She wanted to live and move among people. And people were now surrounding her with attention. Igor followed his mother about like a page, holding himself proudly. No one talked to them of their father, everybody was interested in Yevgenia Alexeyevna as author of the letter about Gorokhov.

"They keep on about Gorokhov," Igor told her, "but they don't know anything about us, do they?"

"No, Igor," his mother replied. "But I would like you to help me again. Do something about Olya, please—she has got right out of hand."

Igor was not slow in doing something. Going over to

the window, he called Olya in from the yard and said to her: "Listen here, Comrade Olya! You've been fooling about long enough!"

Olya made for the door. Igor barred her path. She glanced at him.

"Well?"

"You've got to obey Mother."

"And if I don't want to?"

"Well, I'm your boss now. Understand?"

Olya nodded and asked:

"Are you my boss?"

"Come and see Mummy...."

"And if I don't want to?"

"That won't work," smiled Igor.

"Won't it?" she looked at him slyly.

"No."

With the same expression of indifference she used to wear when leaving her mother, Olya now moved in the opposite direction. Igor felt that she would need a lot of attention.

Her mother's talk was of an instructional character. Olya listened inattentively, but by her mother's side stood Igor, whose silent figure proudly represented the law.

Life was interesting all round. Unexpectedly one evening the flat was invaded by a stout fair-haired man.

"Yevgenia Alexeyevna! You've roused such a rumpus with that Gorokhov.... Everyone's talking about you. I couldn't keep away, I had to come."

"Dear Dmitri Dmitrievich, what a good thing you did," Yevgenia Alexeyevna's pleasure made her look prettier. "Let me introduce my children to you."

"Aha," Dmitri Dmitrievich smiled seriously. "This is Igor, isn't it? Nice face. And this is Olya. She has a nice face too. Now, I've got something serious to talk to you about: the point is, you see, that I want to marry your mother."

The fair-haired man fell silent and stood in the middle of the room, looking questioningly at the children.

"Dmitri Dmitrievich," said Yevgenia Alexeyevna confusedly, "you should have mentioned it to me first. . . ."

"You and I can always reach an agreement, but these are the ones who worry me," said Dmitri Dmitrievich.

"Heavens, what cheek!"

"What cheek!" Olya laughed slowly.

"Well, what do you think, Igor?"

"But what kind of a man are you?" asked Igor.

"Me? There's a question! I'm a loyal, cheerful fellow. I love your mother very much. And I like you. Only with children I'm str-r-rict," he roared suddenly in a deep bass.

"Oh," squeaked Olya joyfully.

"See, she's squealing already, and you haven't even turned a hair. That's because you are a man. Well, Igor, do you like me?"

Unsmilingly Igor answered:

"Yes, I like you. Only . . . you won't leave us, will you?"

"Don't *you* leave me, my dears!" Dmitri Dmitrievich clasped his chest. "Don't desert a complete orphan!"

Olya burst out laughing.

"An orphan!"

"Comrades! What is this about! You've got to ask me, you know," implored Yevgenia Alexeyevna. "Suppose I don't want to."

This roused Igor's indignation.

"But how queer you are, Mummy! He's told us all about himself. You can't treat people like that!"

"That's right," said Dmitri Dmitrievich, backing him up, "people ought to be treated sensitively."

"There, you see? Marry him, Mummy, you arranged it all with him long ago, anyhow. I can tell by your eyes. O-oh, what an artful pair!"

Dmitri Dmitrievich was beside himself with delight.

"Why, they're brilliant kids! And I was fool enough to be scared!"

The story of Yevgenia Alexeyevna is, of course, not the saddest of its kind. There are fathers who are capable not only of deserting their children but of robbing them as well, dragging away to their new abode much of the straw from the family nest.

The overwhelming majority of our fathers know how not to give way to the impressions caused by their first family misunderstanding, are capable of scorning the magnetic attraction of new love and preserving untarnished their contract with their wife, without taking exception to such individual shortcomings as they may find in her after marriage Such fathers carry out their duty to their children more perfectly and deserve our praise on that score too.

But there still are "noble" and ignoble Don Juans, who, with disgusting weakness, pursue their love affairs into other people's homes, scattering herds of semi-orphans everywhere in their wake. Sometimes these people pose as adherents of the cause of free love, sometimes they are ready to show interest in their abandoned children, but at all times they are absolutely worthless as people and have no claim on our indulgence at all.

Injured and insulted mothers and children should at every opportunity transform the "chemical" figure of this kind of payer of alimony into a "mechanical" and simple nought. One should not allow these people to flirt with the children they have abandoned.

And in any case particular delicacy is to be recommended over the question of alimony, so that such money may not corrupt the family.

Wholeness and unity of the family collective is an essential condition of good upbringing. It is destroyed not only by payers of alimony and "only princes," but also by parents' quarrels, the despotic cruelty of fathers and the frivolous weakness of mothers.

He who wishes to bring up his children really well should preserve this unity. It is essential not only for the children, it is essential for the parents.

What is to be done if there is only one child and for some reason you cannot have another?

Very simple: take a strange child into your family, take a child from a children's home, or an orphan who has lost his parents. Love him as your own, forget that it was not you who gave birth to him, and, above all, do not imagine that you have done him a great favour. It is he who has come to the aid of your "one-sided" family by saving it from a dangerous list. *Be sure* to do this, however difficult your material circumstances may be.

Chapter Six

𝔹 EFORE us lies a whole bevy of problems—problems concerning authority, discipline and freedom in the family collective.

In the old days these problems were solved with the aid of the Fifth Commandment: "Honour thy father and thy mother: that thy days may be long upon the land which the Lord thy God giveth thee."

This commandment accurately reflected the relations within the family. The honouring of parents was indeed attended by the acquisition of positive blessings, that is, of course, if the parents themselves possessed such blessings. And if they did not possess them, then one had to fall back on the kingdom of heaven. In the kingdom of heaven the blessings were less tangible, but of better quality. If need be, the Fifth Commandment allowed the acquisition of blessings of a different kind—minus blessings. At divinity lessons the priests would lay particular stress on a version which ran something like this: "Honour thy father and thy mother, and if you do not honour them we shall not answer for the consequences."

Consequences followed in the shape of a strap, a stick and other negative quantities. The priests would bring forward historical examples from which it was obvious that, in cases where parents or elders were not honoured, the Lord was disinclined to mildness. For lack of respect towards his father, Ham paid very dearly at the expense of his descendants, and the group of children who mocked the prophet Elisha were torn to pieces by she-bears. When recounting such a vivid example of the Lord's righteousness, the priests would conclude: "You see, children, how the Lord punishes those who act disrespectfully towards their parents and elders."

We, children, did see. Divine terrorism did not worry us very much: the Lord was, of course, capable of anything, but whether she-bears took such an active part in the performance—we had our doubts. Anyhow, since the prophet Elisha and other important personages rarely crossed our path, we had little reason to be afraid of heavenly vengeance. But even on earth there were enough people anxious to settle scores with us. And for us the Fifth Commandment, sanctified by the Lord and his disciples, was, after all, a fact.

Hence parental authority issued from the Lord's Commandment.

In our modern family things are different. There is no Fifth Commandment, and no one promises any blessings, either plus or minus. And if a father, reverting to the past, does have recourse to the strap, then it is at any rate an ordinary strap without any grace tacked on to it, and the objects of the thrashing have heard nothing of the irreverent Ham or of the she-bears authorized by the Lord.

What is authority? Many people stumble over this problem, but are generally inclined to think that authority is a gift from nature. But since everyone in the family needs authority, a considerable number of parents forgo real "natural" authority and employ substitutes of their own concoction. These substitutes are often to be observed in our families. Their common characteristic is that they are concocted especially for educational ends. It is considered that children need authority and, depending on various points of view about children, various substitutes are concocted.

Such parents' main fault lies in a failure of perspective in educational matters. Authority made specially for children cannot exist. Such authority will always be a substitute and will always be useless.

Authority must be embodied in the parents themselves, irrespective of their relations to children, but authority is by no means a special talent. Its roots are always to be found in one place: in the parents' conduct, including all aspects of conduct—in other words, the whole lives of both father and mother, their work, thoughts, habits, feelings and endeavours.

A pattern for such conduct cannot be given in short form, but what it amounts to is that parents themselves must live the full, conscious, moral life of a citizen of the Soviet Land. And this means that in relation to children they should stand on a certain plane, but a natural, human plane, and not a pedestal created especially for dealing with children.

Thus no problems of authority, freedom and discipline in the family collective can be solved by any artificially devised tricks or methods. The process of upbringing is a constant process, and its separate details find their solution in the *general tone* of the family, and general tone cannot be invented and artificially maintained. General tone, dear parents, is created by your own lives and your own conduct. The most correct, reasonable, well thought-out methods of upbringing will be of no use if the general tone of your life is bad. And, on the contrary, only correct general tone will suggest to you both correct methods of training a child and, above all, correct forms of discipline, work, freedom, play and ... authority.

Father comes home from work at five o'clock. He is an electrician at a factory. Before he has finished pulling off his greasy, heavy, dust-covered boots, four-year-old Vasya is already squatting before his father's bed, wheezing like an old man and peering into the dark space before him with troubled grey eyes. For some reason or other there is nothing under the bed. Vasya flies worriedly into the kitchen, then stamps off quickly into the dining-room and round the big table, getting his feet tangled up in the floor-runner. Half a minute later he returns at a steady trot to his father, brandishing a pair of shoes and blowing out his shining chubby cheeks. Father says: "Thanks, sonny, but put the runner straight."

One more journey at the same steady trot and order is restored in the room.

"That's right," says his father and goes off to the kitchen to have a wash.

His son follows him, dragging along the heavy boots and staring intently at the floor-runner ahead. But it is all right, that obstacle is passed without mishap. Vasya increases speed, catches up with his father and asks: "Did you bring the funnel? Did you bring the funnel for the steam-engine?"

"Of course!" says his father. "After dinner we'll have a go."

Vasya has been lucky in life: he was born in post-revolutionary times; the father he happened to get is handsome—at any rate Vasya likes him very much: his eyes are the same as Vasya's—grey, calm, with a spark of humour in them; he has a serious mouth and a nice moustache, and it's lovely to draw your finger over it because every time you are surprised to find how soft and silky it is, but if you steer your finger even a tiny bit to one side it jumps like wire springs and seems fierce and prickly again. Vasya's mother is beautiful too, more beautiful than other mothers. She has warm, tender cheeks and lips. Sometimes, as she looks at Vasya, she seems about to say something to him and her lips move just a little. And you cannot make out whether Mother smiled or not. At such moments Vasya feels life is something very wonderful indeed!

In the Nazarov family there is also Natasha, but she is only five months old.

Putting on shoes in the morning is a most difficult job. Vasya has long been able to thread a lace through a hole, but when the lace has passed through all the holes, Vasya sees that something is not quite right. Vasya does it again and there you are—it's turned out right this time. Then Vasya looks affectionately at his shoe and says to his mother: "Tie-wy!"

If the job has been done properly his mother ties the knot, but if it is not right she says: "Not like that. Can't you do it?"

Vasya shoots a surprised glance at the shoe and suddenly sees that there really is something wrong. He purses his lips, looks angrily at the shoe and starts work again. It does not occur to Vasya to argue with his mother—he does not know how that is done.

"Is that right? Tie-wy!"

While his mother kneels down and makes the knot, Vasya looks shyly at the other shoe and picks out the first hole through which he will now thread the other lace.

Vasya knows how to wash himself and knows how to clean his teeth, but these jobs, too, demand a mass of energy and concentrated attention. To start with, Vasya smears himself all over with soap and tooth-powder right to the back of his neck, then he begins to form a boat with his little awkward hands. He manages to make the boat and collect some water in it, but while he is bringing it up to his face his palms straighten out too soon and the water splashes away over his chest and tummy. Vasya does not wash off the soap and tooth-powder, he just smears it about with his wet palms. After each such attempt Vasya examines his hands for some time and then again begins to build another boat. With his wet palms he tries to rub all the parts that he suspects of being dirty.

Mother comes up and, without wasting words, takes hold of Vasya's hands, tenderly but firmly bends his head over the wash-basin and unceremoniously goes into action over every square inch of Vasya's little face. Mother's hands are warm, soft and sweet-smelling and they delight Vasya, but he continues to be disturbed by the still unmastered art of washing. There are many original ways out of this situation: one can be naughty and protest man-fashion: "I'll do it myself!" One can also pass over the event in silence, but best of all is to laugh, slip out of Mother's grip and sparkle cheerfully at her with wet eyes. In the Nazarov family the last method is the most applicable, because they are cheerful people. After all, naughtiness does not come from God either, but is learned by everyday experience.

When he has had his laugh, Vasya begins to wash his tooth-brush. That is the nicest job of all: you just pour water over the brush, rub its bristles a bit and it comes clean by itself.

Over a grey cloth in the corner of the dining-room extends Vasya's toy kingdom. While Vasya is putting on his shoes, washing himself and having breakfast, the toy kingdom is a model of peace and order. The trains, steamboats and motor-cars stand by the wall, all facing in the same direction. When Vasya happens to run past them on a job, he stops for a moment to check the discipline in his domain. During the night nothing has happened, no one has run away or offended his neighbour or made a mess. This is because painted wooden Vanka-Vstanka* has stood all night at his post keeping watch. Vstanka has

* *Vanka-Vstanka*—a doll with a weight in the base that keeps it always in a standing position.

broad cheeks and huge eyes and a perpetual smile. Vstanka was appointed a long time ago to guard the toy kingdom, and he carries out this duty faithfully. Once Vasya asked his father: "Can't he ever go to sleep?"

But Father answered: "How can he sleep when he's a watchman? If he's a good watchman he ought to keep watch and not to go to sleep. Otherwise, somebody might drive one of the cars away."

Vasya then looked apprehensively at the car and gratefully at the watchman and ever since then he has always placed Vstanka at his post when he himself goes to bed.

But at present Vasya is not so concerned for the cars as for a precious collection of articles packed in a wooden box. All these articles are ear-marked for the construction of the main building in the toy kingdom. Here there are many wooden bricks and beams, silver paper for covering the roof, a few squares of celluloid for the windows, and a lovely little nut and bolt, the purpose of which has not yet been decided. Apart from this, there are various pieces of wire, washers, hooks, pipes, as well as several window-frames cut out of cardboard with Mother's help.

Today Vasya's plan is to transfer the building materials to the construction site—to the opposite corner of the room. Yesterday evening he was worried about the lack of transport. Couldn't a ship be used? But his father settled that question.

"A ship needs a river. Don't you remember last summer?"

Vasya remembers something of the kind; as a matter of fact, ships do usually sail on rivers. Vasya had a sudden idea of making a river in the room, but he only sighed —Mummy would not allow that on any account. Not so long ago she had taken a very unfavourable attitude towards the plan of building a dock for the steamer. It was she gave Vasya the tin, but when he filled it with water she disapproved.

"Your dock is leaking. Look what a mess you've made!"

Now the tin is full of sand and is going to be a park. Daddy has already brought in a whole branch of pine for the young trees.

Vasya hurries over his breakfast: he has so much work and worry that there is no time to drink a cup of coffee, and his eyes keep wandering towards the toy kingdom.

"Are you going to build the house today?" asks Mother.

"No! I'll be travelling! I'm going to cart the stuff! Over there!"

Vasya points out the construction site and adds: "But I won't make a mess, don't worry!"

As a matter of fact, Mother is not so worried as Vasya himself—building is a very dirty job.

"Well, if you make a mess, you'll have to clear it up," says Mother.

This unexpected turn of events fills Vasya with energy. Forgetting about breakfast, he begins to slip down from his chair.

"Vasya, what are you after? Drink up your coffee. You mustn't leave your cup half empty!"

She is right there. Vasya empties the cup in hasty gulps. His mother watches him and smiles.

"Are you so short of time? Where are you off to in such a hurry?"

"I must hurry," mumbles Vasya.

Already he is in the toy kingdom. The first thing he does is to relieve Vanka-Vstanka.

"Your watchman is on his feet day and night," his mother told him once. "That won't do at all. He must have a rest too. You go to sleep every night, you know."

To be sure, how could Vasya have forgotten about the protection of labour? But this omission was a long time ago. Now Vasya stuffs Vstanka into an old cardboard house and pushes his head down under some building materials. Vstanka makes a fuss and gets out of hand, but what if he does, discipline comes first! And on days-off, when Father is at home, Vstanka languishes for a whole twenty-four hours in the cardboard house, while his post is taken over by a little china fellow in a pink Tyrol hat. This lad, although he is Mummy's present, is a bad worker—keeps on falling over. Father was right when he called him a loafer· "That one in the hat, you can see he's a loafer!"

Because of this Vasya does not like him and tries to do without his services.

The first job Vasya ever did for the community was bringing father's boots and shoes. Vasya's parents give him other jobs too: fetching the matches, putting the chairs in place, straightening the table-cloth, picking up papers, but these are occasional jobs, while the boots and shoes are permanent work—a duty that must not be neglected.

Only once, when a catastrophe occurred in the toy kingdom and the funnel came off the steam-engine, Vasya met his father with the wrecked engine in his hands and was so upset that he forgot all about Daddy's shoes. Father examined the engine, shook his head, clucked his tongue and got right to the bottom of Vasya's grief.

"Capital repair," he said.

These words dismayed Vasya even more. He followed his father into the bedroom, where he stood sadly peering into the engine as it lay on its side on the bed. But suddenly he was struck by the unusual silence in the room, and at that moment he heard his father's voice saying wryly: "So the engine's lost its funnel and I've lost my shoes."

185

Vasya looked at Daddy's feet, blushed, and instantly forgot all about the engine. He dashed into the kitchen and soon the situation was restored. Daddy, smiling rather an unusual smile, looked at Vasya. Vasya carried the boots into the kitchen, and not a thought of the engine entered his head until his father said: "I'll bring you another funnel. A strong one this time!"

When Vasya was six years old, his father gave him a big box, full of little bricks, beams, blocks, girders and other constructional materials. These were for building real palaces. And in the box there was also a book with drawings of the palaces which should be built. Out of respect for his father and the trouble he had taken, Vasya bestowed great attention on the box. Conscientiously he examined each drawing and patiently, with much pursing of lips, picked out the right pieces according to the plan. His father noticed something unusual and asked:

"Don't you like it?"

Vasya did not want to say that he did not like the work, but he could not say anything else. He frowned in silence over the building.

"Don't frown, tell me if you don't like it," said his father.

Vasya looked at his father, then at the building again.

"There's such a lot of houses," he answered. "You build one house, then you pull it down, then you build another one and you pull that down, and there is nothing left. . . . So you go on building and building . . . until you get a headache. . . ."

His father burst out laughing.

"Ah! You're right there! You keep on building and building and you've got nothing to show for it. That's not construction, it's destruction, sabotage "

Vasya stopped building and looked quickly at his father.

"Sabotage? What's that?"

"Well, it's like your trouble—your work is sabotaged. There are some swine...."

"Swine?" repeated Vasya.

"Yes, swine," insisted his father, "they build like that on purpose, and then, do what you like, you might just as well burn it or pull it down, it's no use."

Vasya turned to the drawings.

"You can build another one, one like this, or one like that...."

Taking the model to pieces, Vasya decided to begin a new, more difficult one, so as to give his father at least some pleasure.

Saying nothing, his father watched him complete his work.

"You've not made a bad job of that. But it's just built on air, isn't it? Give it a push and down it goes...."

With a laugh Vasya brandished his arm and knocked the building down. The wonderful palace was reduced to a pile of neat fragments on the floor.

"What did you do that for?"

"It's got to be knocked down anyway, because there's another one to..."

"There you are, you see, you've got nothing to show for your pains."

"Nothing at all," said Vasya, spreading out his arms.

"That won't do."

"No," agreed Vasya, looking with ruthless indifference at the scattered fragments.

"Half a mo." His father smiled and went over to his tool-box. He came back with real treasure in his hands. In the wooden box lay the nails, tacks, screws, bolts, lengths of wire, steel and copper plates and other odds and ends that are part of life for every self-respecting metal-worker. Separately in Father's hand lay some little rods, which jumped up and down when you touched them.

"We'll leave these houses of yours," said Father, "let's build something strong. But what shall it be?"

"Let's build a bridge. Only, there's no river."

"No river? Well, we'll have to make one then."

"Can that be done?"

"It used not to be, but it is now. The Bolsheviks did it. They brought the Volga right as far as Moscow."

"What Volga?"

"The River Volga. Where'd it used to flow? Ever so far away! But they set to and made it flow over dry land."

"And then what?" asked Vasya, not taking his eyes off his father.

"Came like a lamb," replied his father, spreading out his odds and ends on the floor.

"Let's make a Volga ourselves...."

"That's what I was thinking."

"And then we'll build a bridge."

But suddenly remembering what had happened last time he brought up the question of a river, Vasya looked dejected. Squatting in front of his father's box, he began to feel that all these obstacles were getting the better of him.

"We can't build a river, Daddy, Mummy won't let us."

Father raised his brows attentively and also squatted down on his heels.

"Mummy? Yes, that's a serious matter."

Vasya looked up at his father hopefully: suppose Daddy suddenly found a means of combating Mummy. But Father returned his glance uncertainly; Vasya elucidated the situation: "She'll say: you'll spill the water."

"She will. That's the point, she's sure to say so. And we are sure to spill the water!"

Vasya smiled at his father's simplicity: "What were you thinking of then? About making a river and it being dry?"

"Now you listen to me, son. How does a river flow?

It only flows in one place, and all round it's dry. There must be banks. And then, think of it, if you just put a river on the floor, it'll all go through to downstairs. The people living there will want to know what's happening up here. Where's that coming from?—they'll say. And it will be our river that's doing it."

"And didn't any water come into Moscow?"

"Why should it come into Moscow?"

"When they brought up this ... Volga?"

"Well, sonny, there they did things properly, they made banks."

"What of?"

"They found a way of doing it. Out of stone. Out of concrete."

"Daddy, listen! Listen! We'll do that too ... let's make banks!"

And so Vasya Nazarov's great construction project was born. The project turned out to be complicated and demanded much preliminary work. Its immediate result was the complete abandoning of constructional work on temporary palaces. Father and Vasya decided not to build any more palaces because of their complete lack of practical value. Instead they resolved to use the contents of the box on building a bridge. But what was to be done with the book of drawings? Vasya had lost interest in it and Daddy also treated it with some scorn: "What's the use of the thing? Pity to throw it away though. Give it to one of the kids."

"What will he do with it?"

"Oh, he'll have a look at it...."

Vasya did not think much of this proposal, but the following morning, when he went out into the yard, he took the book with him.

The yard was not like a town yard, surrounded by brick walls. It was a large square, with plenty of sky above it. On one side stood a long two-storied building with a

189

full half-dozen wooden porches giving out on to the court-yard. All the other sides were bordered by a low wooden fence, beyond which, as far as the horizon, stretched an undulating sandy district, known in our parts as the "kuchuguri," a land of freedom and mystery very attractive to boys. Only beyond the house and the massive gates nearby did the first street of the town begin.

This house was the home of workers and employees from the carriage-building works—solid, respectable folk, with big families. And the yard was always swarming with youngsters. Vasya had only just begun to get to know yard society. Of the few relationships he had formed last summer he remembered very little, and that winter Vasya had hardly visited the yard once, having caught measles.

At present Vasya's circle of acquaintances was made up almost entirely of boys. There were some girls in the court-yard too, but, being five or six years older than Vasya, they treated him rather aloofly. They were the age when girls develop a proud habit of walking along together, singing, which makes them very inaccessible. As for the youngsters of two and three, needless to say, they were no company for Vasya.

The book of drawings at once aroused general interest. Mitya Kandybin, a lad of Vasya's age, saw the book and shouted: "Where did the album come from? Where'd you get it?"

"It's mine," replied Vasya.

"Where'd you get it?"

"I didn't get it anywhere. Daddy bought it."

"He bought it for you, did he?"

Vasya did not like Mitya because he was too frisky and had too much cheek. His bright little eyes never tired of peeping and peering into everything, and this embarrassed Vasya.

"Did he buy it for you? Was it for you?"

Vasya put the book behind his back.

"Yes, he did."

"Well, show us. Come on, show us!"

Vasya did not want to do any showing. He was not worried about the book, but he felt a desire to resist Mitya's strong pressure. Mitya, however, could hardly stand still and was already trying to get at the book from behind.

"You're too mean to show it, are you?"

Although he was weaker and smaller than Vasya, Mitya was on the point of attacking to get the book, but at that moment his shouts drew the attention of Lyovik.

Lyovik belonged to the older generation and was in the first class of School No. 34. Beaming cheerfully at the aggressive Mitya, he shouted from a distance: "Too much yelling and no fighting! Bash him!"

"What's he keeping it for! The dog in the manger! He won't show anyone!"

Mitya thrust his bare shoulder, covered only with boy's braces, contemptuously towards Vasya.

"Come on, let's have a look!" With cheerful authority Lyovik stretched out his hand, and Vasya gave him the book.

"I say!" exclaimed Lyovik joyfully. "You know what? I lost one just like this. I've got everything else, but the album's gone. What a find! Come on, let's swop!"

Vasya had never swopped anything in his life, and now he did not know how to answer Lyovik. However, it was clear that this was the beginning of an interesting adventure. Vasya looked anxiously at Lyovik's cheerful face as he glanced quickly through the book.

"Fine! Let's go over to my place...."

"What for?" asked Vasya.

"Why, you nut, you've got to see what you want to swop it for."

"I'll come too," said Mitya darkly, still looking rather aggressive.

"Come on then. . . . You'll be there as witness, see. There always has to be a witness when you swop things. . . ."

They went over to Lyovik's porch. When they were already at the top of the steps Lyovik looked round.

"Just don't take any notice of my sister Lalya!"

He pushed the big grey-painted door. In the passage a stench of damp vegetables and beet soup descended on them. When Lyovik shut the door behind him Vasya felt quite scared: the darkness combined with the smell was unpleasant. But another door opened and the boys could see the kitchen. There was not much to see, for the place was full of steam and before their eyes hung some kind of white, pink and blue cloths—probably sheets and blankets. Two of these cloths parted, revealing a rosy face with high cheek-bones and beautiful eyes.

"Lyovik, is that you bringing in those boys again? Look here, Varka, say what you like, but I'm going to give them what for!"

From behind the washing a woman's voice answered faintly: "Why do you lose your temper so, Lalya? What harm will they do you?"

Lalya fixed an angry glance on the boys and, without changing her expression, said very quickly: "What harm will they do? They trample over everywhere, their feet are dirty, their heads are dirty, and there's sand falling out of them. . . ."

She poked her finger into Mitya's shaggy head, then raised it to her eyes: "Oho! The sparrows have been nesting here, I should think! And where does that one come from. Just look what eyes he's got!"

Although the girl was only about fifteen, the impression she made was terrifying, and Vasya took a step back. But Lyovik had already shut the passage door and was saying boldly to his comrades: "Don't take any notice. Come on!"

The boys ducked under the washing and entered a room. The room was small and crowded with furniture, books, curtains and flowers. Only a little passage remained free, and here all three boys halted, one behind the other. Lyovik pushed his two visitors in the chest.

"You sit down on the sofa, or there won't be room to get by."

Vasya and Mitya collapsed on the sofa. The Nazarovs did not possess such a piece of furniture. It was nice to sit on, but the lack of space in the room scared Vasya. There were a lot of strange things here. The piano, several portraits in oval frames, yellow candlesticks, books and music made the room seem very rich and mysterious. In front of them, on a revolving stool sat Lyovik, spinning round and saying: "Swop you four key rings, or you can have a swallow's nest if you like. Then, there's a purse. Look, here's a purse for you!"

Lyovik jumped off the revolving stool, pulled out the drawer of a small desk and placed it on his knees. First of all a little green purse, fastened with a single press-bu'ton, was presented to Vasya. Lyovik pressed the button several times to arouse Vasya's interest. But at that moment Vasya noticed something more interesting than the purse. Along the whole length of the drawer lay a narrow tin box, three fingers wide, and black in colour.

"Oh!" cried Vasya and pointed to the tin.

"The tin?" asked Lyovik and stopped snapping the button of the purse. "Only ... oh well, that's even better."

Mitya jumped up from the sofa and bent over the drawer.

Vasya nodded at the tin: "That's what I need." He looked up at Lyovik with his big eyes, honest, calm grey eyes. And Lyovik looked at Vasya with a pair of experienced and rather cunning brown ones.

"So you'll give me the album for the tin, is that so? Do you agree to that before the witness?"

Vasya nodded his head seriously at Lyovik. Lyovik took the tin out of the drawer and fingered it.

"The tin's yours."

Overjoyed at his luck, Vasya grasped the tin and peered inside. The bottom was strong and there were no cracks showing—that meant the water would not leak through to downstairs. It would be a real, long river! And he would make up the banks with sand. So high! And plant a forest on the banks. The river would flow through the forest and then there would be a bridge.

"Want to see the swallow's nest? I've got one here," offered the host. "I'll show you."

He went off to a third room; Vasya carefully placed the tin on the sofa and stood in the doorway. In the room there were beds, an aquarium and some crowded wooden shelves. Lyovik took down a swallow's nest.

"It's not one of our swallows, it's a Japanese one. See how it's made?"

Vasya cautiously took the dark flimsy ball, with a little opening in it, between his palms.

"Want the swallow's nest instead of the tin?"

"But what's it for?"

"What do you mean 'what's it for'? It's for a collection, stupid!"

"What's a collection?"

"A collection! Well, you get another one like this. Or a different kind. And then you have a collection."

"And have you got a collection?"

"What's it matter what I've got. You'll have one. What's the use of an empty tin!"

But Vasya shook his head.

"I need the tin, but I don't need that."

Vasya remembered the tin lovingly and turned to the sofa. But there was no tin there. He glanced round the room, looked at the lid of the piano, then at a pile of books. No tin.

"Where is it?" he called to Lyovik.

"Who? The swallow?" asked Lyovik from the other room.

"No, where's the tin?"

"But I've just given it to you. I put it right in your hands!"

Vasya looked at the sofa in dismay.

"It was lying here."

Lyovik also looked at the sofa, also glanced round the room, then pulled out the drawer.

"Hold on! Where's Mitya? He must have stolen it!"

"How?"

"How? Why, just pinched it and done a bunk."

"Gone away?"

"Done a bunk! Don't you see? Mitya's not here!"

Vasya sat down sadly on the sofa, then stood up again. He was very sorry about the tin.

"Pinched it?" he asked Lyovik mechanically.

"We swopped square," said Lyovik, pulling a face. "It was an honest swop. I put it in your hands, in front of a witness!"

"What witness?"

"In front of Mitya! That was a witness for you! What a joke! Fine witness!"

Lyovik roared with laughter.

"That was a witness! But what about you? He's cleaned you out. We swopped square!"

In the doorway stood Lalya, regarding her b other's amusement questioningly with her dark slanting eyes. Suddenly she hurled herself into the room. Vasya got up from the sofa in alarm.

"What did you take my purse for?"

Lyovik stopped laughing and moved past Vasya towards the door.

"Did I take it?"

"What's it lying on the table for then?"

"Let it lie there! What's it got to do with me!"

Lalya tugged the drawer open, peered sharply inside and shouted: "Give it back! Give it back at once! Pig!"

Lyovik was now at the door, ready for further retreat. Lalya rushed towards him and collided with Vasya, who had been standing there utterly confused and crushed by the torrent of events. Pushing him head over heels on to the sofa, she crashed at full speed into the door which Lyovik had closed smartly right in her face. A second door crashed to, then a third, the front door. All three doors banged again as Lalya swept through them in pursuit of her brother. At last, just as precipitately, she rushed back into the room, pulled out the drawer again, rummaged in it noisily and burst loudly into tears, leaning on the table. Vasya continued to look at her in amazement and alarm. It was beginning to dawn on him that Lalya's sobbing had something to do with the tin that had just vanished before his eyes. He was about to say something when Lalya, still crying, stepped back and threw her slender body on the sofa beside him. Her shoulders trembled at Vasya's feet. Vasya's eyes opened even wider; plunging his fists into the sofa, he bent over the sobbing girl.

"What are you crying for?" he asked clearly. "P'raps it's about the tin?"

Lalya's sobs stopped abruptly, and she raised her head and glanced angrily at Vasya. Vasya looked at her too, noticing the tear-drops on the tips of her eye-lashes.

"Is it the tin you are crying about?" he repeated, nodding encouragingly.

"About the tin? Aha!" shouted Lalya. "Tell me where it is!"

"Where it is?" asked Vasya, somewhat taken aback by the hatred in Lalya's voice.

Lalya jabbed him on the shoulder and shouted even louder: "Answer me! Answer me where it is! Why don't you speak?! What have you done with it? What have you done with my pencil-case?"

"Pencil-case?"

Vasya did not quite understand. It occurred to him that something else might be involved, not the tin. But he had an honest desire to help this unhappy girl with the beautiful slanting eyes.

"What did you say? Pencil-case?"

"All right, tin then! The tin! What have you done with it?"

Vasya pointed animatedly to the drawer.

"The one that was lying there?"

"Don't try to fool me! Say what you've done with it!"

Vasya sighed and embarked on his difficult story.

"Lyovik said: give me your book and I'll give you the purse. Then he said: have a ring, then he said: have a swallow's nest, only that was afterwards, he gave me the tin before. A black one with a ... with a strong bottom. So I said: all right. And he said: before the witness ... and put it in my hands. So I..."

"Ah, so it was you took it, was it?"

Vasya did not have time to answer. He suddenly saw Lalya's dark-brown eyes quiver, and at that moment his head struck the soft back of the sofa, and he felt a strange unpleasant burning sensation on his cheek. It slowly dawned on Vasya that Lalya had hit him. Vasya had never been hit in his life and did not know that it was insulting. But nevertheless tears bubbled into his eyes. He jumped out from the sofa, clapping his hand to his cheek.

"Give it to me at once!" shouted Lalya rising to attack.

By this time Vasya knew that she might hit him again, and he did not want this to happen, but his mind was really occupied by another thought: how is it she cannot understand that the box is not here. He hastened to explain to her how matters stood.

"Well? Where is it?"

"But it's not here! Not here, you see!"

"What do you mean 'not here'?"

"Mitya took it."

"Mitya?"

"Yes! He ... pinched the tin." Vasya was glad he remembered this word—perhaps it would help Lalya to understand quicker.

"Was it that ginger one? Did you give it to him? Tell me."

Lalya came towards him. Vasya looked round. His only retreat lay through the narrow gap between the piano and the table, but he had no time to use it. Lalya pushed him roughly towards the window, hit him painfully on the head and was again raising her arm. But unexpectedly, both for her and for Vasya, a little fist swept round in a half circle and struck her sharp rosy chin. It was followed by another little fist, then the first came again. Frowning and baring his teeth, Vasya milled away in front of him, striking where he could and missing most of the time. Lalya retreated a little, more from surprise than from the blows, but neither her face nor her stance spelled any good for her adversary. The battle would have gone hard for Vasya had not a thin, long-faced woman in glasses appeared in the doorway.

"Lalya, what is going on here? Whose boy is that?"

"How should I know whose boy he is," said Lalya, glancing round. "Lyovik brought him in. They've stolen my pencil-case! Just look at him now!"

Lalya's brown eyes suddenly smiled for a second, but Vasya was more interested in the older woman's attitude. Probably this was Lalya's mother—now they would both beat him together.

"What, have you been fighting here? Really, Lalya!"

"Let him return the tin! I'll give him some more in a moment. Now then you!"

Lalya came nearer. Vasya moved nearer the table.

Lalya's eyes had grown kinder and he felt calmer in the woman's presence, but he had not forgotten his recent experience.

"Lalya, stop frightening him! What a nice boy!"

"You stop interfering, Varka!" shouted Lalya. "Nice boy! You think everybody is nice. Soft-hearted! Give me the tin, you!"

But at this moment reinforcements arrived. In the doorway appeared a rather short man, plucking at his narrow black beard.

"Grishka!" said the girl, growing more cheerful at once. "Look, she's defending him! This kid got into the house, put my pencil-case somewhere, and Varka defends him!"

"Oh, Varka always defends everybody," smiled the man. "But whose boy is he?"

"Where do you come from? What's your name?" asked Lalya with a smile.

Vasya looked every one over steadily, then he said with serious politeness: "My name is Vasya Nazarov."

"Ah, Nazarov!" cried the girl. She came up to him quite affectionately.

"Vasya Nazarov? All right then. Now be a sport and promise me you'll find the tin. Understand?"

Vasya understood very little: the meaning of "be a sport" was not clear, neither was it clear what "find" meant.

"Mitya took it," he said confidently.

"Really, it's too much," interrupted the woman whose name was Varka. "She beat him."

"Lalya!" said the man reproachfully.

"Oh, Grishka! That tone of voice gets on my nerves! You're as bad as Varka!"

Turning round, the girl tossed her head at Varka and quickly left the room.

"Go along, Vasya, and don't think about the tin," said Varka, "go along!"

Vasya looked into Varka's face and liked it. Ignoring the grinning figure of Grishka, he went out on the steps.

Lyovik was standing nearby, laughing.

"Well? Did you catch it?"

Vasya smiled awkwardly. He had not quite recovered from his terrible adventure and had not had time to consider events. As a matter of fact, he was interested only in separate aspects of his experience. He could not get the tin out of his head—it would have made such a lovely river! From the steps he was already scanning the courtyard for signs of Mitya. Apart from this he must also find out who Varka and Grishka were. And another question: where were Lyovik's mummy and daddy?

He went down the steps.

"Lyovik, where's your daddy?"

"Dad? Didn't you see him?"

"No."

"But he went in. He's got a beard. . . ."

"A beard? But that's Grishka."

"Well, Grishka or Dad—it's all the same."

"No, for Dad . . . people say Father sometimes. Grishka won't do."

"So you think just because he's your father he hasn't any name? What's your dad called?"

"Mine? Aha, you mean what Mummy calls him? Mummy calls him 'Fedya.' "

"Well, your father is Fedya then, and ours is Grishka."

"Grishka? That's what your Mummy calls him, is it?"

"Coo, you are an ass! Mummy and everybody else. He's Grishka and Mummy is Varka."

Vasya was still in the dark, but he did not feel like asking any more. Lyovik was already at the top of the steps, and Vasya remembered that he, too, must go home.

When he reached his own porch and opened the door

he bumped into his mother. She looked at him closely and did not go for water as she had intended, but came back into the flat.

"Tell me, now. What's the matter with you today?"

Without hurrying or getting excited Vasya recounted his adventures. Only at one point words failed him, and here he relied more on mimicry and gestures.

"What a look she gave me! What a look!"

"Well?"

"And then, she hits me such a whack.... Right here."

"Well, then what?"

"Ha! And here.... Then ... I was going to go. And she started again. And how I hit too! And then Varka came!"

"Who is this Varka?"

"I dunno! She's got glasses. And Grishka. Like you call Daddy Fedya, they call each other Grishka and Varka. And Varka said: good boy, go along."

"This is a serious matter, Vasya dear."

"It is," assented Vasya, nodding at his mother and smiling.

Then Father said: "There now! See what a job it is building the Volga! What are you going to do next?"

Vasya sat on his little mat by the toys, and thought. He realized that his father was being artful and did not want to help him in this difficult life. But, for Vasya, Father was a model of wisdom and knowledge, and Vasya wanted to know his opinion.

"But why don't you tell me? I'm still little!"

"You may be little, but you didn't ask me when you went to swop, did you? Didn't ask a thing."

"Lyovik said: let's swop. So I went to have a look and saw the tin."

"Now look a bit further: you made your swop but where's the tin?"

Vasya laughed ironically and made a gesture of despair.

"I haven't got it. Mitya ... pinched it."

" 'Pinched it.' What kind of a word is that? In our language people say 'stole.' "

"What language does Lyovik talk then?"

"Goodness knows what language it is! Thieves talk like that."

"But that's how Lyovik talks."

"Don't you go copying Lyovik. And his sister is studying at the art school, so that tin must be hers, for her paint-brushes. See how it is? His sister gave you a hiding, did she? Well, she was quite right...."

"It was Lyovik's and Mitya's fault."

"No, laddie, the boy to blame is Vasya Nazarov."

"Ha!" laughed Vasya. "But you're wrong, Daddy, I'm not to blame at all."

"Vasya believed Lyovik, somebody he did not know, who was a complete stranger to him. Vasya did not think about anything, let himself be caught napping and accepted the tin, let himself be caught napping twice, with his mouth wide open. And then Mitya Kandybin turned up. And the tin vanished and Vasya got a hiding. Whose fault was it then?"

The more Father talked the more Vasya blushed and realized that it was indeed his fault. He was mainly convinced of this not by the words but by the tone they were spoken in. Vasya sensed that his father was really displeased with him, and that meant Vasya really was to blame. Besides, the words were important too. In the Nazarov family frequent use was made of the expression "to be caught napping." The other day his father had related how an instructor of a group of turners, Mitya Kandybin's father, had been "caught napping," and how in this instance one hundred and thirty parts had "gone west"! Now Vasya recalled Father's story word for word.

He turned away with even deeper blushes, then glanced at his father timidly and gave a weak smile, looking sad and confused. His father was sitting on the chair with his elbows on his knees, laughing as he looked at his son. He now seemed particularly close and dear to Vasya—his soft moustache stirred gently and his eyes were so tender.

Vasya did not manage to say anything. He suddenly remembered that there was nowhere to put the little tin-tacks his father had given him for building the bridge. They were just lying on the cloth in a heap. Leaning on his elbow, Vasya made a thorough examination of the scattered tin-tacks and said:

"But there's nowhere to put the tacks.... Mummy promised to give me a box ... and then forgot...."

"Come on, I'll give you a box," said his mother.

Vasya ran off after his mother, and when he returned his father was already sitting in the bedroom, reading the newspaper and laughing heartily.

"Marusya, come and look at Mussolini all bandaged up, the poor mutt! It's after Guadalajara; he's had to be bandaged up...."

Vasya has heard this strange long word "Mussolini" more than once, but he understood only that it was something bad, something his father did not like. At that moment, however, he remembered Mitya Kandybin. He must get that tin back from him.

After breakfast Vasya was in a hurry to get into the yard. It was Daddy's day-off. Daddy and Mummy were ready to go shopping in the town. Vasya liked to accompany them, but today he was not going. They were taking Natasha with them, but Father said to Vasya: "You are busy today, aren't you?"

Vasya made no reply. He had caught the hint in his father's words—so Daddy knew everything anyway. Vasya's mind was not easy, for he had no definite plan of action.

They all left the flat together. At the gate Father gave Vasya the key to the front door.

"You go for a walk. Don't lose the key, and don't swop it with anyone."

Vasya listened to this command seriously and did not even blush, for he knew the key really was something important that must not be swopped.

When he returned to the yard Vasya noticed a crowd of boys. There was a serious war brewing on the "kuchuguri." It had been talked of for some time and an explosion was imminent. Today it seemed the thunder-clouds must break.

Vasya had been out on the "kuchuguri" several times with his father, but still did not know all the secrets of that wonderful region.

The "kuchuguri" was a broad expanse of open country which, beginning from the last houses of the town, stretched ahead for about three kilometres, and on either side even further. The whole area was dotted with numerous sandy hills, which were quite high and sometimes shaped like real mountain ridges. In places they were overgrown with bushes and elsewhere short stubbly grass grew on them. In the centre of the "kuchuguri" stood a real mountain, which the boys called "Fly Mountain" because people on its summit looked no bigger than flies. Fly Mountain only seemed grand and solid from a distance. In reality it was a jumble of peaks and steep slopes covered with rippling sand. These were cleft by precipices and ravines, overgrown with bushes. All round Fly Mountain, as far as the eye could see, right to the hamlet of Korchagi, which was almost invisible under its thick mantle of green, were scattered smaller mountains with smaller precipices and ravines.

Vasya had seen some boys slide fearlessly right down to the very bottom of the steep slopes, rolling over and over, raising clouds of dust and leaving clearly visible tracks behind them on the smooth surface. It must be a great pleasure to roll down such a slope, he thought, and then to stand triumphantly at the bottom of the ravine, looking up towards the summit and gradually shaking the sand out of your clothes, nose and ears. In his father's presence Vasya hesitated to undertake such a swoop into the abyss, but he dreamed secretly of doing so.

However, at present the "kuchuguri" were no longer available for such peaceful amusements. The area was poisoned with the seeds of war. Vasya had as yet not taken part in the collective operations of the young forces in the locality, but he had already reached "calling-up age" and military matters were of interest to him. For several days now hot debates had been going on among the boys concerning the tense situation in the "kuchuguri." Tomorrow, if not today, war was sure to break out. The yard's acknowledged commander-in-chief was Seryozha Skalkovsky, a fifth-class boy, the son of a works inspector at the factory. Old man Skalkovsky kept his large family on a short rein, but he was a cheery, talkative man with much derisive humour in him. He had the Order of the Red Banner and could remember a lot about partisan times, but never boasted of his successes in that field and, on the contrary, liked discussing military technique and organization. For this reason Seryozha Skalkovsky was also an opponent of the disorderly scuffles taking place on the "kuchuguri," and demanded order.

The enemy was encamped in a big three-storied house near the area in question, half a kilometre distant from Vasya's yard. The boys of this house had long ago made themselves masters of their side of the "kuchuguri" and were now even turning their eyes in the direction of Fly Mountain. It was in the ravines of this mountain that the first clashes had taken place. To begin with they were individual encounters, then groups became involved. In one of the recent clashes a whole detachment under the command of Seryozha Skalkovsky himself had been hurled down by the enemy to the bottom of one of the precipices, and the victors had marched home along the mountain ridges, singing triumphantly. But yesterday evening Seryozha had succeeded in wiping out this disgrace: just before sunset, in the "eastern sector," he had fallen upon a body of the enemy. A battle took place and the enemy retreated, but the real importance of the victory lay in the fact that an unfinished map of the whole territory had been seized from one of the prisoners. This was clear proof of the enemy's aggressive intentions. Vasya appeared in the yard just as Seryozha was saying: "You see, they are already making maps. And here we are without any plan at all. And look, they've drawn in our house and written over it: 'Blue Headquarters.' "

"Oho!" called out someone, "according to them we are Blues, are we?"

"Yes, Blues!"

"And they are Reds?"

"That's what it comes to."

"And they put it down like that on their map," shouted another voice.

"Who gave them the right to do it?"

"Reds! I like that!"

"Now we've got the map we can alter it!"

Indignation rose as the assembled company examined the map. Vasya also squeezed his way up to the offending object, and, although he could not yet read, he saw clearly that the yard had suffered an insult; and as for being called Reds, he had no doubts whatever that only Seryozha's warriors were worthy of that honour.

Vasya listened seriously, looked now at one face, now at another, and suddenly noticed on the other side of the crowd the sharp little eyes of Mitya Kandybin. The fire of war in Vasya's soul died down abruptly and in its stead rose the problem of the tin. Skirting the crowd, he grasped Mitya by the elbow. Mitya looked round and dodged rapidly aside.

"Mitya, did you take that tin yesterday?"

"Yes, I did. What of it? What are you going to do about it?"

Although Mitya put on a bold front, he moved back and was obviously ready to run away. Such behaviour came as a terrible surprise to Vasya. He took a pace forward and said steadily: "Well, give it back!"

"Ooh, you've got a nerve," and Mitya pulled a scornful face. "Give it back! You've got a nerve, you have!"

"So you won't give it back? You stole it and now you won't give it back? Is that it?"

Vasya said this loud and excitedly, with some anger.

In reply Mitya made a horrid ugly face. What happened next no one could say, not even Vasya himself. Anyhow, the council of war was forced to adjourn its discussion of strategic questions, the attention of its members being diverted by a curious sight. On the ground lay Mitya, face downwards, and astride his shoulders sat Vasya, who was asking: "Will you give it back? Come on, will you give it back?"

To this question Mitya would make no reply and kept trying to regain his freedom. His face was smudged with sand, and as it kept twisting rapidly from side to side Vasya kept trying to look on the corresponding side and ask: "Come on, will you give it back?"

The council of war roared with laughter. The funniest thing was that in Vasya's face there was no sign of anger or hostility. His big eyes expressed only interest in whether Mitya would give the tin back or not. He asked his question without any threat, just as an ordinary practical question. At the same time Vasya occasionally squashed his adversary into the earth and pushed his head down a little.

In the end the general attention and laughter caused Vasya to look up. Seryozha Skalkovsky took him by the shoulders and raised him gently to his feet. Vasya smiled and said to Seryozha: "I've squashed him and squashed him, but he won't say anything."

"What were you squashing him for?"

"He took my tin."

"What tin?"

"A big one ... a big tin...."

Mitya stood by, wiping his face with his hand, which did not help to make it any cleaner.

"Why don't you give him back the tin?" asked Seryozha.

Mitya poked up his nose, looked away and said in a dull, sulky bass: "I would have done, only my father took it."

"But is the tin his?"

Mitya nodded with the same indifference. Seryozha, who was a strong, handsome lad with fair, beautifully combed hair, thought for a moment.

"All right. Your father must give it back. After all, it's not his tin." Seryozha turned to Vasya. "So Mitya took it from you, did he?"

"He didn't take it.... It was yesterday ... he ... stole it."

The boys laughed, and Lyovik laughed too. Noticing Lyovik, Vasya shouted: "There's Lyovik, he knows everything."

Lyovik's grin vanished and he turned away.

"I don't know anything about it. It's not my business what he stole from you!"

Then Seryozha acted like a real commander-in-chief and shouted sternly at Mitya: "Did you steal it? Speak up!"

"I took it. What's stealing to do with it?!"

"Very well," said Seryozha, "we'll finish the conference and you two wait here. What's your name?"

"Vasya."

"Well, you watch him, Vasya. He's under arrest!"

Vasya threw a sidelong glance at Mitya and smiled. He was very pleased at Seryozha's way of ordering things, although he did not understand really what it was that pleased him. It was Seryozha's confident strength and the strength of the boys' organization supporting him that appealed to Vasya.

Vasya kept an eye on Mitya, but the latter did not even think of running away—perhaps because he had already felt the grip of his guard, and perhaps he, too, was pleased at being arrested by the commander-in-chief himself. Both combatants stood eyeing each other politely and became so absorbed in the job that they did not even hear the debates at the council of war.

The meeting was attended by about ten boys, including such under-aged participants as Vasya and Mitya, who could not hope for responsible posts, but felt instinctively that in the forthcoming battles no one would hinder them from displaying their energy. The conditions of the war were therefore of little interest to them. But fate was kinder than they had anticipated. Seryozha Skalkovsky's voice suddenly rang out from the centre of the gathering:

"No, we won't touch the main forces. We've got some fine scouts, you know! There's that chap who won the fight today, Vasya, wasn't it? He's a fighter all right! He will be the chief of the reconnaissance."

"No, we need a big'un for chief," objected a voice.

"All right then, but he'll be second-in-command. What's wrong with him anyway?"

Everyone looked at Vasya and smiled. Vasya quickly realized what a career was opening before him, for his father had often told him about reconnaissance work. He blushed with inward pride but made no move to show his excitement and only looked even more fixedly at Mitya. Mitya pouted scornfully and muttered: "What a scout!"

This was said out of envy, but at that moment Seryozha emerged from the circle and, looking about him, began to pull out scouts by their cuffs and elbows and bring them together in a group round Vasya. There were eight of them and the first to enter the group was, of course, Mitya. All were pleased, though in their bearing they lacked the confidence of real scouts.

Seryozha made a speech:

"Now you are scouts, understand? Only see to it that there is discipline and not a free-for-all. Your chief will be Kostya Varenik, and this Vasya here is second-in-command. Understand?"

The scouts nodded their heads and turned towards Kostya. The latter was a slim lad of about thirteen. He had a big cheerful mouth and derisive eyes. Thrusting his hands into his pockets, he viewed his team, then raised a fist.

"The scouts must be fighters, see! Anyone who turns traitor or coward will be shot!"

The scouts opened their eyes wide, gurgling with pleasure.

"Let's go and get organized!" ordered the commander.

"What about the one under arrest?" asked Vasya.

"Oh yes, hold on! Comrade Commander-in-Chief, shall I release the arrested man?"

"Of course not!" shouted Seryozha indignantly. "We're just going to investigate the case!"

Seryozha came out in front and was about to lead them away somewhere when, just at that moment, the heavy gate opened to admit three boys aged between eleven and thirteen. One of them was carrying a stick with a white rag attached to it.

"Oh! Envoys!" exclaimed Seryozha in great excitement.

"They're surrendering!" whooped someone else from behind.

"Attention! No talking!" roared the commander-in-chief wildly.

An alarmed hush descended on the crowd, and everyone waited to see what would happen next. The commander-in-chief was not the only one who broke out in a cold sweat when he saw how well organized the enemy was: one had a white flag, another a Young Pioneer's bugle, the third a golden cock feather stuck in an old cap—he was one of the chiefs. The boys had scarcely recovered from the first shock when the enemy gave an even more spectacular display of organization: the envoys formed up in a line, then the bugler raised his bugle and played something. Even Seryozha was overcome with envy, but recovering himself quicker than the others, he stepped out in front, saluted and said:

"I am Commander-in-Chief Sergei Skalkovsky. We did not know you would be coming and so did not prepare a guard of honour. We beg your pardon."

This relieved the boys, who saw once again that their commander-in-chief knew his stuff.

The chief envoy also stepped forward and made a speech:

"We weren't able to tell you because there was no time. The Red Command declares war on the Blues, but we must agree on the rules and you must return our plan, because you took it against the rules, before the war started. We must make rules about when to fight and what banners the Reds and Blues shall have."

"We're not Blues!" someone in the crowd shouted offendedly. "What's the idea of calling us Blues!"

"Tch!" ordered the commander-in-chief, but himself added: "We don't mind making some rules, only you must not call yourself Reds. That's not right: you can't be just what you like...."

"We thought of it first," said the envoy.

"No, we were the first," came more shouts from the ranks.

Realizing that war might break out before the rules had been made, Seryozha hastened to quieten his forces:

"Hold on! What are you shouting for? Let's sit down and talk things over."

The envoys consented, and all took their seats on a heap of logs by the fence.

Vasya turned to the prisoner.

"Let's go over there."

The prisoner agreed and ran over to the fence. Vasya hardly managed to keep up with him. Together with the other scouts they took their seats on the sand.

After half an hour of argument full agreement was reached between both sides. It was decided to wage war from ten o'clock in the morning until the sound of the factory hooter at four o'clock. At other times the "kuchuguri" territory would be considered neutral, anyone could do what he liked there and no one could be taken prisoner. The victor would be the side whose flag stood on Fly Mountain for three days in succession. Both sides would have red flags, but the flag of Seryozha's army would be lighter in colour than that of the enemy. Both armies would be called Reds, but one would be known as the northern army, the other as the southern. Prisoners could be taken if they were fed, but if not fed they must be released at four o'clock to go where they pleased, because there were not many troops anyway, and if prisoners were held there would not be anyone left to fight. The plan captured by the northerners must be returned to the southerners.

The envoys departed as ceremoniously as they had come. Waving their white flag and playing their bugle, they marched away down the street. Only then did the northerners realize that the war was on and that the enemy was highly organized and powerful. Something must be done at once. Seryozha sent several boys round the flats to carry out mobilization, that is to say, to persuade the stay-at-homes and sissies to enlist in the northern army.

"We have thirty-three good men on our territory, and dozens of scouts, and they're all hanging round their mothers' skirts!"

On hearing these words Vasya thought sadly of the insoluble contradictions of life, because, after all, his mother was the best in the world, but Seryozha said.... Of course, even the skirts of other mothers weren't the same....

Five minutes later one of the mothers came over to the boys, and Vasya took a good look at her skirt. No, it was not a bad skirt, light and shiny, and this mother smelt of scent and looked kind.... With her was her son, seven-year-old Oleg Kurilovsky. Even Vasya had heard a few fables about the Kurilovsky family.

Semyon Pavlovich Kurilovsky was chief of the planning department at the factory. Throughout the whole of the northern army's territory there was no one to compare in importance with Semyon Pavlovich Kurilovsky—a fact that was, incidentally, of great concern to Kurilovsky himself. Vasya's father, however, spoke of him thus: "Chief of the planning department! Of course, he's a big bird. But there are bigger ones in the world!"

Kurilovsky seemed to doubt this. Other people apparently had difficulty in understanding how important he really was. But that was at the factory. In the Kurilovsky family, however, everybody understood, and no one could imagine life not steeped in the greatness of Semyon Pavlovich. Whether the source of this greatness sprang from Semyon Pavlovich's planning work or from his convictions about bringing up children, it is hard to say. But certain comrades who had been honoured with the conversation of Semyon Pavlovich had heard him express opinions of this kind: "The father must have authority! The father must stand at the top! The father is everything! What upbringing can there be without authority?"

Semyon Pavlovich did indeed stand "at the top." At home he had his own, separate study, which only his wife was allowed to enter. All Semyon Pavlovich's spare time was spent in this study. None of his family knew what he did there, nor could they know, they were not even aware of their ignorance, for there were other things, more commonplace than the study, and even these were spoken of with awe: Daddy's bed, Daddy's wardrobe, Daddy's trousers.

On his return from work Daddy did not simply walk through the rooms, he proceeded majestically straight to his study to enshrine his large brown brief-case within its sacred precincts. Daddy dined alone, grim and enveloped in the newspaper, while the children passed the time, shooed away into some distant corner of the flat. Although Semyon Pavlovich did not possess his own "office" car he would often be given a lift home in the factory car. On these occasions the car would plunge strenuously among the waves of the sandy street, its noisy protests echoed round the neighbourhood, all the dogs in the adjoining houses suffered from nervous strain, children rushed out into their front gardens. The whole world stared in astonishment at the car, the irate driver and the pompous figure of Semyon Pavlovich Kurilovsky. Of course, the car was an essential part of Father's authority, and particularly well aware of this were Oleg Kurilovsky—seven years old, Elena Kurilovskaya—five, and Vsevolod Kurilovsky—three.

Semyon Pavlovich rarely quit his exalted sphere to carry out disciplinary functions, but everything the family did, was done in his name or in the name of his future displeasure. Displeasure, mind you, not anger, because even Daddy's displeasure was a terrible thing, and Daddy's anger reached quite beyond the bounds of imagination. Mummy would often say:

"Daddy will be displeased."

"Daddy will find out."

"We shall have to tell Daddy."

Daddy rarely came directly in contact with his subordinates. Occasionally he would share a meal at the common table, occasionally he would toss out a majestic joke at which everyone was obliged to smile delightedly. Occasionally he would pinch Elena Kurilovskaya on the chin and say: "Well?!"

But for the most part Daddy transmitted his impressions and orders through Mummy after she had made her report. Then Mummy would relay the news:

"Daddy agrees."

"Daddy does not agree."

"Daddy has found out and is very angry."

Now Semyon Pavlovich's wife had come out into the yard with Oleg to discover who these northerners were and whether Oleg might take part in their activities, and also to gain a general idea of the ideology and practices of the northerners for her report to Father.

Oleg Kurilovsky was a plump boy with a double chin. He stood at his mother's side and listened eagerly to Seryozha's explanations.

"We are at war with the southerners, they live in that house. . . . We've got to put our flag on Fly Mountain."

Seryozha nodded towards Fly Mountain, the light-yellow top of which was showing in the distance.

"What do you mean 'at war'?" asked Kurilovskaya, casting her eye over the crowd of boys surrounding her. "Do your parents know about it?"

Seryozha smiled.

"Why, what is there to know? We don't keep it secret. But it's only a game. Do you think we ask about every game we play?"

"Of course, about every game. Besides, this is not just a game of yours, it's war."

"Yes, it's war. Only it's a game! Like any other!"

"And what if you wound somebody?"

"How are we going to wound anyone? Do you think we are armed with knives and revolvers?"

"What about those swords over there?"

"They are only wooden swords."

"All the same, suppose you hit someone!"

Seryozha stopped answering. He disliked this conversation which threatened to strip the war between north and south of all its bloody accoutrements. Already he was looking angrily at Oleg Kurilovsky and would not have minded causing him some real misfortune. But Kurilovskaya was bent on getting to the heart of the matter.

"All the same, how will you fight?"

Seryozha got angry. He could not allow further dethroning of the cause of war.

"If you are worried about Oleg, he needn't be in it. Because we won't answer for him: maybe somebody will shake him up in a battle. And he'll run complaining to you! After all, war is war! Look at the little'uns we've got here, they aren't afraid! You aren't afraid, are you?" he asked Vasya, putting his hand on Vasya's shoulder.

"No fear," beamed Vasya.

"Well, there you are, you see!" said Kurilovskaya in alarm, again surveying the boys as if in the hope of finding out who might be guilty of shaking up Oleg Kurilovsky and how dangerous it would be.

"Don't be scared, Oleg!" said a genial voice from the rear. "We've got a Red Cross. If you get your arm or head blown off by a bomb, we'll give you a dressing on the spot. There are girls for that."

The boys laughed uproariously. Oleg livened up and ventured a smile. For him, too, a dressing in place of a severed arm or neck now seemed to have its attractions.

"Good heavens!" whispered his mother and made for the house. Oleg wandered after her. The boys watched them go, winking at each other and grinning widely.

"Ah!" said Seryozha, remembering. "Where's your prisoner?"

"I'm here."

"Come on!"

Mitya bowed his head.

"But he won't give it back anyway!"

"We'll see!"

"Huh! You don't know my father!"

"I wonder!" said Seryozha, tossing his handsome fair head.

The Kandybins lived on the ground-floor. The situation of their flat was similar to that of the Nazarovs, but Vasya could find nothing in common between his home and theirs. The floor had obviously not been swept for several days. The walls were covered with spots. It was hard to say which were the more plentiful on the bare table: scraps or flies. The chairs and stools were jumbled about in disorder. In the next room the beds were unmade and the pillows a grubby-yellowish colour. The sideboard was piled with dirty plates and glasses. Even the drawers of the chest of drawers had for some reason been pulled out and left open. Seryozha, who entered first, at once stepped into a puddle and nearly slipped over.

"Careful, young feller, you ought to be ashamed of falling over on level ground," said a red-faced man with a shaven head.

Mitya's father was sitting by the table, holding a boot upside down between his knees. On the corner of the table beside him stood the black tin. But now it was divided up into compartments, each of which was filled with wooden shoemaker's nails.

"What can I do for you?" asked Kandybin through his nose, taking a fresh nail out of his mouth and placing it in a hole bored in the sole of the boot. Vasya noticed several more such nails between Kandybin's lips and realized why he spoke so strangely. Seryozha nudged Vasya and whispered: "Is that it?"

Vasya looked up and nodded in the same conspiratorial manner.

"What's the idea of coming into somebody else's house and whispering?" mumbled Kandybin with difficulty through the nails.

"They've come for the tin," piped Mitya, taking refuge behind his comrades.

Kandybin struck the boot with his hammer, pulled the last nail out of his mouth and was then able to speak in a normal voice.

"Ah! For the tin? No good coming to me for the tin. Let 'em come to you for that."

Straightening up on his chair, Kandybin looked angrily at the boys, holding the hammer in his hand as if to strike. Kandybin's face was still young but his eyebrows were quite white, like an old man's, and from under them gazed a pair of hard cold eyes.

"Mitya admitted that he took the tin ... stole it, so to speak. And you took it from him. But it belongs to Vasya Nazarov."

Seryozha stood at the table, looking calmly at Kandybin's erect figure.

Kandybin turned his eyes on his son.

"Aha! Stole it?"

Appearing from behind Seryozha's back, Mitya began speaking in a loud aggressive tone with a slight whine in it.

"I didn't steal it. 'Stole,' 'stole'! It was there in front of everybody! And I just took it. They're lying, lying, that's all!"

Vasya looked at him in amazement. Never in his life had he heard such barefaced lies spoken in such a sincere, injured voice.

Kandybin transferred his glance to Seryozha.

"That's not the way, comrades! In you come shouting: he stole it, he stole it! One day you may have to answer for such words, you know!"

From excitement Kandybin began to rummage through the tin, first in one compartment, then in another. Seryozha did not give up.

"All right then, suppose he didn't steal it. But this tin belongs to Vasya ... it isn't yours. So you'll be giving it back?"

"Who to, him? No, I shan't. If you'd come in decent-like, I might have done. But I shan't now. 'Stole it'! Just make him out a thief, that's what you wanted! Off you go now!"

Seryozha tried one more move.

"All right! I said that, but Vasya didn't say anything. So you ought to give it back to him...."

Kandybin straightened himself up still further, boot in hand.

"Now then! You're a bit too young to start teaching me! What right have you got to be here? Barge into my house and start throwing your weight about, would you? Vhat if your father was a partisan! That's nothing to do ith it. You're all much of a muchness as far as I'm concerned. Off with you!"

The boys moved towards the door.

"Where are you going, Mitya?" shouted his father. "No, you stay here!"

Again Seryozha nearly fell over in the doorway. From the kitchen a thin old woman looked out at them indifferently. They went into the yard.

"There's a dirty dog for you!" said Seryozha irritably. But he won't get away with it! We'll have that tin out of him!"

Vasya did not have time to answer, for at that moment the wheel of history started spinning round like a wild thing. Several boys came rushing up to Seryozha, all shouting at once and waving their arms. At last one of them outshouted his comrades.

"Seryozha! Look! They've got their flag...."

Seryozha looked and turned pale. On the summit of Fly Mountain waved a dark red flag, which in the distance seemed black. Seryozha sat down on the steps of the porch, at a loss for words. In Vasya's soul something also stirred—the age-old boyish desire to fight the foe.

Boys kept running up to the commander-in-chief's headquarters, each with the same news and each demanding an immediate crushing offensive against the insolent enemy. With furious treble voices, dirty hands and flashing eyes they all strove to show their leader the shameful spectacle on Fly Mountain.

"What are we sitting here for? Why sit still and let them show off up there? Come on!"

"Attack! Attack!"

Swords and daggers began to thresh the air.

But the commander-in-chief of the glorious northern army knew what he was about. He mounted the steps and raised his arm, thus indicating that he wished to speak. Silence fell.

"What are you shouting about? All shouting your heads off, no discipline! How can we attack when we haven't even got a banner! Are we to go with nothing, is that what you want? And no reconnaissance made! Is that what you are shouting for! As for the banner, I'll provide it myself. Mum promised. I appoint the time for the attack on Fly Mountain—tomorrow at twelve o'clock. But keep it secret. Where's the chief of the reconnaissance?"

All the northerners rushed to look for the chief of the reconnaissance.

"Kostya!"

"Kostya-a!"

"Varenik!"

Some thought of running to his flat. "His mother says we can't go in," they reported when they came back. "He's having his dinner!"

"But there's a second-in-command."

"Oh yes," remembered Seryozha, "Nazarov!"

Vasya Nazarov stood before his commander-in-chief, ready to do his duty. Only in the back of his mind lurked a faint doubt about what his parents would think of his activities as a scout.

"The scouts must go into action tomorrow at eleven o'clock. It's their task to find out where the enemy is, and to report!"

Vasya nodded, then surveyed his men. They were all present, only Mitya Kandybin being detained on domestic affairs.

But just then Mitya's voice was also heard. It was coming from the Kandybins' flat, gifted with extraordinary power and expressiveness.

"Oh Daddy, oh Daddy! O-oh! Oh, I won't do it again! Oh, it's the last time, I won't do it again!"

And another voice thundered on a more independent note:

"Stealing?! You need a tin, do you? It's a disgr-r-race! ... Oh! you little tike!"

A hush fell on the northerners; several of them, including Vasya, went pale. Within a stone's throw one of the warriors of the northern army was being tortured, and they were obliged to listen in silence.

Mitya gave another despairing howl, then suddenly the door opened and he flew out like a cannon ball hurled by his parent's anger right into the northerners' position. His hands were pressed convulsively to those parts of his body through which, according to time-honoured tradition, all good enters a boy. Finding himself among his own kind, Mitya threw a lightning glance back at the scene of torture. His father poked his head out of the door, brandished his belt and announced: "You'll remember, you son-of-a-bitch!"

Mitya listened to this forecast in silence, and when his father retired, fell on the steps at the very feet of the commander-in-chief, crying bitterly. The northern army silently regarded his sufferings. When Mitya stopped crying, Seryozha said: "Don't take it to heart. It's only a personal trouble. Just look what's happening on Fly Mountain!"

Mitya jumped up and glared with his active and, at present, tearful eyes in the direction of Fly Mountain.

"A flag? Is that theirs?"

"Whose do you think it is! While you were having your hiding they occupied Fly Mountain. But what did you get it for?"

"For the tin."

"Did you confess?"

"No, but he said it was a disgrace."

Vasya touched Mitya's trousers.

"Mitya, tomorrow, reconnaissance at eleven ... coming?"

Mitya nodded readily.

"All right," he said, still with a trace of suffering in his voice.

Father said to Vasya: "It's good you are chief of reconnaissance. But it was bad to beat Mitya. And his father beat him too. Poor little fellow!"

"I didn't beat him, Daddy. I only got him down. And squashed him. I told him to give it back, but he wouldn't say anything."

"Well, leave it at that, but it wasn't worth while over a mere tin! You bring Mitya round and make it up."

"How?" asked Vasya in his usual way.

"Well, just say to him: Mitya, come round to our place. After all, he's a scout too, isn't he?"

"Yes. . . . But what about the tin?"

"Kandybin won't give it back? Gives his son a beating

and keeps the tin for himself, does he? Queer fellow! A good turner and a cobbler, and already an instructor, earns good money, but he's got no understanding. Is his place dirty?"

Vasya made a face.

"Dirty as dirty! On the floor and everywhere! But what about the tin?"

"We'll think up something else."

Mother, who had been listening to them, said: "Only mind you, scout, don't get your eye poked in."

"What she really means," added his father, "is don't get taken prisoner, mind that."

The next day Vasya woke up early, before his father left for work, and asked: "What's the time?"

"What is time to you when there's another flag on Fly Mountain," replied his father. "A good scout would have been out on the mountain long ago. And you're still in bed!"

When he had said this, he left for the factory, so it must have been seven o'clock. His words raised a new problem in Vasya's mind. As a matter of fact, why should they not set out on reconnaissance now? Vasya got dressed quickly—no need to put shoes on now, and to pull on his shorts was the work of a moment. Then he dashed to the wash-basin. Here Vasya acted at such whirlwind speed that he attracted his mother's attention.

"Hey! War or no war, you wash yourself properly. Why is the brush dry? What do you think you're up to?"

"Mummy, I'll do it later."

"What's that? Don't ever start that talk with me! And where are you off to in such a hurry? Breakfast isn't ready yet."

"Mummy, I'll just have a look."

"What is there to look at? Look out of the window."

And, indeed, everything that needed to be seen was

visible from the window. The black-looking flag was still hoisted over Fly Mountain and there was not a soul from the northern army about in the yard.

Vasya realized that even the life of a scout was subject to the laws of nature, and obediently began his breakfast. As yet he had not thought over all that reconnaissance work entailed, and knew only that it was a dangerous and responsible job. Dimly his imagination outlined a few possible complications. Vasya is captured. The enemy cross-question Vasya about the location of the northern army, but Vasya is silent or else answers: "Do your worst, I shall say nothing!" His father had read stories to him and Seryozha Skalkovsky had related similar heroic tales of partisans who had been taken prisoner. But Vasya was not merely a dreamer, he was also a realist. And therefore, as he ate his breakfast, his thoughts became tinged with irony and he asked his mother:

"But suppose they do ask where our army is, what difference will it make? They know already, because they came to our yard themselves yesterday evening. With a bugle and a flag and all."

"If they know it already, they won't ask, they'll ask about something else," replied his mother.

"What will they ask?"

"They'll ask how many troops you've got, how many scouts, how many guns."

"Ha! We haven't got a single gun. There's only a few swords. Will they ask about swords too, Mummy?"

"I expect so. But I thought you weren't going to get captured?"

"Then I'll have to run! Or else if you get captured they start questioning you. And what tortures will they use?"

"Depends on the enemy! These southerners are not fascists, are they?"

"No, they're not. They came over here yesterday, just

the same as us, everything the same. Their flag is red like ours, and they're called Reds, only they're southern Reds."

"Well, if they aren't fascists they ought not to torture you."

"They haven't one of those ... Mu...."

"Mussolini?"

"Aha.... They haven't got one."

And so Vasya's first reconnaissance was carried out at home.

When Vasya came out into the yard the troops were already astir. On Seryozha Skalkovsky's porch stood a bright red banner, its solemnity overwhelming the small crowd of young warriors and scouts that had gathered round it. Seryozha himself, Lyovik, Kostya and a few other seniors were discussing the plan of attack. Oleg Kurilovsky was also hanging about the yard, listening to the conversation enviously.

"Well, will they let you come?" Seryozha asked him.

Oleg lowered his eyes.

"No, they won't. Father said I can look on but mustn't fight."

"Come on and be a scout then."

Oleg glanced up at the windows of his flat and shook his head.

Kostya Varenik began to assemble his scouts. Mitya Kandybin was sitting on the logs beside Vasya, looking rather glum. Remembering his father's advice about making up the quarrel, Vasya now examined Mitya's face intently. Mitya's bright little eyes had not abandoned their habit of darting this way and that, but his face was pale and dirty, and his gingery hair was sticking out in little tufts all over his head, like weeds in a field.

"Mitya," said Vasya, "let's make it up."

"Let's," answered Mitya, without changing his expression.

"And we'll be together."

"Together?"

"We'll play and fight together. And you'll come round."

"Where to?"

"To my place."

Mitya stared glumly into the distance and answered with the same lack of feeling:

"All right."

"Did your dad hit you hard? Yesterday?"

"No," said Mitya, making his usual scornful face. "He just waves his belt about, but I know where to dodge and he misses all the time."

Mitya brightened up a bit and even began to look at his companion.

"And does your mummy beat you?"

"Why should she? What's it got to do with her?"

Kostya ran up, counted the scouts, squatted down among them and whispered: "Listen, fellas! See Fly Mountain? That's where they all are probably, those southerners. Seryozha's going to lead ours right round, right round to the rear, along the ravines, so that they won't see. Then he will attack them from behind. Understand?"

The scouts indicated that they understood this strategy.

"And we're going to attack them from the front."

"But they'll see us," objected someone.

"Let 'em. They'll think we are the whole army and won't look behind them."

Mitya was sceptical of such hopes.

"Think they're as daft as that? They'll guess in no time."

"But don't go running out in the open. Keep to the bushes all the time. Then they'll think it's the big ones. Get it?"

Kostya split his men up into two sections. The first column he would lead himself on the left flank, Vasya

226

being ordered to approach with his on the right. If the southerners attacked, the orders were not to engage them but to hide.

In Vasya's column there were five lads, including himself: Mitya Kandybin, Andryusha Gorelov, Petya Vlasenko and Volodya Pertsovsky, all of whom were remarkable for the independence of their opinions and the strident voices they employed in upholding them. At Vasya's first command to form up they at once rebelled.

"There's no need for that. We're scouts. You have to bend down. On your belly, that's how you have to go. He doesn't know what he's talking about!"

But Vasya was inexorable.

"There's no need to crawl. That's when you are on reconnaissance. We are going to attack."

Vasya was vaguely aware of his poor knowledge of military affairs, but the strident voices of the scouts aroused his resistance. He was already beginning to grasp the rebels by their sleeves and shove them into battle order by force. Someone started shouting: "He's got no right to shove us about!"

Help came from an unexpected quarter. Mitya Kandybin was the first to line up.

"That's enough shouting," he bawled. "Vasya's the chief. What he says, goes!"

When they were all in order Vasya led his column towards the field of battle. Marching proudly at the head of his men, he passed the main force assembled round the banner. Seryozha Skalkovsky reviewed the column with approval as it marched past.

"That's the way! Good lad, Vasya! Keep it up!"

Vasya turned to his column, already feeling himself a full-fledged commander, and said: "What did I tell you?"

But the scouts themselves were pleased to have earned the praise of the commander-in-chief.

Vasya's column had taken up its position behind some bushes on a hill within close range of Fly Mountain. On a neighbouring peak to the left of Vasya, Kostya Varenik and his scouts were lying in the sand, while below, on the right, one could catch glimpses of the bright red banner. This was the main force under the commander-in-chief himself, making its outflanking movement.

Fly Mountain was in full view, but its main peak lay partly hidden behind a sandy ridge, above which only the top of the flag was visible. On the ridge stood a solitary black figure.

"That's their sentry," said Volodya Pertsovsky.

"Ah, if only we had some binoculars!" yearned Andryusha.

Vasya felt a sharp twinge of regret. Why had he not thought of asking Daddy for the binoculars! What a pity to miss such a magnificent chance of showing one's authority and military efficiency!

However, one did not need binoculars to see a large force of southerners advancing from behind the peak. The civilian in Vasya stirred uncomfortably at the sight of such a host of enemy troops. Kostya's column got up from behind their bushes and started shouting and waving their arms, whereupon Vasya also waved his arms and let out something like a war-cry. The southern army regarded them in silence. The scouts also subsided. The hush lasted several minutes. But suddenly three of the enemy's men were seen to leave the main force and climb quickly to the summit of the ridge. With a shout of "hurrah," the three southerners leapt at the lone figure, grasped him and dragged him back to their own forces. The figure squealed piteously and began to cry. Their eyes wide with horror, Vasya's scouts looked on at the strange drama being enacted in the enemy's camp—no one could understand what was happening. Andryusha ventured a timid guess: "They've captured one of their traitors."

But Mitya Kandybin, whose eyes were sharper than the rest, said gaily: "Ha-ha! They've bagged Oleg! Oleg Kurilovsky!"

"Is he one of ours? Is he one of ours?" asked several voices.

" 'Course he isn't. He's nobody's. His father wouldn't let him."

"What did they capture him for, then?"

"How do they know who he is?"

Oleg was dragged over to the southern army, struggling and shouting, fit to waken the dead, but the scouts could also hear sounds of laughter, coming, naturally, from the southerners. Oleg was surrounded on all sides.

"Ha-ha!" said Mitya. "Came to have a look and got taken prisoner."

By this time Kostya's column had left the refuge of the bushes and was descending the slope in the direction of Fly Mountain. Vasya grew anxious.

"Come on! Come on!"

Vasya's men also began to climb down from their vantage-point, making forward towards some bushes on the right. The whole ascent up Fly Mountain loomed into view, the enemy flag towering above them to its full height. For some strange reason the enemy did not advance to meet the scouts. They even began to retreat en masse back to their own banner. The foot of Fly Mountain was reached. It only remained to mount the long, steep slope and engage the enemy. But the southern army shouted "hurrah" and doubled off in another direction. Then it vanished altogether, without sight or sound. Only one man remained by the banner—probably a sentry; while on the sand, nearer to the scouts, sat Oleg, crying with fright.

One of Kostya's scouts came running up.

"I'm a messenger! I'm a messenger!" he cried: "Kostya says we are to advance and capture their flag!"

"Fine!" yelled Mitya and was the first to plunge forward up Fly Mountain.

Vasya sighed deeply and began to make the steep ascent.

The slope was rough and trampled by the southerners' feet, making it very hard to walk. Vasya's bare legs sank into the sand up to his knees, and as he followed in Mitya's wake the wind carried sharp, painful little particles of sand into his eyes. On the whole it was a very arduous attack. Vasya drove himself into a lather, but when he raised his eyes and looked ahead it was still just as far to the enemy banner. Vasya noticed that the sentry posted at the banner was growing excited, jumping up and down in a strange fashion and uttering panicky shouts towards the rear.

"Faster! Faster!" Kostya Varenik bawled from the side.

Vasya drove his legs forward with greater energy, tripped over once or twice, but managed to catch up with Mitya. Mitya, who was weaker than Vasya, was falling over at every step and seemed to be crawling rather than running. The other scouts were panting behind, and someone kept treading on Vasya's heels.

Raising his eyes once again, Vasya saw that he was quite near the goal and ahead of all the others. The sentry, who had a strangely unfamiliar and distinctly hostile face, was within a stone's throw. He was a little fellow about the same age as Vasya, but not so sturdy. Staring fearfully at the approaching enemy, he suddenly seized the pole of the banner in his little hands and started tugging it out of the ground. But the southerners' banner was a big one. Its huge dark red folds flapped above Vasya's head. Vasya put on speed, finding it easier to run as the steep rise gave way to a gently sloping summit. At last the southerner uprooted the banner and dashed to make his escape down the opposite slope. Vasya shouted something and ran after him, hardly noticing the pain as he was struck on the head by the banner, which the southerner had not the strength to hold upright. Nor did he notice Oleg Kurilovsky flash past nearby. Vasya swept over the summit, his own impetus carrying him down the other side. He did not lose his wits, however, and was clearly aware of the southerner sliding down beside him. A second later he realized he was leaving his enemy behind. Vasya dug his heels in, steadied himself and looked up just as the southerner with the banner landed right on top of his head. Vasya turned a somersault, slipped quickly to one side and the enemy careered past, dragging the banner in his wake. Vasya hurled himself face downwards on to the pole. It slid along a little under his bare belly; Vasya's left hand buried itself in the cloth. Feeling the joy of victory, he glanced up. Only Mitya was near him, striving to check his descent. Kostya and the other scouts were standing on the summit, shouting something to him and pointing downwards. Vasya looked below and his close-cropped scalp pricked with horror. Strange boys were mounting the slope right in his direction. At their head, coming forward with rapid strides, ran the chief with the cock feather in his cap who had visited them yesterday as an envoy. Behind him scrambled the others, and one of them was clutching the bright red banner of the northern army.

Vasya understood nothing, but sensed the approach of disaster. His eyes starting with fear, he saw Mitya slide right into the arms of the enemy. Vasya made to run up the slope, but a strong hand gripped his leg and a ringing triumphant voice shouted: "No, you don't, you little mouse! I've got you!"

The rout of the northern army was complete. Standing on the summit of Fly Mountain surrounded by enemies, Vasya heard the victorious shouts of the southerners and understood everything. Beside him a full-cheeked, rosy lad with a very pleasant, if alien, face was chattering more than anyone:

"What a victory! How they ran! And that one, that one! Their commander-in-chief!"

"Lucky we had this fellow, or they might have tricked us!" said the befeathered chief, nodding at Oleg Kurilovsky.

"He told them everything," whispered Mitya Kandybin to Vasya.

The enemy revelled in telling each other the secrets of their victory. Vasya realized that they had learnt of Seryozha's plan from Oleg, and this was the reason why they had left their banner undefended while they themselves went to repel the main forces of the northerners. Encountering Seryozha on the edge of the steep slope, they had thrown piles of sand down on the heads of the attackers, hurled them to the bottom and captured Lyovik Golovin together with the northern banner. Lyovik was sitting not far off under a bush, pulling a splinter out of his finger.

"Hey, prisoners!" shouted the chief with the feather. "You're to sit there."

He pointed to where Lyovik was sitting. Beside him on the sand lay the disgraced northern banner. There were three more prisoners besides Lyovik: Vasya, Mitya and Oleg Kurilovsky. They sat on the sand in silence. Lyovik pulled out the splinter, strolled up and down once or twice past the prisoners, then dashed off down a nearby slope, rocketing down its steep incline at terrifying speed. On reaching the bottom he doffed his little yellow skull-cap and waved it cordially in the air: "So long! I'm off to dinner!"

No one followed him. Though this all happened before Vasya's very eyes it seemed like a dream. Vasya could not forget the bitterness of defeat, and now they had to face untold vengeance at the hands of the cruel enemy. After Lyovik's escape one of the southerners suggested:

"They ought to be tied up. Or else they'll all run away."

"That's right," answered another, "let's tie their legs."

"And hands as well!"

"No, hands don't matter."

"But they'll go and untie themselves if their hands are free."

At this moment Oleg Kurilovsky, who had been sitting next to Mitya, leapt into the air with a howl: "Oh-oh-oh! What did you pinch me for?"

The southerners roared with laughter, but their chief reprimanded Mitya.

"You've no right to pinch. You're a prisoner yourself!"

Mitya did not so much as look at him. Whereupon the chief got angry.

"Tie their hands and feet!"

"This one too?" they pointed to Oleg.

"No, he doesn't matter."

The southerners fell upon their prisoners, only to discover that they had nothing to bind them with. Only one of the southerners had a belt, but he refused to surrender it for general use on the grounds that "Ma would make a row."

Vasya stared intensely at the fearsome alien faces of the foe and boiled inwardly with hatred for Oleg, the real cause of the northerners' defeat and Vasya's sufferings. One of the southerners picked up a dirty little strip of rag somewhere and shouted at Vasya: "Give us your legs!"

But from the peak of the mountain came a shout: "Up here! Up here! They're coming! Defend yourselves!"

Like the wind the southerners rushed to repel the northern attack. Only the prisoners were left on the summit of the mountain. The battle raged nearby, on the opposite slope, whence came cheers, shouts of command and laughter. Mitya crawled towards the peak, not, however, to observe the course of the battle. Reaching Oleg he grabbed his leg, and with a desperate shout Oleg slid down beside Mitya towards the bushes. Laughing joyfully Vasya gripped the end of Oleg's shirt and at once mounted astride the traitor.

"Let's bash him," suggested Mitya.

Vasya did not have time to answer. Oleg, who was older and fatter than Vasya, wriggled out of his grip and ran off. At the bushes he was again thrown down. This time it was Mitya's turn. . . . Oleg again wakened the echoes of the "kuchuguri" with awful cries.

"Don't pinch him," said Vasya, "let's take him to Seryozha."

Oleg wept loudly and threatened to tell his father. For this Mitya pinched him once more, whereupon Oleg again gave tongue, this time till his mouth almost reached his ears.

"Let's drag him there!" laughed Vasya. "Come on! Or will you go quietly?" he asked Oleg.

"I won't go anywhere. What have I done?"

"Come on!"

Together they pushed Oleg down the same slope by which Lyovik had escaped. Squealing, Oleg rolled over in the sand. His persecutors scrambled down beside him, digging their heels in. They had almost reached the bottom when victorious shouts were heard coming from the southerners. Oleg howled so loud that it was impossible to conceal their escape. They were easily recaptured.

Yet again the two intrepid scouts had to scramble up the loose sand to the summit. Oleg dragged himself up on hands and knees, crying the while. On the way Mitya contrived to get in one last pinch.

"These fellows are a nuisance! They'll be pitching into that cry-baby all day," said the feathered chief.

"They certainly will," agreed someone else. "What

time have we got for them? As soon as the northerners attack they will start scrapping again."

"All right," said the chief, "we'll let you go, but you must give your word of honour that you'll go home and not back to your army."

"And what about tomorrow?" asked Vasya.

"Tomorrow you can do what you like."

Vasya glanced at Mitya.

"What about it?"

Mitya nodded silently, glancing at Oleg. Oleg refused.

"I'm not going with them. They'll pinch me. I'm not going anywhere."

Sturdy, handsome and gay, Vasya stood facing Oleg, and from the look in his big clear eyes it was plain to everyone that Oleg could expect no mercy on the way home.

The chief lost his temper.

"What are we to do with you then? A big fellow like you!"

"I'll be on your side," moaned Oleg, glancing apprehensively at the scouts.

"He can for all we care, he's not dangerous."

"Well, and you go along," said the chief.

The scouts grinned and set off for home. Before they had time to descend Fly Mountain the alarm was again sounded in the southern camp. They stopped and looked round. Yes, the southerners had run off to engage the attackers.

"Let's creep along behind the bushes," whispered Vasya.

Swiftly they made their way back, panting and stumbling. Behind the last bush lay the northerners' bright red banner, glistening in the sun. Mitya grasped the pole and the banner slid along behind them.

"Now run," he whispered.

"But what about theirs?"

"Their what?"

"Their banner."

"Gosh! But who's that standing there?"

"It's Oleg!"

Mitya was delighted and a gentle smile crossed his face, making him look handsome. He clasped Vasya's shoulders and whispered affectionately: "You take it and leave Oleg to me. All right?"

Vasya nodded silently and they moved swiftly to attack. Oleg squealed deafeningly as he slid down the steep slope at enormous speed. Tugging the banner out of the sand, Vasya glanced downwards: there was no sign either of his own or the enemy's troops, the battle had moved a long way off.

The scouts began their retreat. They got down the slope, but after that the going grew harder. The banners were very heavy. Then it occurred to them to wrap the flags round the poles, so that it would be easier to drag them through the bushes. For some time they went on without looking round, but when they did so they witnessed a scene of terrible confusion on Fly Mountain. Southerners were scurrying hither and thither all over the slopes, peering into every crevice.

"Run, run," whispered Mitya.

They ran on faster. When they looked round again there was no one on the mountain. Mitya looked worried.

"They must be all on our tail! The whole lot of 'em. If they catch us now we're done for!"

"What shall we do then?"

"Know what? Let's turn off here, the bushes are as thick as anything! We'll lie down and stay down. All right?"

They made off to the left. Soon they found themselves deep in such dense undergrowth that it was hard to break a way through. In a tiny clearing they stopped, pushed the poles under the bushes, buried themselves in the sand and lay still. Now they could see nothing, only listen. At the factory the hooter roared triumphantly—four o'clock. After a time they heard the voices of their pursuers, faint at first but growing louder. Soon they could make out the words.

"Here! They're here!" insisted a petulant voice.

"Perhaps they're home by now," replied another, more stolidly.

"No, if they'd gone home we should have spotted them. You can see everything from there!"

"Well, come on, let's search then!"

"Here's where they went! Look at their tracks!"

"That's right."

"See where they dragged the pole!"

Two pairs of bare feet came into view. The scouts held their breath. Examining every yard, the bare feet paced up and down the bushes.

Mitya whispered close to Vasya's ear: "Ours are coming."

"Where?"

"They are, honestly!"

Vasya listened. Sure enough, about a dozen voices were chattering quite nearby, and there could be no doubt that it was their men. Mitya leapt to his feet and gave vent to a strained ear-splitting yell: "Seryozha-a-a!"

The two southerners stopped dead, then threw themselves joyfully at Mitya. But Mitya was no longer afraid and fought back with his fists, his eyes flashing aggressively.

"Keep back! Keep back! Seryozha-a-a!!!"

Vasya jumped out into the open and looked calmly at the enemy. One of them, a very sunburnt lad with vivid red lips, smiled at him.

"What are you shouting for? You're captured anyway. Where are the banners? Tell us where they are," he said, turning to Vasya.

237

Vasya shrugged his shoulders.

"There aren't any. Look! There aren't any!"

Just then some twigs crackled in the undergrowth and voices sounded nearby; the enemy rushed off in the other direction.

Again Mitya shouted: "Seryozha-a-a!"

"What's going on here?" demanded Seryozha, coming out into the clearing. Behind him the whole northern army peered out from the thicket.

"Look!" said Vasya, unfurling the enemy's banner. "And ours too! Ours too!"

"What a feat!" exclaimed Seryozha. "What a heroic deed! Hurrah!"

Everyone shouted "hurrah." Everyone questioned the heroes. Everyone slapped them on the back. Seryozha picked Vasya up in his arms, tickled him and asked:

"How can we thank you? How can we reward you?"

"Mitya too, Mitya too!" laughed Vasya, kicking his legs in the air.

What a wonderful heroic day of victory that was! How fine it was on Fly Mountain, whither the northern army now marched freely and where Seryozha said: "Comrades! Today victory is ours! We attacked three times, but the enemy, armed to the teeth, repelled every attack. Our losses have been terrible. We thought we were utterly defeated. With downcast hearts we had begun to retreat, and then we learned that our valiant scouts, Vasya Nazarov and Mitya Kandybin, had won a brilliant victory on the western front!..."

In conclusion Seryozha said:

"These heroes shall now hoist our banner with their own hands on the top of Fly Mountain! Come on, get hold of it!"

Vasya and Mitya grasped the bright red banner and plunged its pole firmly into the soft sand. The northerners shook the air with their cheers of victory. Not far off skulked a few disgruntled southerners. Some of them came nearer and said: "It's not fair! We have the right to take it down!"

"Excuse me!" answered Seryozha. "Was your banner captured before four o'clock?"

"Well, suppose it was. . . ."

"What time is it now, then?! You pipe down. . . ."

What a wonderful day it was, so full of glory and heroism.

"Let's go to my house," said Vasya decidedly.

Mitya was embarrassed. What had happened to that eternal aggressiveness of his!

"I don't want to," he whispered.

"Come on! We'll have dinner there. And you tell your mummy you are coming to our place."

"What is there to tell?. . ."

"Just tell her you're coming to us!"

"Think I'm afraid of Mum? Mum won't say anything. But. . . ."

"What were you saying this morning then?"

At last Mitya gave in. But when they reached the porch he stopped.

"Know what? You wait here, I'll be back in a sec."

Without waiting for an answer, he ran off to his own flat. Two minutes later he reappeared holding the famous tin. It no longer contained either nails or partitions.

"Here's your tin!"

He was glowing with joy but his eyes wavered.

Vasya was taken aback.

"Mitya! Your father will beat you!"

"Huh, beat me? Think he'll catch me as easy as that?"

Vasya mounted the steps. He had decided that there was only one person in the world who could solve this accursed question of the tin—his father Fyodor Nazarov, the fountain of all kindness and wisdom.

Vasya's mother was surprised to see the boys.

"Ah, you've brought a guest! Is this Mitya? That's good! O my, just look at yourselves! What have you been up to? Cleaning chimneys?"

"We've been fighting," said Vasya.

"Well, you are a sight! Fedya, just come and look at them!"

Father came in and burst out laughing.

"Vasya! Wash yourself at once!"

"There's a war on, Daddy! You know what, we captured their banner, Mitya and me!"

"I don't even want to hear about it. Soldiers ought to wash first and talk afterwards."

He half closed the dining-room door, poked out his head and said with mock severity: "And I won't let you into the dining-room. Marusya, throw them right into the water! And rinse this one as well, phew, what a blackie! And is that the tin? Aha... I see! No, I won't talk to a pair of ragamuffins like you."

Mitya stood rooted to the ground, more scared than in the most desperate battle. With startled eyes he began retreating towards the door, but Vasya's mother put her arm round his shoulders.

"Don't be frightened, Mitya, we'll just have an ordinary wash."

In a little while Mother came out of the kitchen and said to her husband: "Perhaps you'll clip Mitya's hair. It's impossible to wash it...."

"Won't his parents object to the interference?"

"Oh, let them! They don't mind beating the boy, he's all in bruises."

"All right, we'll interfere then," said Nazarov cheerfully, taking the clippers out of the cupboard.

In another quarter of an hour both scouts, clean, rosy and handsome, were sitting at the table ... too full of their adventures to eat anything.

Responding to the boys' stories with expressions of amazement and awe, sympathizing, gasping and laughing in turns, Nazarov lived through all the ups and downs of the soldier's life.

No sooner had they finished dinner than Seryozha ran in.

"Where are our heroes? Come out at once, the envoys will be here any minute. . . ."

"Envoys?" asked Nazarov seriously, straightening his blouse under his belt. "May I come and watch?"

The northern army turned out in strength to meet the envoys. True, they had no bugle, but the northern banner floated on the summit of Fly Mountain!

But before the envoys arrived, Oleg's mother appeared on the scene.

"Where's Oleg? Was he with you?" she asked the northerners.

Seryozha tried to evade the issue.

"You wouldn't let him play."

"No, but his father said he could watch. . . ."

"He wasn't with us. . . ."

"Did you see Oleg, boys?"

"He was hanging around there," answered Lyovik. "They took him prisoner."

"Who took him prisoner?"

"Why, the southerners. . . ."

"Where's that? Where is he now?"

"He's a traitor," said Mitya. "He told them everything and now he's afraid to come back. And he'd better not either!"

Kurilovskaya peered at Mitya in alarm.

Mitya's head now shone like a clean golden apple, and his sharp, determined little eyes no longer seemed insolent, but alive and keen. Nazarov awaited further events with interest, he felt they would develop at break-neck speed. Attracted by the fine evening. Kandybin had also emerged from his flat. He viewed the new, smart Mitya with disapproval, but for some reason seemed in no hurry to assert his parental rights.

Kurilovskaya looked about anxiously, overcome by the indifference of those around her to Oleg's fate. Encountering Nazarov's curious gaze she hastened up to him.

"Comrade Nazarov, tell me what shall I do? My Oleg's disappeared. I'm really terribly worried. Semyon Pavlovich does not know anything about it yet."

"They've taken him prisoner," smiled Nazarov.

"How dreadful! Taken prisoner! Fancy, dragging the boy away like that! Why, he wasn't even playing at all!"

"That's just it, he ought to have been playing. You were wrong not to let him."

"Semyon Pavlovich is against it. He said it was such a dreadful game!"

"Nothing dreadful about the game, it's your attitude that's dreadful. Surely it's not right to put the kid in such a position?"

"Comrade Nazarov, boys get up to all manner of trouble. You can't just follow blindly after them."

"Why blindly? You needn't keep your eyes shut. But children must be allowed to live their own lives...."

Meanwhile the gate had opened to admit a solemn trio of envoys followed by the muddy tear-stained figure of Oleg, looking very sorry for himself. With a gasp his mother rushed over to him. Grasping him by the hand, she led him home moaning and pointing his finger at the boys.

But the boys had no time for Oleg. The southern army was making unheard-of demands: the banner must be returned and the northerners must admit they were defeated. According to the envoys Vasya and Mitya had been released because they had given their word of honour not to fight any more that day; they had been trusted but had not kept their word.

"What do you mean 'word of honour'?" exclaimed Seryozha wrathfully, "war is war!"

"What? You go against the word of honour?" cried the boy with the feather in sincere indignation.

"Perhaps they did it purposely? Perhaps they gave their word of honour on purpose, to trick you!"

"Word of honour?! Oho, that's the kind you are! Oh no, once you gave your word of honour you've got to stick to it...."

"Suppose, f'rinstance, you were captured by fascists? They'd say: give us your word of honour! Well? What would you do with your word of honour then?"

"Oh, that's your line, is it!" The chief brandished his arm skywards. "By fascists! And who are we? What was the treaty we made? Our treaty says we are Reds and you are Reds, and there aren't any fascists. Fascists, I like that!"

Embarrassed by the last argument, Seryozha appealed to Vasya and Mitya.

"Did you give your word of honour?"

Mitya screwed up his eyes contemptuously at the enemy chief.

"We, give our word of honour?"

"Well, didn't you?"

"Of course, we didn't."

"You did!"

"No, we didn't!"

"So I didn't say to you: give us your word of honour!"

"What did you say then?"

"What did I say?"

"Do you remember what you did say?"

"I do."

"No, you don't."

"Oh, don't I?"

"Well, come on, tell us!"

"I'll tell you. But what do you think I said?"

"No, you tell us, if you remember...."

"Don't worry, I remember, but what do you think?"

"Aha? What do I think? You said: give me your word of honour that you won't go back to your own army. Didn't he say that, Vasya?"

"What's the difference?"

But the enemy's card was already lost. The northerners laughed and shouted.

"And how they came in! Word of honour! That's cunning, if you like!"

Even Kandybin, a serious man if ever there was one, burst out laughing.

"Young devils! That cooked 'em! But who's been shaving my kid like that?"

Nazarov made no response. Kandybin moved nearer the boys. Their game was beginning to amuse him. He laughed at great length when he heard the northerners' counter-proposal. His laughter was direct and strong like a child's, at times he doubled up and even bent his knees.

The northerners proposed that their banner should stand for three days on Fly Mountain, and then they would restore the enemy's and begin a new war. And if this didn't please the enemy—"Fly Mountain is ours!"

The envoys greeted this suggestion with derision.

"Yah! Do you think we can't make ourselves a new banner? Why, we'll make a dozen if you like! You'll see whose banner will be standing on Fly Mountain tomorrow!"

"We shall see!"

"And so shall we!"

The farewell ceremony was performed somewhat hastily; the envoys departed in anger, and the northerners shouted after them with no regard whatever for the rules of military etiquette: "Make ten banners if you like, they'll all be ours!"

"Well, tomorrow, look out!" said Seryozha to his men. "We're in for a tough time."

But they did not have to wait till tomorrow.

On the tall flight of steps leading down from his flat appeared the chief of the planning department Semyon Pavlovich Kurilovsky himself, his massive form trembling with wrath. Behind him down the steps stumbled the downtrodden figure of Oleg Kurilovsky.

Semyon Pavlovich raised his hand and said in a peremptory high-pitched tenor which, incidentally, hardly matched his portly figure:

"Boys! Hey there! Wait a minute, wait a minute, I tell you!"

"What's up? What's he shouting for? Who's that?"

"Look how wild he is! He's Oleg's. . . ."

Before he reached the bottom of the steps Semyon Pavlovich was shouting: "Bully! Torture! Rough-handle, would you! I'll show you rough-handle!"

He ran up to the boys.

"Which of you is Nazarov? Where's Nazarov?"

No one spoke.

"Who is Nazarov, I say?"

Vasya looked round in fright at his father, but Father pretended to take no interest in the proceedings. Vasya blushed, lifted a surprised face and said in rather a sing-song voice:

"Nazarov? I'm Nazarov!"

"Aha, so it's you!" bellowed Kurilovsky. "So it was you bullying my son? And the other one? Kandybin? Where's Kandybin?"

Mitya stared over his shoulder at the angry Kurilovsky.

"What are you shouting for? I'm Kandybin, what about it?"

Kurilovsky leapt towards Mitya and grabbed his shoulder so roughly that Mitya spun round him in a circle and landed right in Seryozha's arms. The latter quickly transferred Mitya behind his back, presenting Kurilovsky with his own smiling intelligent face.

"Where is he? Why are you hiding him? Were you bullying together?"

Kurilovsky peered so comically behind Seryozha's back and Mitya hid himself so cleverly that all the boys roared with laughter. Kurilovsky grew purple in the face, looked round and realized that he must retire quickly to avoid making a thorough fool of himself. Another moment and he would probably have run off to give full rein to his anger in his study, but then Mitya's father came up to him.

"Just what did you want with my son?" he asked, putting his hands behind him and throwing his head back, displaying his sharp red Adam's apple.

"What? What do you want?"

"I don't want anything, I'm asking you what you needed my son for? Perhaps you want to give him a hiding? My name's Kandybin."

"Ah, so he's your son?"

"Ooh, he'll hit him in a minute!" said Mitya loudly.

A fresh burst of laughter.

Nazarov walked swiftly over to the two parents, who were already sparring up to each other like a pair of fighting-cocks. Vasya scarcely recognized his father. Not loudly, but in a voice more angry than Vasya had ever heard his father use, Nazarov said: "What's going on here? Stop this at once. Come away and we'll talk the matter over!"

Kandybin did not abandon his pose, but Kurilovsky swiftly realized that this was the best way out of the situation.

"Very well," he agreed with a briskness that he did not feel. "Come to my study."

He made towards his front door. Kandybin shrugged his shoulders.

"Go to the...."

"Come on," said Nazarov, "come on, it will be better if you do!"

"Like hell it will!" Kandybin moved on after Kurilovsky.

The last to mount the steps was Nazarov. As he did so he heard someone in the subdued crowd of boys shout: "Pretty good that! Vasya, is he your dad? That's what I like to see!"

In his own study Semyon Pavlovich could not, of course, shout and make a fuss—after all, here it was not worth destroying his cherished atmosphere of dignity for the sake of a mere boy. With a polite gesture he motioned towards the armchairs; he himself sat down behind his writing-desk and smiled.

"These boys are enough to upset anyone!"

But the host's smile roused no response from the guests. Nazarov looked at him with lowered brows.

"Upset you, did they? Have you any sense at all?"

"What do you mean?"

"You shout at the boys, grab them, shake them. What do you mean by it? Who do you think you are?"

"I suppose I may defend my own son?"

Nazarov stood up and waved his hand contemptuously.

"Defend him from whom? How long are you going to lead him by the hand? All his life?"

"What do you think?"

"Why didn't you let him play?"

At this Kurilovsky also stood up.

"Comrade Nazarov, my son is my own affair. I did not allow him, that is all there is to it. My authority still carries some weight, I hope."

Nazarov moved towards the door. As he went out he turned round.

"Only mind: your son will grow up a coward and a turncoat."

"That's putting it rather strongly, isn't it?"

"It's my way of talking."

During this not very restrained conversation Kandybin had been sitting silently in his chair. He had no desire to go into the fine points of educational theory, but neither could he allow Kurilovsky to man-handle his son. At the same time Kurilovsky's words concerning authority pleased him greatly. He had even found time to say:

"That's right—authority!"

But he could not, on principle, remain behind after Nazarov had left. And as he went down the steps Nazarov said to him: "Listen, Stepan Petrovich, you are a decent fellow and a good workman, and I respect you a lot, but if you strike your son just once more, you'd better leave town, because I'll get you clapped in jail. Take my word for it as a Bolshevik."

"Go on, who are you trying to frighten?"

"I will, Stepan Petrovich."

"What the hell! Why pick on me? What do you mean I beat him?"

"He had a bath in our place today. He's all bruises."

"You don't say?"

"And he's a fine kid. If you go on like this, you'll ruin him."

"You have to keep your authority sometimes."

"Authority, authority, that's a fool's maxim, and you repeat it. You—a Stakhanovite!"

"You are a stickler, Fyodor Ivanovich! What have you got against me? God knows how you ought to treat 'em!"

"Come round to my place and we'll have a chat. There's a drink going and the wife's been cooking jam dumplings today!"

"Hardly the right occasion, is it?"

"It'll do."

In the Golovin family the problem of authority has been replaced by amusement organized round one fixed idea: *Parents and children ought to be friends.*

This is not bad if it is serious. Father and son can be friends, they ought to be friends. But the father still remains a father and the son remains a son, that is, a boy who needs to be brought up; and it is the father who brings him up, thus acquiring certain characteristics besides his position of friend. But if mother and daughter are not merely friends but playmates, and if father and son are not merely friends but bosom friends, almost boon companions, these additional characteristics, the characteristics required for upbringing, are apt, imperceptibly, to disappear.

And they have disappeared in the Golovin family. In this family it is difficult to make out who is bringing up whom. At any rate sentiments of a pedagogical nature are more often expressed by the children, because the parents play fairer and respect the golden rule: a game is a game!

But this game has long since lost its pristine charm. Before, it used to be so nice, such fun: "Bad Papa! Bad Mama!"

What a joy it was to the family, what laughter it caused when Lalya first called her father Grishka! It was the crowning point of the wonderful idea, the acme of pedagogical genius: parents and children were friends! Golovin himself is a teacher. Who better than he is capable of understanding such friendship! And he has understood it. He used to say: "Everything new to the world is always simple, like Newton's apple! Put relations between parents and children on a basis of friendship—how simple, how beautiful that is!"

That joy is now, unfortunately, a thing of the past. Now the Golovins are choking with friendship, it is suffocating them, but there seems to be no way out: just try to bow a friend to obedience!

Fifteen-year-old Lalya says to her father: "Grishka, again you talked a lot of rot at supper at the Nikolayevs'!"

"What rot?"

"What rot? Oh, dragging out all that philosophy: 'Yesenin is the beauty of decay!' I was ashamed to listen. It's so old. That's for little children. What do you know about Yesenin? You, beaks, can't be content with your Nekrasovs and Gogols, now you must have a go at Yesenin...."

Golovin does not know whether to be delighted at the directness and simplicity of their relations or whether to writhe at their obvious vulgarity. Being delighted is on the whole more peaceful. Sometimes he even meditates on this problem but he has already given up meditating on another problem: what kind of a person is he bringing up? The game of friends continues under its own momentum and because there is nothing he can do about it.

Last year Lalya threw up ordinary school and entered the art school. She has no artistic ability, she just thinks the word "artist" is rather chic. Both Grishka and Varka know this very well. They have even tried to speak to Lalya about it, but Lalya rejects their interference.

"Grishka! I don't poke my nose into your affairs, so don't poke yours into mine! What do you know about art anyway?"

And what is Lyovik coming to? Who knows! In any case he is not much of a friend.

Grishka and Varka's life has become sad and helpless. Grishka tries to furnish it up with witticisms, but Varka cannot even do this. Nowadays they never talk about the great friendship of education and look with secret envy at other children who have tasted friendship with their parents in less gigantic doses.

They experience similar envy when meeting Vasya Nazarov.

Just now he has entered the room with the tin under his arm. Golovin abandons his exercise books and looks at Vasya. The sturdy lad with his calm engaging glance is a pleasant sight.

"What do you want, my boy?"

"I've brought the tin. It's Lalya's tin. Where's Lalya?"

"Of course, of course, I remember. You are Vasya Nazarov?"

"Aha. . . . And you are that. . . . What's your name?"

"Me. . . . My name is Grigory Konstantinovich!"

"Grigory Konstantinovich? But they call you something else . . . Gri-shka. Is that right?"

"Y-yes. Very well, sit down. Tell me how you are getting on."

"We are at war now. Over there . . . on Fly Mountain."

"War? And what mountain is this?"

"Look. You can see everything through the window. That's our flag."

Golovin glanced out of the window and saw the mountain with the flag on it.

"Has this been going on long?"

"Two days already!"

"Who's fighting there?"

"All the boys. Your Lyovik's there too. He was taken prisoner yesterday."

"Is that so? Even taken prisoner? Lyovik!"

Lalya appeared from the next room.

"No sign of Lyovik since this morning. He didn't even come in for dinner."

"Must be in the thick of it, eh? Well, Vasya's brought your tin for you."

"Ah, Vasya, so you've brought the tin! You are a sport!"

Lalya put her arm round Vasya and sat him down beside her.

"I need this tin very badly! What a dear you are! Why are you such a dear? Remember how I whacked you? Remember?"

"It wasn't much. It didn't even hurt. Do you beat everyone? Lyovik too?"

"Look, Grishka, what a lovely boy he is. Just look!"

"Well, I'm looking."

"If only you and Varka had a son like him."

"Lalya!"

"Oh, that's all you can say: 'Lalya!' If only I had such a brother, instead of a young urchin. He went and sold my little green purse this morning!"

"Not really, Lalya!"

"He did. To some kid or other, for fifty kopeks. And bought himself a baby-crow with the money. Now he's keeping it under the steps, torturing it. That's your up-bringing!"

"Lalya!"

"Look at him, Vasya! He can't say anything else. Just repeats himself like a parrot!"

"Lalya!!"

Vasya laughed loudly and stared at Grishka as if he really were some strange foreign bird.

But Golovin took no offence, neither did he leave the room, banging the door behind him. He even smiled meekly.

"I'd change you as well as Lyovik for this Vasya here!"

"Grishka! You can talk about Lyovik as much as you like, but this is the last time you speak about me!"

Grishka shrugged his shoulders. What else could he do? . . .

Life went on both in Vasya's yard and on the "kuchugu-ri." In the war between northerners and southerners both sides experienced changing fortunes. There were many victories, defeats and exploits. There were also betrayals. Lyovik betrayed the northerners; he found himself new friends on the enemy's side, and perhaps they were not even friends but something else. When, after three days, he wanted to re-enlist in the ranks of the northern army,

Seryozha Skalkovsky gave orders for him to appear before a military court. Lyovik submitted obediently but nothing came of it; the court, unwilling to forgive such treachery, refused to restore his honour. Lyovik took no offence and did not lose his temper, instead he threw himself into a new amusement. Somewhere on the edge of the "kuchuguri" he began to dig himself a cave, told a lot of tales about it, described what a table and shelves it had, but after that everyone forgot about the cave, even Lyovik himself.

The war did not last long enough to bring about the complete defeat of either side. When military operations were carried to the far south, the opposing armies came across a nice lake with grassy shores, and beyond the lake caught sight of cherry orchards, straw ricks, wells and cottages—the village of Korchagi.

On the initiative of the southerners it was decided to end the war immediately and organize an expedition to explore the new country. The expedition developed on a grand scale when Vasya's father decided to take part in it. Vasya went about the yard several days on end, laughing from sheer joy.

The expedition lasted from four o'clock in the morning till late evening. Its most important achievement was the discovery in Korchagi of an extremely powerful organization, at the sight of which Seryozha Skalkovsky exclaimed: "Here's someone to fight! That's what I like to see!"

The Korchagians had their own football field with real goal-posts. The expedition was literally stupefied at the spectacle of such a high degree of civilization. Some of the Korchagi boys suggested playing a friendly match, but the expedition only blushed in reply to this cordial invitation.

Life marched on, taking Vasya with it. The motor-cars and trains still stood in his toy kingdom; an aged and battered Vanka-Vstanka continued to watch over them; the materials for building the bridge and the little nails in the beautiful box were all in order—but they were already things of the past.

Vasya sometimes stopped in front of the toy kingdom and meditated on its fate, but it no longer roused ardent dreams. Vasya felt an urge to be out in the yard with the boys, where wars were waged, where they built swings, where one heard the new words—"inside-right" and "half-back," and where they were already dreaming of tobogganing down the hills that winter.

One day father and son stood together over the toy kingdom, and father said: "It looks as if you'll be building that bridge, Vasya, when you grow up—then it'll be a real bridge over a real river."

Vasya thought for a moment.

"That'll be better," he replied seriously, "but I'll have to study a lot first ... to be able to build it. But what about now?"

"Now we are going to build a sledge. The snow will be here soon."

"One for me and one for Mitya too."

"Of course. Well, that's that. And now here's something else: you've been getting a bit slack this summer."

"How?"

"You hardly ever tidy up the shelves. The newspapers aren't folded, the flowers aren't watered. And you are a big boy now, we must see about increasing your jobs. You will have to sweep the rooms out in the morning."

"Only you buy a good besom," said Vasya, "like the one the Kandybins have got."

"That's not a besom, it's a broom," corrected his father.

The Kandybin family had been experiencing a veritable renaissance these days. The symbol of this epoch became the broom which Kandybin bought the day after the dumplings and vodka at the Nazarovs'. He would have been more stubborn in that talk with Vasya's father, but how could you be like that if there was a decanter and a large bowl of sour cream on the table and if your hostess kindly put a dozen dumplings on your plate and said: "What a nice boy your Mitya is! We are so glad that Vasya and he are friends."

And so Kandybin tried honestly to be an obedient guest, and he liked what Nazarov had to say. Nazarov did not mince matters.

"Don't you interrupt me! I've more learning than you and I've seen more. Who are you to take advice from if not from me? You ought to treat your son differently, and your household too. A reasonable man, a Stakhanovite like you, ought to uphold our Bolshevik honour. What's the idea of beating such a fine little fellow? Why, it's not decent, understand? It's like going into the street without any trousers on. You eat those dumplings, they're smashing! Pity your wife isn't with us.... Well, another time."

Kandybin ate the dumplings, blushed and agreed with everything. When it was time to go he said to Nazarov: "Thanks for the talk, Fyodor Ivanovich. When you've got a day-off come and see how we live. My wife Polya is a good hand at dumplings too."

The story of Vasya is over. It was not intended to point a moral. Without going into subtleties I simply wanted to represent a very small fragment of life, one of those fragments which pass before our eyes in hundreds every day and which to few of us seem worthy of attention. We have been lucky enough to be with Vasya at the most responsible and decisive moment of his life, the moment when the boy emerges from the warm family nest on to the broad open road of life, when for the first time he becomes a member of a collective, when he first becomes a citizen.

There is no avoiding this transition. It is just as natural and as important as finishing school, as the first day at work, as marriage. All parents know this, but many of them leave their child without help at this decisive moment; and those who do so are the very people who are most blinded either by parental power or by playing at being parents.

A child is a living person. He is by no means a mere ornament to our lives; his is a separate, rich, full-blooded life in itself. Judged by its strength of emotion, its deep impressionability, the purity and beauty of its efforts of will, a child's life is incomparably richer than that of an adult. And therefore its variations are not only magnificent but dangerous. The dramas and joys of the child's life shake the personality more deeply and are sooner able to create both the positive characters among the members of the collective, and its vicious, distrustful, lonely characters.

It is only if you observe and know this full, vivid and tender life, if you meditate upon it, if you participate in it, only then does your parental authority become effective and useful, your parental authority being the power that you have stored up earlier in your own personal and social life.

But if your authority, like a lifeless painted doll, only stands on the outskirts of the child's life, if the child's face, his gestures, his smiles, his thoughtfulness, his tears pass by you unheeded, if your conduct as a father bears no resemblance to your conduct as a citizen—your authority is worth less than nothing, whatever anger or strap it is armed with.

If you beat your child it is for him, in any case, a tragedy, either a tragedy of pain and injury, or a tragedy of habitual indifference and stubborn childish endurance.

But that tragedy is the child's. You yourself, a strong grown-up man, an individual and a citizen, a being with

She darted to her attaché case, and standing over it kept singing with such inspiration that her feet began to dance: "What a goof! What a goof!"

Finally she pulled a packet of five-ruble notes out of the case and rushed back into the bedroom with them.

"My grant! Take it for your shoes!"

When Pavlusha saw his mother, his golden-blue eyes nearly popped out of his head.

"Phew! Mummy! That's a dress!" he gasped.

"Do you like it, Pavlusha?"

"Don't I just!"

"It was given to me as a prize for good work."

"Oh, you are. . . ."

Pavlusha stared at his mother nearly the whole evening with an almost scared expression, and when she caught his glance he would give a broad happy smile.

"Mummy, you know what?" he said at last, gulping excitedly. "You're so beautiful! So. . . . You should always be like that! So . . . beautiful."

The word came right from the depths of his being—not a word, but pure emotion.

Vera Ignatyevna looked at her son with a severe restrained smile.

"That's good. Perhaps now you won't stay out all the evening skating?"

"Of course, I won't."

The last act of the drama took place late in the evening. When he came home from work Ivan Petrovich saw at the table a beautiful young woman in a cherry-coloured silk frock. Before entering the room he even made a movement to straighten his tie, and only at that moment did he recognize his wife. He smiled condescendingly and went up to her, rubbing his hands.

"Oh! Quite a different thing!"

be the outward expression of the technique of family upbringing. Neither you nor your children should have any
doubts as to whether you, as one of the senior, authorized
members of the collective, have the right to give such instructions. Every parent should learn to give instructions
and should be able to keep to them and not take refuge in
parental idleness or domestic pacifism. And then the instructions will become the usual, accepted, traditional
form, and then you will learn to add to them the faintest
shades of tone, beginning with the tone of direction and
going on to tones of advice, guidance, irony, sarcasm, request and allusion. And if you learn further how to distinguish between the real and fictitious needs of your children,
then you yourself will not even notice your parental
instructions becoming the dearest and most pleasant form
of friendship between yourself and your child.

Chapter Seven

Then, too, his form consumes, the toils of love
Waste all his vigour, and his days roll on
In vilest bondage. Amply though endow'd,
His wealth decays, his debts with speed augment,
The post of duty never fills he more,
And all his sick'ning reputation dies.
Meanwhile rich unguents from his mistress laugh,
Laugh from her feet soft Sicyon's shoes superb;
The green-ray'd emerald o'er her, dropt in gold,
Gleams large and numerous, and the sea-blue silk,
Deep-worn, enclasps her, with the moisture drunk
Of love illicit. What his sires amass'd
Now flaunts in ribands, in tiaras flames
Full o'er her front, and now to robes converts
Of Chian loose, or Alidonian mould,
...Hence, by the muse forewarn'd, with studious heed
Shun thou the toils that wait, for easier far
Those toils to shun, than, when thy foot once slides,
To break th' entangling meshes and be free.

LUCRETIUS, *De Rerum Natura*

J MET Lyuba Gorelova by chance when she came to see me over a small matter. While I was writing out the required slip, she sat quietly in her chair, sighing now and then, her hands crossed in her lap, her gaze directed somewhere far into the distance. She was about nineteen years old, and one of those neat girls who even in their saddest moments never forget to keep their blouses ironed.

"What are you sighing so sadly for?" I asked. "Are you in trouble?"

Lyuba raised her prim little head with a jerk, sighed pianissimo and smiled piteously.

"No ... it's nothing much. I *was* in trouble, but it's all over now."

I have had plenty to do with girls' troubles in my lifetime and am used to discussing them.

"All over, and you are still sighing about it?" I questioned further.

Lyuba gave a shiver and looked at me. A flame of interest had leapt into her earnest brown eyes.

"Would you like me to tell you all about it?"

"Yes, do."

"It's a long story."

"Never mind. . . ."

"My husband has left me. . . ."

I looked at her in surprise: her long story seemed to be over. And as for the details—you could see them in her face: the small pink mouth trembled in a smile and tears were sparkling in her eyes.

"Left you?"

"Aha," she assented in a whisper, nodding childishly.

"Was he a good man . . . this husband of yours?"

"Yes . . . very good! Very, very good!"

"And did you love him?"

"Of course. Why not? I still love him!"

"Are you unhappy over it?"

"You know . . . I am, awfully!"

"So your troubles are not quite over, then?"

Lyuba gave me a challenging suspicious look, but my sincere manner reassured her.

"Yes, they are. . . . It's all over. What can I do about it?"

Her smile was so naive and helpless that I, too, began to wonder what she could do.

"What indeed? You will have to forget your husband and begin again, right from the start. You'll get married again. . . ."

Lyuba pouted scornfully.

"Who to? They're all alike. . . ."

"But your husband wasn't so marvellous if it comes to that. He left you, didn't he? As a matter of fact, he's not really worth loving."

"What do you mean not worth loving? You don't even know him!"

"Why did he leave you?"

"He fell in love with someone else."

Lyuba said this calmly, almost with a touch of satisfaction.

"Tell me, Lyuba, are your parents alive?"

"Yes, they are. Daddy and Mummy! They keep on telling me off for having got married."

"Quite right too."

"No, it's not. What's right about it?"

"Of course, they're right. You're still a child and already married and divorced."

"Well.... What about it! What's that got to do with them?"

"Aren't you living with them?"

"I have a room of my own. My husband left me and went to live with his ... and the room is mine now. And I earn two hundred rubles. And I'm not a child! How can you call me a child?"

Lyuba looked at me in angry surprise, and I saw that she was quite serious about this game she played in life.

Our next encounter took place under similar circumstances. Lyuba was sitting in the very same armchair. She was now twenty.

"Well, how are your family affairs?"

"Too good for words!"

"Ah! So you found someone better than your ... that...."

"Nothing of the kind. I got married to the same one ... for the second time!"

"How did that happen?"

"It just happened. He came to me and cried. And said I was better than anyone else. But that isn't true, is it? I'm not better than anyone else, am I?"

"Well ... tastes differ, you know. ... What's so bad about you anyway?"

"There you are! That means he loves me. And Mummy and Daddy said I was being foolish. But he said: 'Let's forget everything.'"

"And have you forgotten everything?"

"Aha," said Lyuba in the same quiet whisper as before, and nodded just like a child. Then she looked at me with serious curiosity as if she wanted to test whether I understood her game in life.

The third time I met Lyuba Gorelova in the street. She appeared suddenly out of a side-turning with some big books in her arms and ran to catch a tram, but, on seeing me, exclaimed: "Oh, hullo! What a good job I met you!"

She was just as young, just as neatly groomed, and the blouse she wore was just as fresh and beautifully ironed. But there was a trace of dullness, a kind of inward tiredness in her brown eyes, and her face had grown paler. She was twenty-one.

She walked along beside me, repeating softly:

"What a good job I met you."

"What makes you so glad? Do you need me for something?"

"Aha. I haven't anyone else to tell things to."

And she sighed.

"Are you in trouble again?"

She spoke quietly, her eyes fixed on the road.

"I was in trouble. Such trouble! I even cried. She sent an application to the court, you know. And the court passed judgement and now we have to pay 150 rubles a month. Alimony. Not that it's so very much. My husband gets five hundred rubles a month and I get two hundred and fifty. Only it's such a pity. And you feel ashamed some-how, you know! Honestly! But they're wrong. It wasn't his child at all, but she brought in witnesses. . . ."

"Listen, Lyuba, send him packing."

"Who?"

"That husband of yours."

"How can you say such a thing! He's in such a diffi-cult position. And he hasn't got a flat. And there's the money to pay, and everything. . . ."

"But you don't love him."

"Don't love him? What do you mean? I love him very much. You don't know how good he is! And Father says he's a waster! And Mother says: 'You aren't registered, so leave him!' "

"But aren't you registered?"

"No, we aren't. We didn't get registered before and now it's too late."

"Why too late? You can always register."

"I know. But it means getting a divorce and all that. . . ."

"You mean your husband has to? From the one who's getting the alimony?"

"No, he never registered with her. From another one."

"From another? Who's she then . . . his old wife?"

"Why old? He registered with her quite recently."

I stopped dead.

"But I can't understand it at all. This must be his third then?"

Lyuba did her best to explain.

"Yes, I suppose, if you count me, she's the third."

"But when did he have time? How could he?"

"He didn't live with her long, the one who gets the alimony. . . . He wasn't long with her. And then he kept going about until he met this other one. And she had a room. So they started living together. But she said she didn't like it and they must get registered. She thought it would be better that way. So he got registered as her husband. But after that they only lived ten days together...."

"And then what?"

"Then, as soon as he saw me in the metro ... with a comrade ... he suddenly felt so sorry. And he came to me and cried so hard."

"Perhaps he was lying all the time and was never registered with anyone...."

"No, he didn't say anything about it. It was she, the one he was registered with, came and told me everything...."

"And did she cry?"

"Aha," said Lyuba quietly and gave a childish nod. And she looked at me attentively. I lost my temper and shouted out for the whole street to hear: "Throw him out on his neck, at once! You ought to be ashamed of yourself!"

Lyuba clasped her big books tighter and turned away. Probably there were tears in her eyes. Then she said, addressing not me but the other side of the street: "How can I throw him out? I love him."

I met Lyuba Gorelova for the fourth time in a cinema. She was sitting in the lounge in the corner of a big sofa, nestling against a young man, a handsome, curly-haired young man. He was whispering something in her ear and laughing. She was listening with strained attention, staring away somewhere into the distance with happy brown eyes. She seemed just as neat as ever and I did not notice any dullness in her glance. Now she was twenty-two.

She was delighted to see me. Jumping up from the sofa, she ran over and grasped my sleeve.

"Come and meet my husband!"

The young man smiled and shook my hand. He really did have a pleasant face. They sat me down between them.

Lyuba was indeed glad to see me and kept plucking at my sleeve and laughing like a child.

"I've heard a lot about you. Lyuba tells me you are her destiny. As soon as she saw you she said: 'There's my destiny,' " said her husband in a restrained manly way.

"Isn't it true, isn't it true?" shouted Lyuba, attracting everybody's attention. She hid behind my shoulder and with mock severity commanded her husband: "Go along. Go and have a glass of lemonade! Well, what are you waiting for? I want to tell him what a good husband you are. Go away!"

Reaching behind my back, she pushed him with her hand. He shrugged his shoulders, smiled awkwardly at me and walked away to the buffet. Lyuba took possession of both my sleeves.

"Tell me, is he good?"

"Lyuba, how can I say whether he's good or not?"

"But you've seen him. Can't you tell?"

"He looks all right, but ... if you remember all his deeds ... well, you yourself realize...."

Lyuba's eyes grew several times larger.

"Stupid! Do you think he's that one? Nothing of the kind! He's another man altogether! He's the real one, you see ... the real one!"

I was dumbfounded.

"How do you mean, 'the real one'? And what about the other? Your 'true love'?"

"He was no true love! He was such a rotter! I'm so happy. If only you knew how happy I am!"

"But do you love this one? Or are you ... mistaken again?"

She fell silent, suddenly losing all her liveliness.

"Do you love him?"

I was expecting her to nod in her childish way and murmur: "Aha."

But she sat beside me, subdued and tender, stroking

my sleeve, and the look in her brown eyes seemed to be centred deep within her.

At last she said quietly: "I don't know how to say: I love. I can't say it ... it's so strong!"

She looked at me, and her glance was that of a woman who loved.

Teaching young people to love, teaching them to know love, teaching them to be happy means teaching them self-respect and human dignity. No educational trips into the autonomous republic of Venus will help you here. In human society, especially in socialist society, sex education cannot be physiological education. The sexual act cannot be isolated from all the achievements of human culture, from the conditions of life of man in society, from the humanitarian course of history, from the triumphs of aesthetics. If a man, or woman, does not feel himself a member of society, if they have no feeling of responsibility for its life, for the beauty and reason of it, how can they love? Where are they to find self-respect, confidence that they possess some intrinsic value above that of mere male and female?

Sex education is first and foremost the cultural education of the social personality. And if in bourgeois society this education is blocked at every turn by such obstacles as the class division of society, poverty, coercion and exploitation, in our State the road lies wide open for such education. In the humblest Soviet family, as soon as that family realizes to the full what an important and decisive part it plays in the life of the state, as soon as it learns to feel the unity it has with society not only in the great moments of history but in every detail of daily life, the problem of sex education solves itself, for such a family is already in the fairway of the cultural revolution.

Not so long ago the problem of sex education presented itself to many people who had nothing better to do, in this form: how should one explain to children the secret of child-birth? The problem arose in liberal guise, it being considered liberal not to doubt that the secret of child-birth must be explained to children. Scorn was heaped on the old outrageous dodges—storks were hated, cabbage despised. People were convinced that storks and cabbages must be the cause of manifold disasters and that by timely explanation these disasters could be averted.

The most daring and liberal demanded complete abolition of all "veils" and complete freedom in sex discussion with children. In various ways and all kinds of voices stories were told of the dreadful tortuous paths by which modern children learned the secret of child-birth. To sensitive people it may well have seemed that the child confronted with the secret of child-birth was in a tragic quandary similar to that of King Oedipus! One could only wonder that these unfortunate children did not indulge in mass suicide.

In our day there is not such a desire to explain the secret of child-birth to children, but in some families conscientious parents do still suffer over the question of what to do about this secret and how to answer their children if they ask about it.

It should be noted, however, that far more talk than practical action has been expended on this pressing question, urgent as it may be. I know of only one case when a father set his five-year-old son to watch his mother give birth to her child. Like every other case of idiocy, this incident merits only the attention of a psychiatrist. Far more often it has happened that honest parents have in fact embarked on various "truthful" attempts at explanation. But no sooner had they begun than they found themselves in an almost hopeless position.

In the first place a violent contradiction emerged between parental liberalism and parental idealism. It suddenly became quite clear—no one knew why—that the problem of sex, in spite of all their explanations, in spite of all their heroic truthfulness, was determined to remain the problem of sex and not the problem of cranberry jelly or apricot jam. Because of this, it could never be tackled without going into details that even by the most liberal standards were quite unbearable and needed hushing up. In its desire to reach the light the truth appeared in such a shape that even the boldest parents felt rather like fainting. And this happened most often of all with those parents who had risen from the rank and file, who were in closer company with "ideals," who were actively striving for betterment and perfection. As a matter of fact, they wanted to "explain" the sex problem in such a way that it would somehow become no longer sexual but something else, more pure and lofty.

Secondly, it came out that even with the best will in the world, even with the most scientific approach, parents nevertheless told their children just what they would have heard from those "terrible boys and girls" whom the parental explanation was designed to forestall. It came out that there are no two versions of child-birth.

In the long run people remembered that right from the very beginning of the world not a single case had been recorded of young people who married not having sufficient idea of the secret of child-birth, and, as everybody knows ... always the same version, without any very noticeable deviations. The secret of child-birth seems to be the only sphere of knowledge where there are neither controversies, nor heresies, nor doubtful points.

Alexander Volgin lives on the fourth floor of a new block of flats. Alexander's father Timofei Petrovich Volgin works in the People's Commissariat for Internal Affairs. He wears two silver stars on the sleeve of his tunic and there are two little stars on his crimson buttonhole tabs. These stars mean a lot in Alexander's life. But more important still is the revolver. The revolver Father carries in his holster is a No. 2 Browning. Alexander knows very well that the Browning is a better weapon than the Nagant, but he also knows that his father keeps the revolver he likes best in the drawer of his desk, and that this "old favourite" is a Nagant—a battle companion about which Father can tell many stirring tales that were enacted in the days when there was no clean cosy flat in the new house, when there was not even Alexander himself, nor Volodya Uvarov, nor Kostya Nechiporenko. The stories one hears at school about those times are very short and all of them come out of books, and they are told by teachers who have never seen the real thing and do not really know anything about it. Now, if they had heard the story of how twenty Cheka* men, when riding out of town over the beaten snow of a wintry road, ran into a whole gang of bandits, how the Cheka men took cover behind the last fences of the town, how for four hours they fought the bandits first with rifles, then with Nagants, how each man left one cartridge for himself— then they would know the importance of that Nagant which now rests peacefully in the drawer of Father's desk. But teacher just goes on telling those school-book stories, and if you showed her a real Nagant she would most likely scream and run out of the class-room.

Alexander Volgin is proud of his father and proud of his revolver and his stars. Alexander knows that there are certain special rights and laws in his father's fighting life which he, Alexander Volgin, must observe. But as for other circumstances—Father's calm deep gaze, his silent clever eyes, and his balanced masculine strength—Alexander is no more aware of them than people are aware of being healthy. He has somehow left all that right out

* *Cheka*—abbreviation for the Extraordinary Commission to Combat Counter-Revolution, Sabotage and Profiteering that existed during the first years after the Revolution.—*Tr.*

of his estimation. Alexander is convinced that he loves his father for his fighting activities.

Now—Mummy. Mummy will not scream or run away if you show her a Nagant. When she was living in Ovruch she herself fought off the bandits while Father was away at a Party meeting. Nadya was there too, but she was only one year old then and did not come into that story. Nadya is now seventeen. Alexander loves her, but that is not the point. Mother. Of course, Mother is not a fighter although she did have to use a gun at Ovruch. In the first place she works in some Department of Public Education or other; secondly, she hasn't got a revolver, nor any stars, nor the rank of Senior Lieutenant of State Security; and thirdly, she is very beautiful, very kind and tender, and even if she did have a revolver and all the ranks in the world, who knows what place they would hold in Alexander's imagination. Alexander Volgin loves his mother not for any particular services rendered, he simply loves her, and that's that!

Alexander Volgin reached these conclusions about love the year before last, that is, the time when he found some real friends in life, not mummy's darlings who could not do anything except dress up like tailor's dummies, but real comrades with experience of life and minds of their own. Perhaps they, too, love their parents, but they don't make up to them in public and, anyway, they have no time to bother with parents. What with the problems life springs on you every day, it's enough to make you forget your dinner, let alone your parents, and it takes a lot of strength and knowledge to solve these problems: think of the match between Locomotive and Dynamo, for instance, of flying affairs, or the pulling down of that house in the next street, or the way they're asphalting the main road nearby, or radio. And at school, too, there is so much to do, so many problems, such a tangled web of relations, so many conspiracies, so many events that even Volodya Uvarov sometimes loses his head and says: "That's a fat lot of good to me, I must say. They can go to the devil! I can't be bothered!"

And Volodya Uvarov never laughs. Volodya Uvarov really is like an Englishman, everyone knows that. He never laughs. Others have also tried this business of keeping a straight face, but no one can manage it for more than a day: the second day they always show their teeth and laugh like monkeys. But Volodya Uvarov only curls his lip once in a while—you can't call that laughter. That's his way of expressing scorn. Alexander respects Volodya Uvarov's stern manners but has no intention of imitating him. His own fame is based on wit, infectious laughter and an unfailing talent for making facetious remarks. All the boys know that it is wiser to keep clear of Alexander's tongue. The whole of the fifth class knows it. And the teachers know it, too. Yes ... even the teachers.

When it comes to teachers, of course, it's a bit more awkward. Some teachers have a habit of starting trouble.

A few days ago the Russian Language teacher Ivan Kirillovich announced that he would be making a start on Pushkin. Before this, Volodya Uvarov had brought *Yevgeny Onegin* into class and demonstrated a few lines. And then Ivan Kirillovich said he would be making a proper start on Pushkin. "Proper" he called it, but in fact he left out the most interesting parts. Loudly, but politely, Alexander Volgin asked: "What does this mean: 'That which to glances e'er affords such invaluable rewards....'?"

Alexander Volgin had well-chiselled features and an expressive mouth. He grinned shamelessly at Ivan Kirillovich and waited for an answer. The boys' eyes lighted up because the question really was an interesting one. Everybody knew what "that" referred to—a foot, a woman's foot; Pushkin wrote about it in detail and the boys liked it. They had shown these lines to the girls and observed with great interest what impression they made. But with the girls this passage had fallen rather flat. Valya Strogova glanced at it, did not turn a hair and even laughed. And the mere recollection of what she said made you feel ashamed.

"Huh, the milksops! Never seen that before!"

The other girls laughed too. Alexander felt embarrassed and looked at Volodya. Not a muscle moved in Volodya's plump face.

"Never mind when we saw it, you just explain what it means," he ground out between his teeth.

Volodya brought that off beautifully, and one might have expected him to come out the victor in this encounter. But the final result was much sadder.

Valya Strogova looked keenly at Volodya. What superiority and disdain flashed in that glance. Then she said: "Those lines aren't a bit difficult to understand, Volodya. But you are still a baby. When you grow up you'll understand."

Not everyone can bear such trials calmly. Thus tested, fame perishes, influence disappears, prestige collapses, ties that have taken years to build up are snapped in an instant. And so everyone waited with bated breath to hear Volodya's reply. But Volodya did not have time to reply, for with a toss of her bobbed head Valya Strogova walked proudly to the door. Nina and Vera linked arms with her, and all three marched off looking even more unapproachable than ever, throwing careless glances over their shoulders and patting their hair into place. Volodya Uvarov watched them go in silence, curling his full lips contemptuously. No one spoke except Kostya Nechiporenko, who said: "You want a job bothering with them."

Kostya Nechiporenko was top of the class and felt very satisfied with himself; he could permit himself the luxury of an individual opinion. All the others were agreed that Volodya had suffered a defeat and that immediate decisive action was required of him. Delay was impossible. Volodya sat at his desk and wrapped himself in a frigid English silence. Alexander Volgin spent all the time between classes cracking jokes on the most trivial excuses. Picking on thin, short-sighted Misha Gvozdev, he asked: "Why do men wear trousers and women wear skirts?"

Misha realized that this innocent remark was the beginning of some painful joke and tried to slink away without answering. He had a cowardly, cautious way of moving, and his face wore a scared expression. But Alexander grabbed him by the elbows, and repeated loudly for the whole class to hear: "Why do men wear trousers and women wear skirts, eh?"

Misha struggled feebly, staring sullenly at the floor.

"Leave him alone, he'll start blubbing in a moment," said Volodya through his teeth.

"No, let him tell us!" laughed Alexander Volgin.

Misha leaned weakly on the desk. He was indeed on the verge of tears. When Alexander released his arms he crept away into the far corner and sat there in silence, his face turned to the wall.

"There's a queer bird for you!" laughed Alexander. "So that's what he's thinking of, the low-minded fellow! But it's quite simple really.

> *"So that Misha shouldn't lose his head*
> *And get married to a man instead."*

Then Misha burst out crying and jerked his elbow petulantly, although for all anybody cared he might just as well have kept it still. But Volodya Uvarov frowned in disgust, and he was right: no amount of banter could take away the unpleasant taste of that conversation with the girls. There were many in the class who even before this had treated Volodya and his friend Alexander Volgin with silent disapproval. And it was particularly depressing to see the cold disdainful air of independence with which the girls came into the class and took their places at their desks. They were pretending that the back desk did not exist, or that if it did, it had no interest for them. They were trying to make out that they knew everything and that their knowledge made them a lot higher and better than any of those Volgins or Uvarovs. The girls kept putting their heads together, whispering and laughing. How could a fellow guess whom they were laughing at and why they thought so much of themselves?

Something had to be done quickly. The question put to the teacher was designed to restore the situation, and Alexander Volgin awaited Ivan Kirillovich's answer with a solemn smile. Even the thorough softies, even the swots and hard-workers were hushed and paying proper attention to this interesting duel. The teacher was still very young and it looked as if he would not escape from his awkward position.

And indeed Ivan Kirillovich was taken aback, and mumbled, blushing: "Well, er ... that's another question, you know ... er ... a question of ... er ... other relations. I don't understand why you ask?"

Alexander Volgin made a heroic effort to achieve a proper studious face and the result, it seems, was not too bad.

"Well, when you read that 'invaluable rewards' you can't understand it. You can't make out what rewards he means."

But the teacher suddenly climbed out of the mire, and climbed out very well indeed.

"We were discussing something else. There's no need to make a diversion. I will call at your home in a day or two and explain the matter then. Your parents will listen, too."

Alexander Volgin went pale and lapsed into a state of polite and utter helplessness. "Please do," he mumbled.

274

Volodya gave Alexander a murderous glance and, without standing up, said:

"If the question was asked in class why should it be answered at home?"

But the teacher pretended not to hear and went on talking about Pushkin's story *The Captain's Daughter*.

Alexander was about to say something else, but Kostya Nechiporenko tugged at his shirt and pulled him forcibly down into his seat.

"Don't be a hooligan! Or you'll catch it," he advised good-humouredly.

The honour of the back desk was saved, but at what a cost!

Three days later Alexander Volgin still remembered this incident with alarm. At home he responded nervously to every ring at the door, but the teacher still did not come. Alexander was doing his home-work particularly well now, keeping quiet in class and trying not even to look at Volodya. If that Ivan Kirillovich did come round telling tales to Father, who knows how it would all end. So far Alexander had had no clashes with Father over school matters. Alexander got good marks and there were no rows. At home he had tried to discuss school as little as possible, thinking this would be more convenient all round. And now this affair had turned up.

On getting into bed at night Alexander would meditate on what had happened. Everything was quite clear. Father would not say anything about his asking side questions in class, but when it came to those "invaluable rewards," dash them, he would get into a row for that. At this point Alexander would heave rapidly from side to side, doing so not because he would get into a row but because there was something even more terrible in the offing. The row could be as bad as you liked, that was not the point. What kind of a row would it be anyway? Would

Father give him a hiding? No, he wouldn't do that. But how could a fellow talk to his father about all these things: rewards, feet—horror! What an awful, shameful, impossible subject!

Volodya Uvarov asked:

"Did he come?"

"No."

"What are you going to do when he does?"

"I don't know."

"You tell him you really didn't understand anything."

"Tell who?"

"Your father, of course. Just say you didn't understand. Who can understand the damn things anyhow!"

Alexander shook his head.

"Huh, think it's so easy to kid my dad? He's seen plenty like you and me, you know."

"Well, I think it's not bad ... passable ... I would tell mine that."

"And he'd believe it?"

"Who cares whether he believes or not! A nice thing I must say! How old are we? Thirteen. Well? We aren't even supposed to understand anything of the kind. So we don't—that's all there is to it."

"May be we don't, but why pick such a ... you know what I mean."

"Just picked it.... Happened to be doing Pushkin ... and that turned up...."

Volodya sincerely wanted to help his friend. But for some reason Alexander hesitated to tell Volodya the truth. The truth was that Alexander could not deceive his father. Somehow he just could not do it, no more than he could talk to him "about such questions."

The storm broke from an unexpected quarter: Nadya!

"Nadya tells me..." that was how Father began.

This was so overwhelming that even the theme itself lost some of its edge. Father talked; Alexander was in a queer state, the blood in his organism flowed up and down where and how it wanted, his eyes blinked in senseless confusion, and his head drummed with the unexpected and unforgivable discovery: Nadya! Alexander was so depressed by this news that he did not even notice his tongue babble on its own initiative: "But she doesn't know anything. . . ."

He took a grip on himself and checked his tongue. His father looked at him seriously and calmly, but as a matter of fact Alexander was not in a fit state to notice how his father looked. He could see before him only his father's sleeve and the two silver stars on it. His gaze wandered aimlessly over the embroidery of the stars. His father's words penetrated his ears and did something inside his head; anyhow some kind of order began to appear there. Clear, understandable and somehow acceptable thoughts came spinning towards him; like his father's sleeve they gave off a kind of warmth. Alexander realized that these were his father's thoughts and that in them lay salvation. Nadya suddenly dropped out of his consciousness. His throat ached, the waves of shame stopped playing havoc with his circulation, a warm friendly glow kindled his cheeks, and kindled his soul. Alexander raised his eyes and saw his father. Father had a firm, muscular mouth; he was regarding his son with a steady understanding gaze.

Alexander rose from his chair and sat down again, but could not wrench his eyes from his father's face and could not stop his tears—dash those tears.

"I understand now, Dad. I'll do as you say. All my life I will! You'll see!" he groaned.

"Calm yourself," said his father quietly. "Remember what you have said: all your life. Mind now, I believe you, I shall not check on you. And I believe you are a man, not just a . . . good-for-nothing."

Father stood up quickly and Alexander caught a glimpse of his smooth belt and unbuttoned empty holster.

Father went out. Alexander sank his head on his arms and fell into a dazed happy state of repose.

"Well?"

"Well, he said it."

"And what about you?"

"Me? Nothing. . . ."

"And you probably started crying and saying: oh, Daddy, Daddy!"

"What's crying got to do with it?"

"Well, didn't you cry?"

"No."

Volodya looked at Alexander with an air of lazy confident reproach.

"You think as he's your father he must be right. According to them we're always to blame. But they don't say anything about themselves, it's always us. Mine's the same when he starts: you ought to know, you ought to understand. . . ."

Alexander listened to Volodya with a dismal heart. He could not betray his father, yet Volodya demanded betrayal. And on Volodya's side there was undoubtedly some kind of honour that could not be betrayed either. A compromise was needed and Alexander could find no respectable form for it. Volodya would have to climb down. And why shouldn't he? They had both gone too far, anyway.

"So you think my father was all wrong?"

"I do."

"But perhaps he was right?"

"What's right about it?"

"Another one would have gone about it differently. He would have said: How dare you! You ought to be ashamed! And all that."

"Well?"

"He didn't say that, did he?"

"Well?"

'It's all right for you to keep on saying 'well', but if you had heard him...."

"Well, suppose I had.... Well, go on anyhow. Only you think they always talk like that: 'You ought to be ashamed,' 'You ought to be ashamed'? Don't worry, they know how to put it on too."

"Why should they put it on? Was he putting it on?"

"Of course, he was, and you thought it was grand: secrets, secrets, everyone's got secrets!"

"He didn't say it like that at all."

"How then?"

"Quite differently."

"Well, how?"

"You see, he says: in life there's something mysterious and secret. Everybody knows about it, he says, men and women, and there's nothing dirty about it, it's just secret. People know. What of it? They know, but they don't go dragging it about in public. That's culture, he says. And you, he says, are a lot of milksops, you've only just found out and your tongues are wagging like the cow's tail. And then he said...."

"Well?"

"Then he said: a man needs his tongue for important things, but you just use yours to swat flies."

"Is that what he said?"

"Yes, it was."

"That was clever of him."

"And you think...."

"But it's just words of course. Why did Pushkin write it down then?"

"Oh, he said something about Pushkin too. Only I've forgotten how he put it."

"Quite forgotten?"

"No, not quite, only ... I understood then, but the words he used ... you see...."

"Well?"

"He says: Pushkin was a great poet."

"That is news, I must say!"

"No ... hold on, the point isn't that he was great, but that you have to understand...."

"Nothing hard to understand about those lines."

"Of course not, but that's not the point. What he said was, aha, I remember: it's quite true, quite true, that's what he said: it's quite true!"

"Drop it: 'quite true'!"

"But that's what he said: it's quite true, this poetry speaks of that ... of that ... well, you know...."

"All right, I understand. What then?"

"Then he went on: Pushkin said it in poetry ... in such wonderful poetry, and then ... yes, there was another word, aha—tender poetry. Tender poetry! And then he says: that is what beauty is!"

"Beauty?!"

"Yes, and you, he says, don't understand anything about beauty. You keep wanting to make it into something else."

"Nothing of the kind! Who wanted to make it into something else?"

"Well, that's what he said: you want to make it into ... the talk, no, the language of a drunken lout. Pushkin's not what you need, what you need is scribbling on the fence...."

Volodya stood erect and listened carefully, beginning to curl his lip. But he kept his eyes lowered as if in thought.

"Was that all?"

"That was all. And he said something about you too."

"About me?"

"Yes."

"That's interesting."

"Shall I tell you?"

"Think it matters to me what he said?"

"To you, of course not."

"You let him pull the wool over your eyes."

"I did not."

"He got round you properly, I must say. But what did he tell you about me?"

"He said: Your Volodya plays at being an Englishman, but as a matter of fact he's just a young savage."

"Me?"

"Yes."

"And he said 'plays at'?"

"Yes."

"A savage?"

"Yes, that's what he said: 'a savage.' "

"Very nice! And what did you say?"

"Me?"

"You were glad, of course?"

"No I wasn't."

"So I'm a savage, and you, I suppose, are a man of culture!"

"And he said another thing: Tell your Volodya that in a Socialist state there won't be any savages like him anyhow."

Volodya smiled contemptuously, for the first time during the whole conversation.

"He got round you nicely, I must say! And you swallowed it all. It'll be dangerous being friends with you now. Now you are a 'man of culture.' And your sister will pass everything on. The girls will tell her, of course. It'll be impossible to say anything in class! And what do you think she's like? Do you know what she's like herself?"

"What's she like? What do you mean?"

Alexander really could not understand what Volodya meant. Nadya was above suspicion. True, Alexander had not yet forgotten the first staggering shock he had experienced when it came out that Nadya had given him away, but for some reason he could not be angry with his sister, he was just angry with himself for forgetting that she would find out all about it. Now he looked at Volodya and it was obvious that Volodya knew something.

"What is she like then?"

"Oh! You don't know anything? She said all that about you, but she's the one!"

"Tell us."

"Can't tell you! You're such a cultured man!"

"Come on, tell us."

Volodya drew himself up in an attitude of frigid haughtiness, but vague meditation still hovered on his plump face. And instead of the lofty idleness that had been there before, a cluster of tiny needles glinted in his eyes. Such needles always appear when wounded vanity comes in conflict with a boy's eternal nobility and love of truth.

And now vanity gained the upper hand. Volodya said:

"I'll tell you all right, only there's one thing more I must find out."

Thus a compromise was achieved. Nadya was in the tenth class and her interference did not interest the friends, but her double-dealing could not be tolerated.

Nadya Volgina studied in the tenth class of the same school that our friends attended. It was clear enough through what channels the Pushkin affair had achieved publicity. These girls had a manner of making proud looks and various ways of tossing their heads fit in perfectly with whispering and gossip, and now it was known what they had been whispering about. They had jumped at this chance. If one remembered that the question about Pushkin's lines had been put in an extremely cultured form, and that, in fact, nobody had ever thought of making his poetry into the language of louts, and that everyone, not only the girls, realized the lines were beautiful, and that the teacher ought to have explained them properly in the first place—if one remembered all that, the low cunning of these girls came right to the fore at once. They had made a show of discussing *The Captain's Daughter* and the teachers had been taken in. But they had told Nadya about Pushkin's lines. And that was what they had been talking about at the lesson.

And Valya Strogova was only so proud when she was in class. But she went home with Goncharenko, a boy in the eighth class, on the excuse that they lived in the same house. And they went to the ice-rink together. And left the ice-rink together. As far back as the autumn Volodya Uvarov had sent her a note:

"To Valya Strogova.

"Don't think we don't understand anything. We understand everything. Kolya Goncharenko, oh, what a handsome clever boy! Only it's nothing to show off about."

They had seen Valya Strogova receive the note during a Grammar lesson and read it under the desk, and they had seen how she sat there angrily through all the lessons and breaks. And during the last lesson Volodya had received an answer.

"To Volodya Uvarov.

"You silly fool. When you get some brains, let us know."

It took Volodya three days to recover from that insult. He sent another note but it returned in a shameful state with the inscription on top: "This was written by Uvarov, so it need not be read."

And still she went about with Goncharenko. And the teachers thought that as she was a girl she was above suspicion. And not only Valya. There were plenty like her. They all had secrets, they all had some kind of mysterious intrigues, while the fifth class had to put up with their airs and graces. And all the threads of these secrets led away into the upper regions, the distant heights of the eighth, ninth and tenth classes. With their good looks and sprouting moustaches the seniors got in everywhere. And what goings-on the girls had in these upper regions it was impossible to imagine.

Volodya Uvarov held very sceptical views on the subject. He would tell the most improbable stories about the older girls, and was not even very concerned that he should be believed. The truth of his stories did not interest him, he was interested in themes, possibilities and details. The others did not contribute anything. Volodya was not believed, but his tales were listened to with interest.

The girls of the ninth and tenth classes! Just think of them! Even Volodya was scared. Could it ever enter his head to write one of them a note? How could he? What would he write about? The girls in the senior classes were incomprehensible creatures. It was even rather frightening to look at them. Suppose she noticed and glanced at you—just what could a chap say? Only the most daring spirits allowed themselves sometimes, as they dashed down the corridor, to brush the thigh or breast of one of the senior girls. But that was a poor form of amusement. Such things were done in fear and trepidation; the risk was enormous. If you were caught, if she looked at you, if she said something, what escape was there on the hard unyielding floor that would not open and swallow you up at will. Last year the class did have a reckless young tough like that, one Ilya Komarovsky—he had been expelled. What of it? Among the boys he used to talk about things that set the very desks blushing, while his listeners would look round more than listen. And yet even he, talk as he did, if he played a loutish trick and met the girl's eye, he was finished. He would shut up and try to smile. And she only said to him: "Wipe your nose. You've got a handkerchief, haven't you?"

And they expelled Komarovsky not for that at all, but for playing truant and studying badly. And when he went no one was sorry, it was even a relief.

Deep down, Alexander Volgin had nothing against the senior girls; but that was a terrible secret, it was such a secret that its real meaning did not occur to him even in dreams, and if it did there was no unravelling it. But he was in a better position than others, for in their flat itself, with him and his parents, lived Nadya—a being he could not understand but whom he liked and felt attached to. Nadya's friends in the tenth class came to the flat. Like her, they were gentle girls, with killing eyes, soft chins and wavy hair that was absurdly clean, and certain things about their figures that it was better not to think about either in dreams or reality. Alexander was sometimes admitted to their company, he was admitted not quite on disinterested grounds. In their company he behaved easily, talked loudly, cracked jokes, and rushed at lightning speed for ice-cream and cinema tickets. But that was all on the outside. Inwardly his heart murmured faint protests and his soul stirred uneasily. It was this self-confidence of the girls that confused him, this kind of wise power they had, that was in charming contradiction with their apparent weakness and lack of manly skill. They did not know how to throw a stone properly, but when Klava Borisova once took Alexander's cheeks in her soft warm hands and said: "This boy will make a handsome man one of these days," a strange noisy wave of emotion rushed over Alexander, stinging him and taking his breath away. And when he dragged himself out of that wave and opened his eyes, he saw that the girls had already forgotten about him and were discussing something quietly among themselves. Then he had a dim feeling that somewhere very near lay the boundary line of human happiness. That evening in bed he recalled this incident calmly, and when he closed his eyes the girls floated in his imagination like high white clouds.

He did not know how to think about them, but in his mind they were always linked with joy. And neither Volodya's sarcasm, nor the crudities of Ilya Komarovsky could prevent that.

And so he did not want to believe the stories the boys were telling about various escapades in which the girls were said to have taken part. It was the same now that Volodya was making hints about Nadya. Where was Volodya's proof?

"What did you want then? For them to do everything in front of your nose?"

"No, but what proof have you got?"

"Have you ever noticed how your Nadya goes home?"

"What about it?"

"And how many dandies there are after her?"

"What do you mean 'how many'?"

"Haven't you ever counted them? There's Vasya Semyonov, and Petya Verbitsky, and Oleg Osokin, and Taranov, and Kisel, and Filimonov. Haven't you seen them?"

"Well, what about it?"

"Do you think they go after her for nothing? Do you think they're such fools as that? You keep your eyes open."

Alexander kept his eyes open and saw that they actually did go about together, that they were cheerful and laughing, and that Nadya walked among them, her eyes lowered. He saw Klava Borisova in the same dazzling setting, but apart from a little sad jealousy no suspicions awakened in his soul, although the "dandies" did seem very unpleasant.

Spring came; the sun did longer duty in the sky; the chestnuts bloomed in the streets. Alexander had more to do: matches, and boating, and swimming, and various exams. Nadya was preparing for the exams even harder than usual. The girls would gather in her room every day. In the evening they would come out pale and serious, and Alexander's chaff made no impression on them at all. Sometimes young men came to study as well, but all this had such a solid tenth-class appearance about it that even

Volodya would not have found it in him to say something rotten.

And just then, at the very height of the exams, something happened. After supper, late in the evening Father said: "What's become of Nadya?"

Mother glanced at the clock on the wall.

"I was wondering that myself. She went out at four to go and study at a friend's."

"But it's past one."

"I've been worrying for a long time," said Mother.

Father picked up the paper, but anyone could see he did not feel like reading. He noticed his son concealed behind a copy of *Ogonyok*.

"Alexander! Why aren't you in bed?"

"It's a holiday tomorrow."

"Go to bed."

Alexander slept in the dining-room, on the divan. He undressed quickly and got into bed, turning his face to the wall, but of course could not go to sleep. He lay and waited.

Nadya came home close on two. Alexander heard her timid ring and the quiet opening of the door as she entered, and realized that she had done something wrong. A subdued conversation took place in the hall. He heard Mother say: "Do you think it's only a matter of explaining?"

Then there was some talk in the bedroom. Father was there too; what they were talking about remained a mystery. Alexander could not get to sleep for a long time—he was overcome by a strange mixture of curiosity, alarm and disillusion. Sleep had already laid its fingers on him when for the last time he saw the faces of Nadya and Klava, and the other girls, and around them swirled some disgusting, unbearable but at the same time rather curious thoughts.

The next day Alexander peered keenly into Nadya's

face and noticed a few details. There were dark shadows under her eyes. She had grown paler and was sad and thoughtful. Alexander regarded her with sympathy, but the thing that worried him most was to find out what had happened last night.

He told Volodya nothing. He still remained his friend; together they discussed school affairs, got up to trivial little pranks, went fishing and criticized the girls. But still he did not feel like talking about Nadya.

At home Alexander with persevering energy poked his nose into every chink he could find in the family's life. He would pretend to be asleep, he would hide for hours on end in the study, listen to the conversation of his father and mother, keep watch on Nadya, her moods and the way she spoke.

On the day-off he had a stroke of luck. His father went out on a hunting trip at dawn, rousing the whole family by his departure. Alexander also woke up, but lay with closed eyes and waited. Out of the corner of his eye he saw Nadya, half-dressed, make her way to her mother's bedroom to have "another hour." She always did that when Father left home early or was on duty at work.

Soon a conversation began in the bedroom. Much of it did not reach Alexander: some he did not hear, some he did not understand.

His mother said: "Love should be tested. A person may think he has fallen in love when it's not really so. One doesn't buy butter without testing it, but we just pick up our feelings in an armful and rush off with them blindly. It's very foolish really."

"It's very difficult to test," whispered Nadya almost inaudibly.

Then silence. Perhaps they were whispering so quietly, and perhaps Mother was affectionately stroking Nadya's tousled head. And then Mother said:

"Silly, it's very easy to test. You can always tell a good, real feeling."

"Like good butter?"

A smile sounded in Mother's voice.

"Even easier."

Most likely Nadya hid her face in the pillow or on Mother's lap, because her voice came very faintly.

"Oh, Mummy, it's so difficult!"

In his irritation Alexander was just about to turn over, but remembered that he was supposed to be fast asleep and so only pouted discontentedly: just a lot of sob-stuff! And what had butter got to do with it! Queer folks these women, why couldn't they talk business!

"That's right, one must have a little experience. . . ."

And he missed the rest of what his mother said. They were a pair for whispering!

Nadya started talking in a quick excited whisper.

"Mummy, it's all very well for you to say: a little experience! Suppose I haven't got any, not even a little, what then? Tell me, how does it come about: experience of love? Is that what you need? Experience of love? Oh, I don't understand at all."

"Now she'll start crying," decided Alexander and let out something like a sigh.

"Not experience of love, dear me, no! Experience of love—that sounds rather unpleasant somehow. Experience of life."

"What experience of life have I got?"

"You? Seventeen years. That's quite a lot of experience."

"Tell me something! Do tell me something, Mummy."

Mother seemed to be collecting her thoughts

"Won't you tell me?"

"You know yourself, don't pretend."

"Me, pretending?"

"You know what womanly self-respect and pride are. No man thinks much of a woman who hasn't that pride. You know how easy it is to keep a rein on yourself and not give way to the first impulse."

"But suppose you want to give way?"

Alexander was beginning to grow quite downcast: when would they speak of that evening? And what had happened? All this book talk: giving way, impulses!

Mother said sternly and much louder than before: "Well, if you are as weak as all that, give way perhaps. A weak person always loses and gets into a mess everywhere. It's weakness makes people drink their happiness away."

"But why was it so strict before? And now why is there so much freedom: marry when you like, get divorced when you like? Why does Soviet rule allow such freedom?"

Mother answered just as sternly: "Soviet rule counts on real people. A real person knows himself how to act. But sloppy things always need packing up to stop them oozing out all over the place."

"Do you think I'm a sloppy thing?"

"Why?"

"You know how it is: I'm in love . . . almost in love. . . ."

Alexander even raised his head from the pillow to be able to listen with both ears.

"Almost or really, I'm not afraid of that. You're my clever girl, and you've got self-control. That's not why I'm cross with you."

"Why then?"

"I never expected such faint-heartedness from you. I thought you'd got more pride, more of a woman's self-respect. And there you go meeting a man only for the second time and staying out with him until one in the morning."

"Oh!"

"That is weakness, of course. That's not doing yourself justice."

There was silence. Probably Nadya had her face in the pillow and felt too ashamed to speak. Even Alexander felt rather uncomfortable. Mother came out of the bedroom and went to the kitchen to wash. Nadya had subsided altogether.

Alexander Volgin stretched loudly, coughed, yawned, and gave various other signs that he had only just woken from deep sleep and was meeting the day with a light heart. At breakfast he examined the faces of his mother and sister, and delighted in his knowledge. There was nothing much to be seen in Nadya's face; she carried it off pretty well, even joked and smiled. But her eyes, of course, were red, and her hair was not arranged quite as well as usual, and in general she was not so beautiful as she had been before. Mother poured out the tea, looking into the cups with a rather dry little smile that may have expressed sadness. Then she glanced at Alexander and smiled a real smile.

"What are you making faces about?"

Alexander gave a jump and hastily restored order to his face, which really had been conducting itself in a way its owner had never agreed to.

"I'm not making faces."

Nadya shot a cheerful mocking glance at her brother, shook her head slightly two or three times and . . . said nothing. That was rather high and mighty of her and perhaps it would have passed yesterday, but today it was an insulting challenge to Alexander's knowledge of the facts. He could so easily fell her. . . . But secrecy was dearer than honour, and Alexander contented himself with a formal rebuff.

"Well, well! And what was that look for?"

Nadya smiled.

"You look as if you had got an 'excellent' for Geography."

There was a hint of mockery in those words, but it did not have time to work properly on Alexander. Suddenly his mind was taken up with Geography: rivers and canals sparkled, figures and the names of towns invaded his memory. And with them came a host of other things: honour, and Father, and a "satisfactory" for the third term, and the competition with 5-B. Today was the exam. Alexander forgot his sister and dived for his Geography book.

But on his way to school he kept remembering the morning conversation. The background was pleasant: Alexander Volgin knows the secret and no one as much as suspects it. This background was decorated with various images, but Alexander could not yet see them all as a whole. Now one would stand out, now another, and each spoke only for itself. There was a pleasant image saying that his sister had done something wrong, but just by, there was another that kept worrying him—it was unpleasant that something had happened to his sister. And right near was that whole girlish realm of theirs, outlined with broad vivid strokes, just as enchanting as before, like high white clouds. And without any clouds at all capered dwarfish caricatures suggesting that the girls were only putting it on and Volodya was perhaps right after all. Then all that faded out and was forgotten, and Alexander remembered his mother's words early that morning, rather unusual, important words that he kept wanting to think about but did not know how to think about; he could only recall their wise, fond strength. He remembered the words about a man's not thinking much of a woman. There was something interesting there, but what it was he could not understand, because the view was blocked by a big familiar word "man." A man—that was him, Alexander Volgin. That word had often turned up since the talk with his father. It was something strong, stern, enduring and very mysterious. Then this image, too, was obliterated, and shameful thoughts pushed their way to the surface, Ilya Komarovsky's crude stories and Volodya Uvarov's unrelenting cynicism. But this, too, disappeared, and again there were high white clouds glistening in the blue sky, and pure gentle girls smiling tenderly.

All this hovered round Alexander's soul, tapping on the walls, each telling its own story, but inside lay only the gift from his father—a man stands for strength and nobility.

Alexander arrived at school early. The exams were to begin at eleven and it was now only a quarter past ten. Several pupils were already at work round the maps. Volodya Uvarov was walking about the school square, showing off with his hands behind his back. Was he really so well up in geography? Volodya asked a few mundane questions about Alexander's mood, about the Sandwich Islands, about the chances of getting an "excellent," stated carelessly that he himself was only trying for a "satisfac," and suddenly asked: "Has your sister got married now?"

A shudder passed right through Alexander, and he stared at Volodya with wide-open eyes.

"What?"

"Ho! She's got married and he doesn't know! I like that!"

"What do you mean? Got married? How?"

"What an innocent young calf! He doesn't even know how people get married. Very simple: one, two, and in nine months there's a kid."

Volodya stood with his hands behind his back, his handsome round head held high.

"You're lying!"

Volodya shrugged his shoulders like a grown up and gave one of his rare smiles.

"You'll see."

And he walked off to the building. Alexander did not follow him; he sat down on a bench and began to think. It was hard to think and he could not reach any conclusions, but he remembered that he must be a man. Luckily Geography went off excellently, and Alexander ran home in a joyful mood. But when he saw his sister his joy vanished instantly. Nadya was sitting in the study, copying out something into her note-book. Alexander stood in the doorway, then to his surprise found himself moving towards her. She raised her head.

"Well, how did Geography go?"

"Geography? I got an 'excellent.' But you just tell me something."

"What do you want to know?"

Alexander heaved a sigh and blurted out: "Look here, have you got married or not?"

"What?"

"Tell me . . . are you married or not?"

"Am I married? What are you raving about?"

"No, you tell me."

Nadya looked at her brother keenly, stood up and grasped his shoulders.

"Wait a minute. What does this mean? What are you asking about?"

Alexander lifted his eyes to her face. It was angry and hostile. She pushed him away and ran out of the room. From the bedroom came the sound of her bursting into tears. Alexander stood by the desk and thought. But it was hard to think. He wandered into the dining-room. At the door he bumped into his mother.

"What horrid things have you been saying to Nadya?"

And so once again Alexander Volgin sits facing his father and again he can give the silver stars a close examination. But this time Alexander is calm, he can look his father straight in the eye, and his father replies with a smile:

"Well?"

"I promised you. . . ."

"You did."

"I told you I would be a man."

"That's right."

"Well, so I have been ... in everything."

"You only went wrong over one thing."

"Didn't I act like a man?"

"No. You need not have asked Nadya."

"Who then?"

"Me."

"You?!"

"Come on, tell me all about it."

And Alexander Volgin told his father everything, even the conversation he had overheard that morning. And when he had finished he added: "I want to know whether she's got married or not. I must know."

Father had listened attentively, nodding from time to time without asking a single question. Then he walked round the study, took a cigarette from a box on the desk, enveloped himself in a cloud of smoke, and waved the match out. And meanwhile he asked with the cigarette between his teeth:

"What must you know that for?"

"So that Volodya won't say it."

"Say what?"

"So that he won't say she's got married."

"Why mustn't one say that?"

"Because he's lying."

"Lying? Well, let him lie."

"But he'll keep on lying."

"What harm is there in what he says? Is it bad to get married?"

"He says she's married, but...."

"Well?"

"But he says ... he says dirty things."

"Ah ... so you understand now."

"Yes, I understand."

Alexander nodded, affirming to himself that he had indeed understood.

His father came up close to him, took hold of his chin and looked into his eyes seriously and sternly.

"Yes. You are a man. Well, from now on always understand. That's all."

The next day Alexander did not come near Volodya and sat at another desk. During the break Volodya put his hand on Alexander's shoulder, but Alexander threw it off sharply.

"Keep off!"

Volodya sneered.

"Think I need you?" he said.

The story really ends here. Volodya Uvarov and Alexander Volgin parted company for a long time, perhaps for ever. But there was one day, not more than a fortnight later, the last day of the school year, when their paths once again crossed for a minute.

In a group of boys on the same square Volodya was saying: "Klava in the tenth class is the first...."

The boys were listening to Volodya with their habitual grudging attention.

Alexander pushed through the crowd and confronted the story-teller.

"That was a lie! You lied on purpose!"

Volodya treated him to a lazy glance.

"Well, what of it!"

"You always lie! And you always have done!"

The boys caught something new in Alexander's tone, a new cheerful ring. They drew closer. Volodya frowned.

"I've no time to listen to your rubbish...."

He moved away. Alexander did not stir.

"No, don't go away!"

"Oh, why not?"

"I'm going to beat you!"

Volodya reddened, but, still trying to play the Englishman, compressed his lips and snapped: "I'd like to see you."

Alexander Volgin swung his fist and struck Volodya on the ear. Volodya answered the blow at once. It was the start of one of those good boyish fights where it is always hard to know who is the winner. Before one of the seniors arrived on the spot both combatants' noses were bleeding and several buttons had flown off.

"What's the fight about," asked a tall lad in the tenth class. "Who started it?"

One lone voice said conciliatorily: "Just a fight, that's all. They both started it."

The crowd buzzed disapprovingly.

"Both! Hark at that! He's been asking for it a long time!"

The good-natured voice of Kostya Nechiporenko cut calmly through the general murmur.

"They're not both to blame. There's a great difference between them. Volgin was beating that snake for spreading tales, and he was hitting back ... he had to!"

The boys laughed loudly.

Volodya wiped his nose on his sleeve, glanced round quickly and made off to the building. They all watched him go: there was nothing English in his walk.

No talks with children about the "sex" problem can add anything to the knowledge that will come of itself in good time. But they do cheapen the problem of love, they rob it of that restraint without which love is called lewdness. The revealing of the secret, even when done in the wisest fashion, intensifies the physiological side of love, encourages not sexual feeling but sexual curiosity, making it simple and accessible.

The culture of feelings of love is impossible without restraint organized during childhood. And sex education should consist in fostering that intimate respect for questions of sex that is known as chastity. The ability to control one's feelings, one's imagination and one's desires is a most essential ability, the social importance of which is not sufficiently appreciated.

Many people, when they speak of sex education, imagine the sexual sphere as something completely isolated and separate, as something that one should have confidential dealings with. Others, on the contrary, make sexual feeling a kind of universal foundation for the whole personal and social development of man; in their view a person is always, primarily, either a male or a female. Naturally, they, too, arrive at the idea that education must be, primarily, sex education. Both the one and the other, in spite of the contrast between them, hold that direct and deliberate sex education is useful and necessary.

My experience says that special, deliberate so-called sex education can only lead to regrettable results. It will "educate" sexual feelings as if man had not experienced a long cultural history, as if lofty forms of sexual love had not already been attained in the time of Dante, Petrarch and Shakespeare, as if people had not practised the idea of chastity long ago in ancient Greece.

Sexual feelings cannot be correctly educated in the social sense if they are considered as existing apart from the whole development of the personality. But at the same time the sexual sphere must not be looked upon as the basis of all human psychology and made the focal point of the educator's attention. The cultivation of the sexual life is not the beginning but the conclusion. By educating the sexual feeling separately we still do not educate a citizen; yet in educating a citizen we do also educate the sexual feeling, but a sexual feeling already ennobled by the basic trend of our education.

And therefore love cannot be nurtured simply out of animal sexual attraction. The power of "loving" love is to be found only in the experience of non-sexual human affection. A young man will never love the woman he has chosen to be his wife, if he has not loved his parents, his comrades, his friends. And the broader the scope of his non-sexual love the more noble will be his sexual love.

A man who loves his country, his people, his work will not become a profligate, he will not look on a woman merely as a female. And the reverse conclusion is equally true: the man who is capable of treating a woman with vulgar and shameless cynicism does not deserve to be trusted as a citizen; his attitude to the common cause will be just as cynical, and one cannot put complete trust in him.

The sex instinct is a tremendous driving force; left in its original "savage" state or intensified by "savage" education, it can become only an anti-social phenomenon. But restrained and ennobled by social experience, the experience of unity with other people, of discipline and continence—it becomes one of the pillars of the very highest aesthetic appreciation and the most beautiful human happiness.

The family is a most important sphere, where a man takes his first steps in social life! And if those steps are organized correctly, then the sex education will also proceed correctly. In a family where the parents are active, where their authority comes naturally from their life and work, where the life of the children, their first contact with society, their study, play, moods, joys and disappointments are constantly heeded by the parents, where there is discipline, good management and control, in such a family the development of the children's sex instinct, too, is always correctly organized. In such a family the need never arises for any forced and spasmodic tricks, because, in the first place, parents and children have between them the absolutely necessary bond of delicacy and silent trust. Given this bond, mutual understanding is possible without resort to naturalistic analysis and bald statements of fact. And in the second place, on this basis there will be significance and wisdom in every word that is spoken at the right time, in every concise and serious word about manliness and chastity, about the beauty of life and its dignity, every word that will help to give birth in the future to great love, the creative force of life.

In every healthy family, sex education proceeds in such an atmosphere of restraint and purity.

The more wisely and the more reservedly we talk of love with our children, the more beautiful will their love be in the future, but that reserve must go hand in hand with constant and regular attention to our children's conduct.

No philosophy, no speechifying will do any good if the family has no correct system, no proper bounds of conduct.

The old intellectual "Russian" impetuousness was able to combine, it would seem, two incompatible things. On the one hand, thinking intellectuals could always come out with the most radical and rational ideas often exceeding the bounds of plain reality, while at the same time they always exhibited a passionate love of slovenliness and disorder. Perhaps they had a special taste that could discern in this disorder a gleam of something higher, something attractive, something that touched them deeply—a precious gleam of freedom. In the Bohemian muddle of their everyday life they were able to see some high aesthetic meaning. In this love there was something of anarchism, of Dostoyevsky, of Christianity. But the fact is that in this slipshod "leftish" way of living there is nothing except historical poverty and nakedness. Some people even today, at the bottom of their hearts, still despise accuracy and orderly movement, a mode of living that pays proper attention to details.

A slovenly attitude to life cannot fit in with the style of Soviet life. With all the means at our disposal we should exorcise that belated Bohemian spirit which only by a great misunderstanding is considered by certain comrades a token of poetic taste. In scrupulous accuracy, in collectedness, in strict and even severe consistency, in the thoroughness and thoughtfulness of a human action there is more beauty and poetry than in any "poetic disorder."

Slovenliness in the everyday life of the family, where no one is accustomed to keeping exact times, to a strict system, to organization and prudence, does great harm and more than anything else upsets the normal sexual experience of the young. How can one talk about upbringing if the son or daughter get up and go to bed when they think they will or just when they have to, if in the evenings they "go out walking" no one knows where, or spend the night "at a girl-friend's" or "with a comrade," whose address and family circumstances are simply unknown. Here one is up against such domestic laxity (and perhaps not only domestic but also political laxity) that any kind of upbringing is simply out of the question— everything is fortuitous, haphazard and irresponsible.

From the very earliest age children should be trained to keep exact time and clearly defined bounds of conduct. On no account should the family allow any "nights-out" at a strange family's, except in cases that are absolutely clear and reliable. What is more, all the places where a child may have to stay for a few hours even during the day should be well known to the parents. If it is the family of a comrade, only parental idleness can prevent father or mother from getting to know it better.

A strict time-table for the child's day is an essential condition of upbringing. If you have no such timetable and you do not intend arranging one, your time is utterly wasted reading this book, or any other book about upbringing.

The habit of keeping exact hours is a habit of making an exact demand on yourself. An exact hour for rising is most essential training for the will, it is salvation from molly-coddling and from day-dreaming under the bed-clothes. Punctual arrival at table is respect for mother, for the family, for other people, it is respect for oneself. And all punctuality means being in reach of discipline and parental authority; thus it is also sex education.

And as part of the same everyday culture a large place should be given in every family to the doctor, to his advice, to his hygienic and prophylactic guidance. At certain periods girls particularly require this attention of the doctor, who should always have the help and support of the mother. Medical responsibility should, of course, lie mainly on the school. Here there is a place for serious talks on questions of sex, for acquainting the boys with questions of hygiene, continence, and in the older ages, with the danger of venereal diseases.

It should be noted that correct sex education within the limits of one family would be considerably facilitated if society as a whole devoted great active attention to this problem. The voice of public opinion and public morality should make still stronger and more insistent demands on society itself.

From this point of view we must, in particular, touch on such a "trifle" as bad language.

Highly cultured people, people holding responsible posts, who have perfect command of the Russian language, sometimes discover in swearing a kind of heroic inspiration, and resort to it on every possible occasion, contriving at the same time to keep extremely cultured and intelligent expressions on their faces. It is hard to understand the cause of this stupid and abominable tradition.

In the old days, swearing perhaps served in its own way as a remedy for a poor vocabulary and tongue-tied illiteracy. With the help of the standard expletive one could express any primitive emotion—anger, delight, surprise, condemnation, jealousy. Yet for the most part it did not even express any emotion at all, but served as a means of linking up disjointed phrases and ideas—a universal parenthetical phrase. In this case the formula was pronounced without the slightest feeling, showing only the confidence of the speaker and his fluency of speech.

In twenty years our people have learnt to speak. That is everywhere apparent, and can be seen at any meeting. Tongue-tied illiteracy is not in the least characteristic of our people. That has happened thanks not only to the wide spread of literacy, of books and newspapers, but mainly thanks to the fact that the Soviet man has had something to talk about; thoughts and feelings have existed that needed to be, and could be, expressed. And our people have learnt to speak their mind on any question without swearing. Before, they could not manage it and made do with the universally accepted, interchangeable formulae:

"Oh, the ...!"
"What the ...!"
"A ... fine thing!"
"You can ... well ... yourself!"

Even connected speech was, in fact, connected rather in this way:

"I ... goes up to him, and he, the ..., says: go to the ...! Oh, you ..., I thinks! A ... lot I ... care! I've ... seen ... thousands like you...."

Swear-words in our country have lost their "technical" significance, but they still remain in the language, and it can even be asserted that they are quite wide-spread and have currency in the speech even of cultured people. Now they express bravado, "an iron character," decisiveness, simplicity, contempt for the elegant. Now they are a kind of coquetry, the aim of which is to please the listener, to show him one's daring approach to life and lack of prejudice.

Certain chiefs are particularly fond of using them when talking to their subordinates. The effect is stylish beyond expression: an enormously responsible and powerful man sits at a huge desk in a monumental atmosphere of official stillness and luxurious furnishings, surrounded by telephones and diagrams. How is he to talk? If he talks in a concise, polite, business-like way—what will happen? People may say: the fellow's a bureaucrat. But suppose that, for all his power and pomp, he lets fly with a thunderous, or joking, or tight-lipped oath, then on the one hand his subordinates will tremble more, and on the other give him more respect. They will run off into their own office and rhapsodize: "What a man! What a man!..."

And instead of being a bureaucrat, he becomes one of the boys, and from there it is not very far to "our favourite chief."

Women, too, do not escape such charms. In front of them, of course, expression is not open but, rather, symbolic.

"If it weren't for Anna Ivanovna here, I'd be talking to you differently!"

And Anna Ivanovna smiles lovingly because she, too, has the confidence of the chief. "Our favourite chief!"

And since there is always someone over someone else, everyone expresses himself in keeping with his capabilities and authority. If he comes last in the hierarchy and does not rule over anyone, he takes it out of inanimate objects at his disposal: a lost file, a recalcitrant arithmometer, a bad pen, blunt scissors. Under particularly favourable conditions he takes it out of the next man, his fellow-worker, or the next department, or, lowering his voice by seventy-five per cent, the "favourite" chief.

But not only people in authority embellish their speech with such genuinely Russian ornaments. Very many people, particularly between the ages of 20 and 22, like to show off with bad language. It would seem that one had to spend very little mental energy to realize that Russian revolutionary zest is something diametrically opposed to the Russian zest for drinking, but not everyone realizes it! Not everyone realizes the simple and absolutely obvious fact that the swear-word is a cheap, wretched, utterly petty foulness, a sign of the most savage, most primitive culture—the cynical, insolent, ruffianly denial both of our respect for woman and of our striving for profound and genuinely human beauty.

But if for women that loosely used obscene word is only insulting, for children it is extremely harmful. With amazing light-mindedness we tolerate this thing, we tolerate its existence side by side with our great and active aspirations for education.

It is essential that we begin a resolute and persistent struggle against foul language, if not from aesthetic considerations, then from purely educational ones. It is difficult to calculate, and even more difficult to portray, the terrible harm this Rurikovian inheritance brings to our children, to our society.

For a grown-up person a swear-word is simply an extremely insulting coarse word. When saying or hearing it, the grown up experiences only a mechanical shock. An obscene word rouses no sexual images or feelings in him. But when a boy hears or speaks that word, it does not come to him as a relative term of abuse, it brings with it its inherent sexual meaning. The essence of this misfortune is not that the secret of sex is unveiled before the boy, but that it is unveiled in the most ugly, cynical and immoral form. The frequent uttering of such words trains him to pay exaggerated attention to sexual matters, to perverted day-dreaming, and that leads to an unhealthy interest in woman, to limited and blind visual sensitivity, to the petty, wearisome sadism of catchwords, dirty stories and bawdy jokes. A woman appears to him not in the full splendour of her human charm and beauty, not in the full harmony of her spiritual and physical tenderness, of all the mystery and strength of her being, but merely as a possible object of violence and utility, merely as a humiliated female. And such a youth sees love from the back yard, from the side where human history has long ago dumped its primitive physiological standards. It is on this garbage heap of cultural history that the boy's first vague conception of sex is fed.

It is unnecessary, of course, to exaggerate the unfortunate results of this phenomenon. Childhood, life, the family, school, society and books give the boy and the youth a large number of pushes and impulses in the opposite direction; our whole way of life, practical and comradely association with girls and women bring new food for higher feelings and more valuable conceptions.

But neither should they be underestimated.

Every man who denies himself the use of swear-words, who encourages a comrade to do the same, who demands restraint from any and every rampant "hero" he happens to meet, will bring enormous good both to our children and to the whole of our society.

Chapter Eight

*V*ERA IGNATYEVNA KOROBOVA worked in the library of a
big factory that had sprung up on the edge of the town.
Usually she returned home about five. But today she, her
assistants and sympathizers had stayed on longer—they
had been preparing for a conference. The conference would
be held tomorrow. A writer, a well-known literary figure,
was to take part. The readers liked his books, so did Vera
Ignatyevna. Today she had busied herself joyfully with
the show-case. With loving care she put out all the critical
literature about the writer on the shelves, arranged notices
of recommendation nicely beside the pages of the magazines, and in the centre of the show-case pinned up a portrait of the writer. It was a good portrait, an unusual one;
the writer's gaze was full of a good-natured, homely sadness, which made the whole show-case seem friendly and
somehow very intimate. When the work was finished it
was a long time before Vera Ignatyevna could bring herself to set off home—she still wanted to do something
more.

Vera Ignatyevna was particularly fond of her library
at this evening hour. She loved to gather up the books
returned by the readers and put them back on the shelves
with a specially tender care, tidy up the card index, and
see to it that old Marfa Semyonovna dusted properly
everywhere. Under her supervision a cosy, restful order-
liness came over the library, and then she could go home.

But it was even better, as it had been today, to stay and work with a little company of enthusiasts like herself.

In the shadowy passages between the shelves only a few of the books show up in the light of the lamp over the table. These books look as if they were out for a walk on a brightly lighted street at night. Further away, other books dream peacefully in the shadows, or softly whisper something to each other, glad not to be left standing by themselves this evening. In the far dark corners those old fellows, the magazines, are fast asleep; they are fond of a nap during the day, too, for the readers rarely trouble them. Vera Ignatyevna knows her book kingdom well. In her imagination each book has its own face and special character. This character is rather an intricate combination of the outward appearance of the book, the general outline of its contents and, most of all, the kind of relations it has with readers.

Take, for example, *Our Acquaintances* by Gherman. That is a buxom, young-looking woman with a pretty face, talkative and witty, but somehow not serious, a bit eccentric. She is to be found mainly in the company of girls between seventeen and eighteen. In spite of her being far older than they, they are on very familiar terms with her, and, judging by their faces, this buxom matron tells them something that is not even written in the text. Men return this book with ironic expressions on their faces and seem to say: "Hm ... yes!"

How the Steel Was Tempered is a sacred book, you must not drop it carelessly on the table, you feel you should not say angry words in its presence.

The Road to the Ocean is a serious gloomy comrade; he never smiles, on principle never takes any notice of girls, and only keeps company with rather dry, thin men in horn-rimmed spectacles. *Power* is a book with a melancholy character, a quiet stick; she glares hostilely at the reader, and the reader is afraid of her; if he has anything to do with her he is extremely polite and keeps strictly to business. *The Nineteen* is an old and famous doctor who has a queue of visitors and receives them with the tired kindly expression of a man who has worked hard and well. The reader returns this book with an air of calm gratitude, confident that it has done him good.

Even in Vera Ignatyevna's hands, as she takes a book in, or lets it out, books behave themselves differently. Some wait submissively to be registered, others leap out of her hands, drawn by the eager glances of the reader, yet others are stubborn and want to get up on the shelf— that is because the reader greets them with a cold unfriendly eye.

In Vera Ignatyevna's imagination the books all have their own interesting and intelligent lives, which she herself even envies a little, but still loves.

Vera Ignatyevna is thirty-eight. There is still very much youth in her face, her shoulders and her white neck, but Vera Ignatyevna does not know this, for she never thinks of herself. She thinks only of books and of her family, and there are always so many of these thoughts that they crowd confusedly into her mind and cannot keep in the queue.

Pleasant as it is to stay on at the library in the evening, her thoughts turn towards home. Vera Ignatyevna sweeps various nick-nacks quickly into her bag and hurries out to the tram. In the crowded car she stands for a long time, clinging to the back of a seat, and meanwhile the restrained whispering life of the books gradually dies away, and domestic affairs take its place.

This evening she will be back late, so it will be a very busy evening, too. While she is still in the tram the worries of the evening take over her mind and begin carving up her time with some pleasure. Where that pleasure comes from she does not know. Sometimes it seems to her that it is from love. Very likely it is. When the face of

Pavlusha or Tamara rises in her mind's eye, Vera Ignatyevna no longer sees the passengers or the streets flying
past, no longer notices the jerks and stops, nor feels her
own body, and the strap of her hand-bag and her tram-
ticket stay between her fingers only because of a long-
established habit. Pavlusha has a lovely fresh face, and
his eyes are brown, but in the whites there is so much
blue that Pavlusha seems to be golden-blue all over.
Pavlusha's face and eyes are such a captivating vision
that Vera Ignatyevna cannot even think about him, all
she does is see him. About Tamara, however, she can think,
though Tamara is also a real beauty. Vera Ignatyevna
always sees something uniquely charming, womanly and
tender in her. There is so much of these qualities in her
long eye-lashes, in the dark curls round her temples and
down her neck, in the deep mysterious glance of her
serious eyes, and the inexplicable charm of her movements. She often thinks of Tamara.

The life of Vera Ignatyevna herself for ages past had
flowed on in the same old channel. This straight steady
line had been carved across plains of labour and monotonous daily care—a dull lace-work of trivialities, which never left her throughout the day but just went on around her
in the same old loops, circles and crosses all the time.
The Revolution thundered past Vera Ignatyevna in a
rumble of sound and fury, she felt its hot breath, she saw
the old life, the old people, the old customs caught up and
borne away on the blast. As a working-woman, she rejoiced at this life-giving whirlwind, but she could not tear
herself away from the lace-work, not even for a minute,
because that lace-work was needed by someone. Vera Ignatyevna never thought of it as a duty, she simply could
not imagine how it was possible to break one of the loops
if Tamara, or Pavlusha, or Ivan Petrovich was going to
shout the house down over it. Even her marriage to Ivan
Petrovich had been like making another piece of lace-

work. She could not have refused: Ivan Petrovich might have whimpered, to say the least.

Vera Ignatyevna had never complained once in her whole life. Everything had turned out all right in the end, and now she could look at her children with joy, and think about them. And besides, books lent her existence an added charm. As a matter of fact, Vera Ignatyevna had never gone in for analyzing her life—she hadn't the time. It was hard to tell the good and the bad in it But when her thoughts turned to Tamara they began to work in a very unusual way. There was no doubt that Tamara's life ought to be different. Now Tamara was at the Institute of Architecture, studying something; on her desk lay a drawing she had started, some sort of "orders" and capitals, some lions with very complicated tails, like bunches of flowers, and bird-like beaks. Of course, Tamara's destiny did not lie in these lions, but in something else. That something was not quite clear, but in books it was called happiness. Happiness Vera Ignatyevna imagined as a woman walking in radiant beauty, as the fiery pride of her glance, as the joy issuing from her. Everything showed that Tamara was born for that kind of happiness and that she herself did not doubt it.

Vera Ignatyevna pushed her way mechanically to the exit and hurried the short distance to her house. Tamara opened the door. Vera Ignatyevna dropped her hand-bag on the window-sill in the hall and glanced into the living-room.

"Has Pavlusha had his dinner?"

"Yes."

"Has he gone out somewhere?"

"I don't know. I think he's skating."

That everybody had had dinner and that Pavlusha had gone skating was quite plain. Scraps of food were scattered over the table among the dirty plates. The floor in the hall was stained with mud and littered with pieces of wire and string.

With a habitual gesture Vera Ignatyevna pushed her straight hair off her forehead, looked round and picked up the broom in the hall. Tamara sat down in a big armchair, undid her hair and fixed her lovely eyes dreamily on the window.

"Well, what's to be done about my shoes, Mummy?"

Sweeping under Tamara's chair, Vera Ignatyevna said quietly: "Perhaps you can make them do, Tamara, dear?"

Tamara pushed her chair back with a crash and tossed the comb on the table; her eyes suddenly lost all their loveliness. She waved her pink hands at her mother, her silk dressing-gown flew open and the pink ribbons of her underwear also peeped out angrily at Vera Ignatyevna.

"Mother! How can you talk like that! It's infuriating! A brown dress with pink shoes! Just look at the things!"

Indignantly Tamara kicked out a small foot clad in a pretty pink shoe. At the moment she had everything to match: a pink dressing-gown and pinkish stockings.

Vera Ignatyevna paused with her broom for a moment and glanced sympathetically at Tamara's foot.

"Yes ... we'll have to buy you a pair. When pay-day comes round."

Tamara let her gaze follow the work of the broom. By all the laws of physics and geometry her glance should have fallen on her mother's battered, shapeless, faded shoes, but for some reason that did not happen. Tamara looked round the room, her eyes tired with suffering.

"I'm fed up," she said, "how many pay-days have I waited for already!"

Tamara sighed and departed into the bedroom. Vera Ignatyevna finished tidying the living-room and went to the kitchen to wash the dishes. She took an old calico overall out of the kitchen-cupboard and put it on. The Korobovs had no one to help with the house. There was an agreement by which the yardman's wife Vasilisa Ivanovna came in at two and made dinner for Tamara and Pavlusha. Ivan Petrovich and Vera Ignatyevna preferred to have their dinner at work—it was more convenient and took less time.

Vera Ignatyevna had a wonderful primus stove, she never tired of admiring it. She had only to give it two or three little pumps and with cheerful readiness it would roar away, giving a steady efficient flame. And the water in the saucepan would boil in fifteen minutes. As with other things, Vera Ignatyevna had a liking for the primus, and recognized in him a nice friendly character and above all ... such a worker.

Vera Ignatyevna also knew how to read the expressions of the dirty plates. It even made her smile to look at them —they had such a funny lovable air. In silent trusting expectation they would watch her bustling about, and wait impatiently to be bathed in hot water. They must have itched with impatience.

Vera Ignatyevna loved the life of the things around her, and when she was alone with them she felt happy and at ease. Sometimes she even talked to them. While at work, Vera Ignatyevna's face would liven, sparks of wit would dance in her eyes, and her full lips even break into a homely smile. But with people, even close relations, all this whimsical liveliness disappeared: it was awkward to play the fool in front of other people, awkward and silly, Vera Ignatyevna was not used to it.

Tonight, as she washed the dishes, she only joked a tiny little bit, and then remembered Tamara's shoes and went on thinking about them all the rest of the time.

She studied this whole question of the shoes very thoroughly. Perhaps it had been a mistake to buy pink shoes just because the dressing-gown was pink, and in any case one should not buy shoes to match a dressing-gown. But it had happened now, and there was nothing one could do about it. Then there was that rather drawn-out affair with the brown dress. The dress was a silk one, and actually was a soft shade of brown. It went very well with Tamara's hazel eyes and dark curls. But somehow this problem of brown shoes had taken her by surprise: she *had* thought the brown dress was the last thing on the list. The day before yesterday, when she was at home alone, Vera Ignatyevna had made a comparison. The dress was a fawny-brown and the shoes pink, not rose-pink, a little darker and not so vivid. For the merest instant Vera Ignatyevna had an idea that one could wear a brown dress with such shoes. And the shoes themselves at that moment seemed to have nodded agreement. But that was only a moment of weakness. Vera Ignatyevna tried not to remember it. Now she remembered only Tamara's troubled face, and it hurt her.

There was a knock on the front door. Vera Ignatyevna shook her hands over the basin and went to open it. To her surprise she found Andrei Klimovich Stoyanov standing in the doorway.

Andrei Klimovich Stoyanov loved the library and its books no less, perhaps, than Vera Ignatyevna. But he was not a librarian, he was a milling-machine operator, and rather a special one at that, for the other operators never mentioned his name except in double form:

"Stoyanov-Himself."

"Even-Stoyanov."

"Only-Stoyanov."

"Oh!-Stoyanov."

"Stoyanov's-the-man."

Vera Ignatyevna was not so good at understanding animate objects as inanimate ones, so she could not grasp what was so special about Andrei Klimovich as a milling-machine operator. True, enthusiastic reports reached her from the workshops that Stoyanov's team had overfulfilled its quota by 170-190 per cent, that in Stoyanov's team they had thought up some marvellous "conductor," that Stoyanov's team had planted a whole flower-bed round their machines; there were even jokes that the team would soon be renamed "The Andrei Stoyanov Milling-Machine Nursery-Garden." And yet, all Vera Ignatyevna could see in Andrei Klimovich was a book-lover. She found it difficult to understand how he could cope with his milling-machines if he really was so much in love with books. Andrei Klimovich had taken the evening shift on purpose, and at the factory trade-union committee elections had himself asked:

"Fix me up with something to do in the library."

Andrei Klimovich had his own way of liking books. To him, books were people between book-covers. He sometimes expressed his surprise as to why there were descriptions of nature, of rain or forests, in books. He would come to Vera Ignatyevna's room and say:

"People are hard to understand, there's something hidden in people; a writer can tell what it is, and we can find out if we read. But rain—well, it's just rain. If I look at rain, I see straight away—it's rain. And I can tell what kind of rain, a shower or a storm, harmful or harmless. It's the same with forests. A writer can never describe what you can see."

On the other hand, the people described in books always roused Andrei Klimovich's keen attention. He liked talking about these people, knew how to spot contradictions, and always took offence if a writer was unjust towards people.

"I don't like Dostoyevsky. They say he's a good writer, but I don't like him. He can say things about people, it makes you ashamed to read. Take that Raskolnikov, now. He murdered the old girl, didn't he. Well, try him and give him a proper punishment. But here you get a whole novel written about it! And I keep on reading and reading, and darn me if I don't begin to feel sorry for him. And it makes me angry: why should I be sorry, and it's all because he torments the man too much, you can't help feeling sorry."

And now here was Andrei Klimovich, standing smiling in the doorway. His smile was a little shy, a gentle beautiful smile—more like a young girl smiling than a forty-year-old milling-machine operator. And at the same time there was much courage and personal dignity in it.

"Do you mind if I come in, Vera Ignatyevna, there's a little matter I'd like to see you about."

Andrei Klimovich had been round about books before—he lived in the same street—but this time he seemed to have come about something rather special.

"Still busy with the housework?"

"Oh, it's not really housework. Just a few dishes. Come into the living-room."

"No, let's talk here, in the kitchen, in the shop, so to speak."

"But why?"

"Vera Ignatyevna, this matter, you know, is ... kind of secret!"

Andrei Klimovich smiled slyly, and even glanced into the living-room, but did not see anyone there.

In the kitchen Andrei Klimovich sat down on a wooden stool, looked ironically at the pile of clean, but still wet plates, and asked:

"You didn't use all that crockery for your dinner, did you?"

Vera Ignatyevna wiped her hands on the towel.

"No, the children did."

"The children? I see! I've come on behalf of the factory trade-union committee, so to speak. There's a problem to be settled."

"Is it about tomorrow's conference?"

"No, it concerns you personally. We've decided to give some people prizes for their cultural work. It should be

316

at the New Year, but as there's going to be a kind of celebration at the library we decided to give you yours now. Usually they give money prizes, but that's where I put my oar in: You can't award Vera Ignatyevna a money prize, I said, nothing'll come of it, just a lot of fuss, that's all."

"I don't understand," Vera Ignatyevna smiled.

"Well, it's very simple really. Money's a slippery thing: in one pocket today, in someone else's tomorrow, and the next day not a trace of it anywhere. Money won't do for you, you haven't even got any pockets. It's got to be some definite thing!"

"What thing?"

"Think it over."

"A thing? I see, all right, then. But do I deserve a prize?"

"That's been decided at a higher level. You don't come into that. Well, what's it to be?"

"I need a pair of shoes, Andrei Klimovich. Really I do, very much!"

Andrei Klimovich glanced cautiously at Vera Ignatyevna's shoes, and even more cautiously she moved up to the wooden stool where the dishes were lying.

"Shoes, these ones ... ye-es! Shoes would be a good thing. We can give you a pair of shoes."

"Only...."

Vera Ignatyevna blushed.

"Only brown... they must be brown, Andrei Klimovich!"

"Brown?"

Andrei Klimovich looked aside with a kind of sad smile.

"Well, I suppose we can get brown.... Only shoes, you know ... you can't buy shoes without trying them on. We'll go to the shop together and get them fitted.

Sometimes the arches are wrong, and you have to look at the style, or they may give you Lord knows what!"

Vera Ignatyevna blushed and smiled. He glanced up at her out of the corner of his eye, and the toe of his shoe tapped the floor meditatively.

"Let's go tomorrow and buy them?"

"But why should you go to all that trouble, Andrei Klimovich? I never try shoes on. I just tell them the size."

"The size? What size do you take, Vera Ignatyevna?"

"What size?... Fours."

"Fours? Won't they be a bit small?"

Vera Ignatyevna remembered that it was time the dishes were wiped, and turned round for the drying-cloth.

"You can't get away with that, Vera Ignatyevna," said Andrei Klimovich cheerfully.

Vera Ignatyevna picked up the first plate, but even the plate was looking at her with a broad platish grin.

"What can't I get away with?" said Vera Ignatyevna, for appearance' sake.

"Size four. That's what you can't get away with!"

Andrei Klimovich gave a loud laugh, rose from the stool and shut the door firmly. Standing with his back to it, he raised his eyes to the ceiling and began declaiming: "Your young lady won't get anything this time ... not now that I've been specially appointed to this job. She won't get one of her brown shoes. She's beautiful enough without them!"

Vera Ignatyevna did not know how to say: "What business is it of yours?" and in any case you could not be rude to someone like Andrei Klimovich. She lapsed into a confused silence. Andrei Klimovich again bestrode the stool.

"Don't be angry with me for interfering in your household. It's necessary sometimes, believe me! Something's got to be done about you. Acting on behalf of the factory trade-union committee, I have the authority of the State behind me, you know. And that's what I said: we are awarding this prize to Comrade Korobova; and that daughter of yours, the young dress-me-up, can get her prizes out of her father!"

"Whatever makes you say that! She's not a dress-me-up! A young girl. ..."

Vera Ignatyevna looked angrily at her guest. Why, indeed, did he say such things: dress-me-up! And that was about Tamara, about her beautiful daughter with the long eye-lashes and lovely curls, about a beautiful woman whom the future was to bring great happiness. Surely Andrei Klimovich was not an enemy of her daughter, thought Vera Ignatyevna suspiciously. She had seen few enemies in her life. Andrei Klimovich had a curly moustache that nodded pleasantly over his gentle smile, and that, of course, contradicted his hostile words. Yet he might be an enemy.

"Why do you speak of Tamara like that?"

Andrei Klimovich ceased to smile and stroked the back of his head worriedly.

"Vera Ignatyevna, let me tell you the truth."

"What truth?" Vera Ignatyevna suddenly felt she did not want to hear the truth.

"Yes, I'll tell you the truth," said Andrei Klimovich seriously, smacking his knee. "Only stop wiping those plates for a minute, and listen!"

He took the wiped plate out of her hands, carefully placed it on the dry pile, and even passed his hand over it as a sign that everything was in order. Vera Ignatyevna sat down on a stool by the window.

"There's no need to be afraid of the truth, Vera Ignatyevna, and don't be offended. It's your own affair, of course, and so is your daughter, I know that. The only thing is we're very fond of you as one of our workers. And we notice things. Look how you dress, for instance. We've noticed it. This skirt now ..." Andrei Klimovich carefully took a fold between two fingers. "... Anyone can see you've only got one. It does for work, and it does for the conference, and it does for washing up in. But that skirt's past its time by the look of it. It's a good job it's black, or ... it'd have been finished long ago! I won't mention your shoes. Is it poverty? With your husband earning, and yourself earning, and your daughter's grant, and you've only two children. Isn't that so? Only two. Well, the thing is that young lady of yours is too mighty fond of dressing up! Look at her. Even the women engineers can't keep up with her. She comes to the club—all dressed up to the nines, now it's blue, now it's black, now it's some other colour. But that's not the point, let her dress up if she likes; people are talking about you apart from that. And why do you have to wash up the dishes!"

"Andrei Klimovich! I'm a mother—I may take care of my family if I wish to!"

"You're a mother—well I never! My Elena Vasilyevna is a mother too, but just you look how my daughters work. They don't mind, they're young, they'll have plenty of time to get their fun. And my Elena hasn't got hands like yours, even though you're an intellectual worker, as they call it. It's shameful, I tell you straight. You've got lots of life in front of you, you're still young, and a handsome woman, why should it be like this, why?"

Vera Ignatyevna lowered her eyes, and was about to pluck at the knee of her skirt, as women always do in such cases, but remembered how Andrei Klimovich had just been running it down, and remembered, too, how darned and patched it was. She took her hand off her knee, and gradually began to get annoyed with Andrei Klimovich.

"Andrei Klimovich, everyone lives his own life. I like the way I live."

But Andrei Klimovich gave her an angry look, and even his curly moustache bristled angrily.

"But we don't like it."

"Who doesn't?"

"We don't, the people. How is it: our librarian, whom we all respect, dresses like ... I don't know what. And your husband doesn't like it either."

"My husband? How do you know? You've never seen him."

"For one thing, I have seen him, and for another, if he's a husband—husbands are all alike, you know—one day he'll go and ... these men, you know what they are, you have to keep an eye on them."

Andrei Klimovich smiled condescendingly and rose from his stool.

"To cut a long story short, we've decided to give you a prize of a dress length. It's going to be silk, some kind of bourgeois name it's got, a real tongue-twister. My wife can say it all right, but no man can. And it's got to be made at our factory dress-maker's, that's so you'll have it made your own size. I've got the money!"

He clapped his hand to his pocket. Vera Ignatyevna looked up at him, then looked at the unwiped plates, and sighed quietly. There was a grain of justice in his words, but it ripped apart violently some necessary loop in the lace-work of her life, and that was rather frightening. And she could not reconcile herself to Andrei Klimovich's hostility towards Tamara. The whole thing was strange somehow. But at the same time Andrei Klimovich loved books, and he was a member of the factory trade-union committee, and she liked his plain convincing manner.

"Well, what do you say?" asked Andrei Klimovich cheerfully, standing by the door.

She was about to answer, but at that moment the door flew open, and they were confronted by a charming sight: Tamara with her dressing-gown wide apart, showing stockings, ribbons, shoes and all. She uttered a piercing squeal and vanished, the door slamming behind her. Andrei Klimovich stroked his moustache sideways.

"Hum. . . . What do you say, Vera Ignatyevna?"

"Well, I suppose . . . if it's necessary . . . I'm very grateful to you."

That evening was not quite the same as usual, although events proceeded normally enough. Vera Ignatyevna finished the washing up, tidied the kitchen and began to prepare supper. Then in came Pavlusha, lively, flushed and wet to the skin. He put his head into the kitchen and said:

"I'm as hungry as a crocodile! What's for supper? Porridge and milk? What if I don't want porridge and milk? No, I want just porridge and just milk, separately."

"Where did you get so wet?"

"I'm not wet, we were just throwing snow at each other."

"Whatever for? Are you wet underneath?"

"No, only in one place, just here."

Vera Ignatyevna hurriedly set about changing her son's clothes. Apart from the "one place," that constituted his whole back, he was wet in many other places, and his socks had to be wrung out. Vera Ignatyevna wanted Pavlusha to slip into bed and get warm, but this plan did not appeal to him. While his mother was hanging his clothes out in the kitchen, he dressed himself up in his father's shoes and Tamara's blue working overall. Then the first thing he did was to show himself to his sister in this array. He was richly rewarded.

"Give it back!" shouted Tamara and flung herself in pursuit of the overall. Pavlusha ran through the rooms, first into the living-room, then the bedroom. After jumping twice over his father's bed, he again arrived in the living-room. Here Tamara would have caught him, but he neatly swivelled chairs in her path, roaring with laughter at his success. Tamara shouted "give it back," bumped into the chairs and hurled them aside. The crashes alarmed Vera Ignatyevna. She ran in out of the kitchen. Still in pursuit of her brother, Tamara did not notice her mother and knocked her roughly against the cupboard. Vera Ignatyevna hit her arm painfully but did not have time to feel it before she was stunned by the crash of breaking glass: in falling, she herself had knocked a jug of water off the sideboard. By that time Pavlusha was already laughing in Tamara's arms and obediently pulling off the blue overall. Tamara snatched the overall away from her brother and smacked his shoulder with her pink hand.

"If you dare take my overall again, I'll give you such a thrashing."

"Ooh, thrashing! You are strong, aren't you!"

"I'll do it now!"

"Come on then, just try! Come on!"

Noticing her mother bending over the remains of the jug, Tamara shouted:

"Mama! It's too much! He's always taking my things! What is this! If I need any clothes I have to ask for them three years on end. I can't even have a pair of shoes. But when it comes to grabbing and tearing things, no one must say anything! Oh, why is life so ... horrible!"

Tamara choked out the final words with a sob, flung the overall petulantly on the table and turned away to the sideboard, but instead of sobbing any more, stood staring in silence at the sideboard. Usually, in this attitude she appeared so wronged and unhappy that her mother would immediately be overwhelmed with pity for her. But this time Vera Ignatyevna did not glance in her direction —she was too busy with the tedious work of gathering up the pieces of the broken jug. Tamara gave her mother a sharp look and again turned her attention to the carved edge of the sideboard. Her mother said nothing and carried the broken glass away into the kitchen. Tamara gazed after her in some surprise, but hearing her footsteps, once more adopted her former position. Vera Ignatyevna returned from the kitchen with a rag and, bending down over the spilt water, said quietly and seriously:

"You're treading in the water ... move aside."

Tamara stepped over the puddle and retired to her desk, but from there continued to watch her mother.

As a matter of fact, events were proceeding quite normally. There had been merry games like this before, and similar breakages. In the same normal atmosphere Vera Ignatyevna put the supper on the table. Pavlusha, half-undressed, made a rush for the porridge. For some time he mixed butter into the porridge with one hand, keeping a tight hold on a glass of milk on the table with the other—he was very fond of milk. Tamara never ate porridge, she liked meat, and now there were two warmed-up cutlets waiting for her on her plate. But Tamara had become a fixture at her drawing desk, and was ignoring both her mother and the cutlets. Vera Ignatyevna glanced at her daughter, and pity wakened in her maternal heart.

"Tamara, sit down and have something to eat!"

"All right," whispered Tamara, shrugging her shoulders bitterly, as one who is aweary of life.

But life flowed on normally. At eleven Ivan Petrovich came home. It was a long-established convention that Ivan Petrovich always came from work, and so for several years past the question of where he had come from had never arisen. Even when he returned wrapped in the vapour of State Distilleries, Vera Ignatyevna worried more about his health than the breaking of office regulations. The convention was always so scrupulously observed because Ivan Petrovich was remarkable for his wonderfully steady character that justly roused the envy of many wives. People who knew Vera Ignatyevna often said to her:

"What a wonderful husband you've got! It's not often one meets a husband with such a character! You are so lucky, Vera Ignatyevna!"

These words always had a pleasant effect on Vera Ignatyevna—no one usually envied her in life, except for one trivial occasion when somebody had said to her:

"What a wonderful primus you have! It's not often you can find such a good one as that!"

Ivan Petrovich was a senior planning expert, but unlike other senior planning experts, who, as everyone knows, are a bad-tempered race given to the analysis of market conditions and frequent changes of job, Ivan Petrovich had an equable temper and no inclination to analysis, and he had kept the same job for upwards of fifteen years. True, he never told his wife anything about his work, and Vera Ignatyevna only knew that he was a planning expert somewhere because she remembered it from her young days.

Ivan Petrovich wore a well-cut suit, his face was clear and full, and he had a perfectly trimmed little beard. Vera Ignatyevna only looked after his suits once they were made; how they were made she had not the faintest idea. Ivan Petrovich took care of that without her advice. Every month he gave Vera Ignatyevna three hundred rubles.

As always, when he came home, Ivan Petrovich sat straight down to table, and Vera Ignatyevna gave him his supper. While she was doing so he supported his beard on his folded hands and nibbled at the joints of his fingers. His eyes roamed calmly round the room. Plates appeared before him, he assumed a rather dignified air and tucked the corner of a napkin into his collar. He never ate without a napkin and in general he was a very neat man. He could talk only when he had had a bite to eat.

Today everything proceeded normally. Ivan Petrovich ate his cutlets and reached for the stewed fruit. As he did so, he asked:

"Well, Tamara, how's your architecture going?"

From her desk Tamara gave a polite shrug. Vera Ignatyevna sat down on a chair by the wall and said:

"Tamara is very upset. We can't seem to buy her that pair of brown shoes."

Ivan Petrovich broke a toothpick off his match-box and burrowed into his teeth with it, helping it with his tongue and sucking appreciatively. With an effort he turned his eye on Tamara. Then he attentively examined the tooth-pick, and said: "Shoes, that's serious. Why, haven't we enough money?"

"You've never enough when it comes to me," observed Tamara sadly.

Ivan Petrovich stood up at the table, put his hands in his trouser-pockets and began to think of something, staring down at his empty plate. In this thoughtful attitude he raised himself on his toes and then lowered himself again two or three times, then started whistling the duke's song from *Rigoletto*. He seemed to be thinking about the shoes. But apparently he did not think up anything very good. Making a last tiptoe, he walked slowly into the bedroom and there, too, could be heard whistling the song of the duke. Tamara turned in her chair and hurled an angry glance at the bedroom door. Vera Ignatyevna began to clear the table.

And so that evening, too, passed normally—an evening in the life of Vera Ignatyevna. And yet it was different from other evenings. Ever since Andrei Klimovich had left, something had been stirring faintly in Vera Igna-tyevna's soul.

It was not the first time Vera Ignatyevna had thought of interesting things while she was doing her housework. Usually she would remember her work in the library, running over in her mind the books that had been received, her conversations with readers and the advice she had given. She liked to recall successes, witty remarks and warm words of encouragement. When some inspiring or remarkable expression occurred to her several times, she

326

would examine it with an inward smile, attend to its finest shades of meaning, and rejoice.

That evening, but for Andrei Klimovich, she would have thought of tomorrow's conference, recalled the show-case and the portrait of her favourite writer, and thought of his books in their handsome grey-blue bindings. His books had a young, laughing note in their character; it was pleasant to remember them.

But that evening she thought of none of these things. While she prepared the supper, and while she gathered up the fragments of broken glass, and again while she was wiping the plates when everybody else had gone to bed, Vera Ignatyevna kept thinking of what Andrei Klimovich had said. For some reason only one subject came to the fore: Andrei Klimovich's devastating remarks about her skirt. It was very disappointing to learn that all her efforts and labours and hopes had been in vain. How many evenings she had spent on repairing that skirt, and always, when she had finished, she had been sure she had achieved her aim, and that she would go out to work next day looking very respectable; and now and then, for a fleeting instant, it had even seemed to her that her appearance would be not merely respectable but even elegant. And it had turned out quite the reverse. "People are talking about you." So everybody had noticed and they were all laughing about it. And tomorrow? Tomorrow would be the conference.

After finishing the dishes and tidying up, Vera Ignatyevna cleared away, took off her skirt and spread it out on the table. The skirt obediently displayed its old wrinkles. Vera Ignatyevna took a close look at it, and unexpectedly her eyes filled with tears; she felt so sorry for the old lady. The skirt looked up at her with such a sad and weary expression of decrepitude; you could see it so badly needed to rest, to lie down somewhere in a warm corner of the chest of drawers, and have a good sleep.

Once upon a time it had been made of silk. It had been very womanly and playful then. Now the silkiness of the cloth could only be seen if one looked very closely, but even that silkiness had turned grey. And among these frail and trembling grey threads everywhere there were wrinkles and the scars of old wounds received in life. The places that had been darned long ago held together somehow, but the latest rents were just a fine network of darning, through which gleamed the white top of the table.

Vera Ignatyevna plugged in the iron. With great care, trying not to press too hard, she passed it a few times over the skirt. Where the iron had been, the wrinkles smoothed out and disappeared, and the old lady began to look forlorn and tender.

When she had finished ironing the skirt, Vera Ignatyevna held it up and inspected it. No, there was no deceiving oneself now: even ironed, it did not promise elegance. But Vera Ignatyevna smiled bravely: never mind, we've spent our lives together and we'll answer for it together.

Vera Ignatyevna's feelings began to relax, and when she sat down to put her shoes in order, it seemed particularly cosy in the stillness of the kitchen, and she no longer thought of the skirt, nor of what she would say at the conference, but of herself.

It was characteristic of Vera Ignatyevna that she did not feel lonely now. In the first place, the skirt was lying ironed and at ease on the table, secondly, Andrei Klimovich's moustache was smiling at her somewhere in the distance. She was not annoyed with him any more. Well, she must consider what he had said.

With a thick needle and waxed thread Vera Ignatyevna sewed up the sole of her shoe, and meditated, smiling. She smiled because she felt she had grown younger, and that was unusual and rather funny. She imagined herself in a new silk dress, and that, too, seemed ... strange and ... funny. Through the fog of her domestic cares she perceived that this new dress was inevitable, but it was not only a dress ... outrageous, shameful thing to think— there was something young about it. Vera Ignatyevna even shook her head in surprise. She went cautiously up to the misty mirror over the sink. This time she was really amazed by a pair of young smiling eyes and by full merry lips that seemed to be whispering something. There was no rosiness visible in the mirror, but Vera Ignatyevna could feel it flushing warmly over her cheeks. A chance thought reminded her of Ivan Petrovich. She turned away from the mirror and again sat down on the stool, but her hand holding the thick needle did not resume its work. It came to her clearly: what kind of wife was she? How could she be the wife of this well-dressed, clean-shaven, self-confident man? She had not been his wife for a long time, and could not be. Ivan Petrovich did not see her undies, her stockings, there was much that he did not see....

Vera Ignatyevna came to herself with a jerk. Her fingers set to work hurriedly on the shoe. Frowning to herself Vera Ignatyevna hastened to finish her job and go to bed to avoid thinking of anything else.

The conference went off very interestingly. The readers spoke with sincerity and emotion and, as they left the platform, shook the writer's hand and thanked him. Vera Ignatyevna greeted every speaker with an anxious attentive glance, and watched them go, feeling relieved and joyful. Both old and young knew how to speak, as well as how to feel; that was a great triumph, and Vera Ignatyevna knew that it was a triumph of the whole people. Before her and behind her she could feel a new delightful country that could speak and feel.

Andrei Klimovich also took the floor and said briefly:

"The books of our comrade here that I have read have been a danger to my life, and that's a fact: I didn't sleep for two nights running. He shows such fine people! Daring people, you know, young people, full of gaiety. Come what may, people like that are devoted to their cause! And it's true. You read the book at night, then you wake up in the morning and have a look round you, and you really do see such people. Why, I'm one of them myself...."

The audience laughed loudly. Andrei Klimovich realized that he had gone too far and confusedly stroked his moustache sideways. Then he made a recovery.

"We need more culture, of course, that's true enough, and you were quite right to mention it. Well, culture is what we're striving for. Look at the library we've got here, and this fine club, and the way writers and scholars come to visit us. And thanks to Soviet power for putting such comrades on the job as Vera Ignatyevna Korobova."

A warm burst of applause swept the hall. Vera Ignatyevna looked round at the writer, but the writer was already standing at the table, smiling at her and clapping. Many people in the hall had stood up, everyone was looking at Vera Ignatyevna, the roar of applause grew louder and louder. Vera Ignatyevna was about to make for the door in fright, but the writer gently put his arm round her and propelled her carefully towards the table. She sat down and, to her own surprise, put her arms on the back of the chair, dropped her head on her arms and began to cry. A hush fell on the hall at once, but Andrei Klimovich waved his arm in mock despair, and everyone laughed kindly and affectionately. Vera Ignatyevna raised her head, quickly brought her eyes under control, and laughed too. A wave of talking swept through the audience. Andrei Klimovich picked up a piece of paper and read out that the Party organization, the factory trade-union committee and the management had made a decision to reward chief librarian Vera Ignatyevna Korobova for her energetic and devoted work by presenting her with a prize of a length of crêpe de Chine. This last word Andrei Klimovich pronounced with some uncertainty and even nodded his head to show how difficult it was; nevertheless the word was greeted with fresh applause. Andrei Klimovich took a light package tied round with blue ribbon out of his bag, put it in his left hand and stretched out his right to shake hands. Vera Ignatyevna was about to take the package but realized that that would be wrong. Andrei Klimovich caught her hand and shook it warmly; the people in the hall applauded and laughed joyfully. Vera Ignatyevna blushed scarlet and gave Andrei Klimovich a look of sincere reproach. But Andrei Klimovich smiled loftily, and patiently went through all the necessary ceremonies. At last the crêpe de Chine, wrapped in tissue-paper and tied round with blue ribbon, was deposited on the table in front of her. At that moment she remembered her old skirt, and hastened to draw her feet under the chair so that her shoes should not be seen by the audience.

But it was not all over yet. The writer took the floor and made a good speech. He thanked the trade-union committee for taking the opportunity afforded by the conference to reward the work of so fine a person as Vera Ignatyevna Korobova. In writing circles many people knew Vera Ignatyevna. It was not enough just to write a book, once a book was written it had to be brought into personal contact with the reader, and that was great work of political, cultural and moral enlightenment. Round such people as Vera Ignatyevna a new socialist culture was growing and spreading. Today's conference was no less an achievement than the building of a new factory, than raising fertility, than constructing roads and railways. And in our Soviet Union there were many such conferences, such manifestations of a young and deep socialist culture. We should all be proud of that, and proud of such people as Vera Ignatyevna. While in the fascist states books were being burned on bonfires, the best representatives of humanism hounded and persecuted, in our country books were treated with love and gratitude, such creative library-workers as Vera Ignatyevna were honoured. On behalf of the writers, he thanked her for her great work and wished her strength and health to be able to carry on working for a long time on the education of the Soviet reader....

Vera Ignatyevna listened attentively to the writer's speech and realized with surprise that she was indeed performing a great task, that her love of books was by no means a secret personal feeling, but something great and useful and important. She came face to face with something she had not noticed before—the social significance of her job. She examined this idea intently and suddenly grasped its whole meaning all at once: she saw tens of thousands of books read by people; she saw the people themselves, who not so long ago had been naive and timid, staring awkwardly at the lines of books and titles and asking: "Give us something about bandits," or "Something, you know ... about life." Then they had started asking for books about the war, about the Revolution, about Lenin. And now they no longer asked for anything, but put down their names thirty-fifth or fifty-fifth on the list for a certain book, and grumbled:

"What do you think of that! A library like this and only five copies! This is no good!"

But she had known all this before! There were eight librarians working under her, and they all knew it, and often in the library of an evening they would talk about books, about readers, about methods. She knew the work of other libraries, too, she had been to many conferences, read critical and bibliographical articles and journals. She knew everything, she had taken part in everything, and yet she had never felt such a great pride, such a sense of having created something as she did today.

And the writer seemed to answer the question that was already in her mind:

"People like Vera Ignatyevna are terribly modest, they

never think of themselves, they think of their work, they are too taken up with its message. But we, you and I, think of them, we shake their hands in the warmest gratitude, and it was an excellent idea on the part of your factory organization to reward Vera Ignatyevna with an expensive dress. And we say to her: No, you think of yourself, too. Live happily, dress well, you have deserved it; that was just why we made our Revolution, so that every real toiler should live well."

That remarkable day was remarkable to the very end. After the conference a party was organized in the library for the library-workers and the regular readers. The tables were laid with wine, sandwiches and cakes. The young workers sat Vera Ignatyevna down beside the writer, and till evening they recalled their victories, their difficulties and doubts, and talked of their mutual friends: readers, books and writers.

But when they parted Andrei Klimovich carefully took the parcel tied with blue ribbon from under Vera Ignatyevna's arm and said:

"You needn't take this home. We'll just lock it up here in the drawer, and tomorrow, with any luck, it'll be at the dress-maker's."

Even the writer burst out laughing, and Vera Ignatyevna meekly gave up the parcel.

When she got home Vera Ignatyevna set about her usual jobs. Pavlusha had gone out skating again, leaving the same tracks behind him in the hall. Tamara, apparently, had been at home with her hair uncombed all day; the same design still lay on her desk and nothing had changed there, except for one lion's tail that had now been inked in. Tamara was not on speaking terms with her mother: that meant the beginning of one of those effective sieges that always followed a rapid but abortive attack.

Before, Vera Ignatyevna had always taken this strategy as a sign not only of her daughter's annoyance but of some fault on her own part; and yet today, for some reason, Vera Ignatyevna could not feel she had committed any fault. And it was very sad to see Tamara suffering, and very painful to look at her pretty, unhappy face, and a great pity to think that the present was so black for this sweet young life; but for all that it was quite clear that the person to blame for this was not Vera Ignatyevna. Her thoughts ran on to Ivan Petrovich. Very likely he was to blame. She could not help remembering that duke's song. Ivan Petrovich really should have taken some interest in Tamara's shoes. And ... three hundred rubles a month was very little. What salary was he getting? Before, he used to get seven hundred, didn't he? But that was a long, long time ago. . . .

As she thought of these things Vera Ignatyevna was still under the influence of her wonderful triumph that day, and for that reason her mind worked better and more boldly. She could not forget either the wave of popular love and attention, or the sweeping picture of her great work that the writer had drawn. And her home now seemed to her poor and deserted.

But no one had done away with domestic cares. They were there today as on any other day, and they still had to be attended to as usual, with the same thoughts and worries, the same emotions fixed through decades of habit. Once more Vera Ignatyevna served Pavlusha and Tamara their supper. Tamara gazed at the cutlet with such sadness in her eyes, her fork gathered up the pieces of food on her plate with such touching helplessness that Vera Ignatyevna could not feel at ease. A lump rose in her throat, and suddenly she remembered the parcel tied with blue ribbon. That parcel signified nothing but plain greedy egoism. While this beautiful girl could not even put on her favourite dress, Vera Ignatyevna was hoarding away her expensive crêpe de Chine. And then she would have a dress made and flounce about in it like some actress, and who would help this poor girl? In her imagination Vera Ignatyevna could already see the door of the commission shop, and there she was going inside and offering ... but she had nothing to offer, the parcel was still in the keeping of Andrei Klimovich. For a fraction of a second the idea flitted through her mind that she could take the parcel, but just as quickly Andrei Klimovich gave a smile with his curly moustache, and the commission shop disappeared. The lump in Vera Ignatyevna's throat grew bigger, and she was still ill at ease when Ivan Petrovich came home.

When Ivan Petrovich had started his supper, Vera Ignatyevna said from her chair by the wall:

"We had a conference today, and, would you believe it, after the conference they presented me with a prize."

Tamara opened her eyes wide and forgot her sufferings. Ivan Petrovich asked: "A prize? That's interesting! Did they give you much?"

"Material for a dress."

Ivan Petrovich placed his two fists, armed with knife and fork, one on each side of his plate, and went on masticating in an appreciative, business-like manner.

"Old-fashioned sort of prize," he said, tapping the handle of his knife on the table.

Tamara came up to the table, lay half over it and fixed a lively interested gaze on her mother.

"Have you got it yet?"

"No ... it's there ... at the dress-maker's."

"So you've already got the material?"

Vera Ignatyevna nodded her head and looked shyly at her daughter.

"What material is it?"

"Crêpe de Chine."

"Crêpe de Chine? What colour?"

"I haven't seen it ... I don't know."

Tamara's head and all its accessories: her pretty eyes,

rosy lips, and sweet little nose, broad at the base and pointed at the tip, rested neatly in her palms. Tamara surveyed her mother keenly, seeming to consider what she would look like if arrayed in crêpe de Chine. Her eyes lingered on her mother's knee, dropped to her shoes, then lifted once again to her shoulders.

"Are you going to have a dress made?" asked Tamara, continuing her examination.

Vera Ignatyevna felt even more ashamed and said quietly, with an effort:

"Yes ... I think so ... my skirt's too old now...."

Tamara cast a final glance over her mother, straightened up, put her hands behind her back, and looked up at the lamp.

"I wonder what colour it will be."

Ivan Petrovich drew up his plate of curd fritters and said: "At our office gifts for prizes have been out of date for a long time. Money is more convenient in all respects."

But it was not until the next day that the new dress came into its own. During the dinner-hour Andrei Klimovich called in at the library and said:

"Well, let's go and dress up."

"What have you come for? Do you think we can't manage without you?" retorted Marusya, gay and dark-eyed, from the top step of the shelf-ladder.

"I came on purpose. Vera Ignatyevna and I are going to the dress-maker's together."

Vera Ignatyevna put her head out of her little room. Andrei Klimovich nodded towards the door.

"Where do you think you'll go? Who'll let you in there? It's a lady's tailor's. We'll manage without you."

Marusya jumped down from the ladder.

"You mustn't go."

"Marusya, come over here. I've a word to say to you in secret."

They walked away to the window. Andrei Klimovich began whispering, and Marusya laughed and exclaimed: "I should think not!—Of course!—Why, what's so secret about that?! We know that without you telling us. We've known it for a long time!—Don't worry!—No-o! No, we understand."

They came back from the window, well pleased with each other, and Marusya said:

"Come on, give me that prize."

Andrei Klimovich departed to the farthest corner of the library. His second accomplice, Natasha, just as gay, but fair-haired, dashed after him, her overall flying.

"It's under lock and key! You'll never open it by yourself!"

They returned with the famous parcel. Vera Ignatyevna was working at her desk, surrounded by bills. With a fond attentive gesture Natasha took away her pen and placed it on the inkstand, then pushed away the bills, and in sweet girlish solemnity placed the ribboned parcel before Vera Ignatyevna. Her two fingers pulled at the knot, and in a second the blue ribbon was adorning her shoulder. Then from the wrapping of white tissue-paper came the first joyous gleam of silk.

"Cherry!" cried Natasha, clasping her hands as if in prayer. "How lovely!"

"Cherry! Really now!" exclaimed Vera Ignatyevna in embarrassment. "You shouldn't have done it!"

But Natasha's hands had already swept up the superb folds of material and draped them over the breast and shoulders of Vera Ignatyevna, who snatched protestingly at Natasha's fingers and blushed to the roots of her hair.

"How beautiful," Marusya was squealing. "How it suits you! Isn't it lovely! Just the colour for your complexion! What a wonderful choice! Cherry-coloured crêpe de Chine!"

The girls besieged Vera Ignatyevna, rejoicing sincerely over the deep dark red waves of silk, Vera Ignatyevna's embarrassment and their own friendly enthusiasm. Marusya pulled Andrei Klimovich by the shoulders.

"Did you choose it? Yourself?"

"I did."

"All alone?"

"All alone."

"And you chose cherry?"

"I did."

"I don't believe it! You couldn't have done! You took your wife with you."

"Why should I need my wife? If I myself, from early childhood, so to speak, was brought up, so to speak... in these silks. ..."

"What silks? Where was that you were brought up?"

"Why, in these here, what-do-you-call-it ... cream-doo-sheens! Of course, I was!"

Andrei Klimovich stroked his moustache and put on a serious air. Marusya regarded him distrustfully.

"What were you then... an aristocrat?"

"What do you think! When my mother used to hang out the clothes to dry... after washing, it was a real picture: silk all round you—cherry, apple, apricot!"

"A-ah!" cried Marusya. "To dry! Whoever thought of washing silk?"

"Well, don't they?"

"No, they don't!"

"In that case I take my words back."

The girls squealed and laughed, again draped the material over Vera Ignatyevna's shoulders, then over their own shoulders, and even over Andrei Klimovich's. And he kept up his former line: "What about it? I'm used to this kind of thing."

The same rejoicing continued at the factory dress-maker's. The question of styles roused such a battle that Andrei Klimovich shook his head resignedly and took himself off, only pausing at the door to say:

"What a crazy lot of people!"

Vera Ignatyevna was insisting on the very simplest style.

"An old woman can't wear a thing like that."

Such words would take Natasha's breath away, and she would again drag Vera Ignatyevna up to the mirror.

"All right, then, let it be plain! But you must have a flounce in here."

The experienced grey-haired tailor would nod his head.

"Yes, that will be better," he would say, "that'll give fullness to it."

Vera Ignatyevna felt as if she had been brought there to take part in a game for little children. Even in the far-off days of her youth she could not remember such a commotion over the making of a dress, and now all this fuss seemed even more out of place. But there was no stopping the girls. Once they had started on fashions, they went on to hair styles and began suggesting the most radical reforms in that field. Then came the turn of stockings, shoes and underwear. In the end Vera Ignatyevna chased them off to the library on the plea that the dinner-break was over.

When she was left alone with the tailor she insisted firmly on a simple style, and the tailor agreed that it would be most suitable. After fixing the time, she went back to work. On the way she found herself, to her surprise, making a firm resolve to obtain and wear a beautiful dress. And along with this a new picture of herself had arisen. It was a new Vera Ignatyevna. In the mirror at the dress-maker's she had seen her new figure adorned in cherry-coloured silk, and her new face illuminated by it. She was pleasantly surprised to find in this new picture nothing loud, nothing foolishly coquettish, nothing absurd. Above the dark red folds her face did indeed seem more beautiful and young and happy, but at the same time it had much dignity and a great truth.

As she reached the door of the library Vera Ignatyevna remembered the writer's speech. She glanced down at her shoes. There was no doubt that such trash could discredit both herself and the cause she served.

Vera Ignatyevna returned home that evening, feeling unusually tranquil. As before, she fondly imagined to herself the faces of Pavlusha and Tamara, and as before, she admired them; but now she wanted more to think about them, and could do so without being alarmed by trivial worries. They appeared to her now more as interesting people, than children under her protection.

At home she found the usual uncleared table. She gave it a habitual glance, but the habitual urge to set about the task of clearing up did not waken as promptly as before. She sat down in the armchair beside Tamara's desk and felt how pleasant it was. Throwing her head back, she lapsed unresistingly into a half-doze in which her thoughts did not sleep but danced untrammelled through her mind in a free and blissful crowd.

Tamara appeared from the bedroom.

"Didn't you go to the institute today either?" asked Vera Ignatyevna.

"No," said Tamara sadly, walking to the window and looking out into the street.

"Why don't you go these days?"

"I haven't anything to go in."

"Tamara, what can we do about it?"

"You know what ought to be done."

"Are you still on about the shoes?"

"Yes."

Tamara turned to her mother and burst out:

"You want me to go about in pink shoes and a brown

dress? You want people to laugh at me? Is that what you want? Well, say it then."

"But you have other dresses, Tamara, dear. And you've got black shoes. They're old ones, of course, but they're sound. Surely not all your students are so particular about having everything to match."

"The black? The black shoes?"

Tamara dashed to the wardrobe and returned holding a black shoe. She pushed it indignantly in front of her mother's nose.

"Am I supposed to wear this? Is that what you call a pair of shoes? Perhaps you don't call that a patch? Perhaps you think that's not sewn up?"

"But, Tamara, look what I wear!"

Vera Ignatyevna said this quite mildly, in the most friendly confiding way. She wanted to soften the reproach as much as possible. But Tamara did not even notice any reproach. She was only concerned with the illogicality of the comparison.

"What are you saying, Mother? Do you think I ought to dress like you? You've had your life. But I'm young, I want to live!"

"When I was young I had much less than you ever have. I often went to bed hungry."

"Now she's started! What do I know about what you had and what you didn't have. That was under tsarism, it's nothing to do with me! Things are quite different now! And parents ought to live for their children now, everyone knows that—except us. But when I'm old I won't grudge things for my daughter!"

Tamara stood leaning on the table and went on shouting and waving the shoe, but could see neither the shoe nor her mother. Her tears were rising. She stopped to take a rest, and Vera Ignatyevna managed to put in:

"Surely I'm not so old that I must give up everything and go about in these rags?"

"Am I forcing you to go about in rags? Go about in what you like, but don't make me into a laughing-stock! I'm sure you're having a new dress made for yourself, aren't you? Of course you are. You can have anything, but I can't. You are having a new silk dress, aren't you?"

"I am."

"There you are, you see? I knew it! You can dress yourself up. Who have you to dress up for? For Father?"

"Tamara! But you have a dress!"

"Couldn't you sell it! You could sell the brown dress for me. And what's the colour of that... prize? What colour is it?"

"Cherry."

"You see: cherry! How many times have I asked for cherry! I've asked and asked, but you've always forgotten."

Tamara could no longer restrain her tears, her face was wet.

"Whatever do you want?"

"I want it! Why shouldn't I? Brought me into the world and now won't give me anything to wear. But you dress yourself up, you ought to be ashamed to try and look young at your age! Ashamed!"

By this time Tamara was in hysterics. With another cry of "ashamed!" she rushed into the bedroom. Her sobbing, though muffled by a pillow, could be heard all through the flat. Vera Ignatyevna froze to the armchair. A black cloud of gloom bore down on her; perhaps she really did feel ashamed. There was a knock at the door. Still wrapped in the black cloud and listening to Tamara's sobs, she went to open it.

It was Andrei Klimovich. As he came in he gave a look in the direction of the sobbing, but immediately smiled.

"I thought I'd bring these in on the way home. They're the coupons for free dress-making."

"Come inside," said Vera Ignatyevna mechanically.

This time Andrei Klimovich expressed no desire to talk in the kitchen, and willingly came through to the living-room. Vera Ignatyevna hurried to shut the bedroom-door, but was too late. Tamara appeared in the doorway, brandished something big and dark, and flung it down at her mother's feet. Light black waves swept through the air and subsided on the floor. Tamara watched their flight only for a second, then rushed back into the bedroom, and the brown dress alighted at her mother's feet.

"Go on! Wear them!" shouted Tamara. "Deck yourself up! I don't want your adornments."

Tamara noticed Andrei Klimovich but she was past caring. She stamped angrily into the bedroom, slamming the door behind her.

Vera Ignatyevna stood in silence over the scattered garments. She could not even think. She was not insulted, and felt no shame on account of her visitor. Human anger always paralyzed her.

Andrei Klimovich placed some papers on the table, then bent down quickly, picked up both dresses and laid them over the arm of the chair. He did this in a conscientious manner, and even straightened out one of the sleeves. Then he faced Vera Ignatyevna inquiringly, his hands behind his back, and asked: "What's this? Are you afraid of that sh——?"

He said this loudly, obviously wishing to be heard in the bedroom. And indeed the bedroom became quiet as the grave.

Vera Ignatvevna started at the coarse word, clutched at the back of the chair, and suddenly ... smiled.

"Andrei Klimovich! What are you saying?"

Andrei Klimovich stood in the same attitude, looking severely at Vera Ignatvevna. His lips were pale.

"I haven't said much, Vera Ignatyevna. It isn't enough just to say things. We respect you a lot, that's a fact, but we can't forgive a thing like this. Who are you fostering here? Who? Are you fostering enemies, Vera Ignatyevna?"

"What enemies, Andrei Klimovich?!"

"Just think, what use are such people to anyone! Do you think it's only unpleasant for you, just a family matter? There she is, had her dinner, but the washing-up's not done, and she, the dirty hussy, instead of clearing up after her, what does she do? Throws her rubbish in your face! Things that you paid for with your honest labour! If she feels like that towards you, what's her attitude to Soviet power? And I expect she belongs to the Komsomol. Doesn't she?"

"I do. What about it?"

Andrei Klimovich glanced round. In the doorway stood Tamara, looking at him scornfully and shaking her head.

"You do, do you? Well, I'd like to see you wash up the dishes, you dolled-up slut!"

Tamara did not glance at the dishes. She could not tear her hate-filled gaze away from Andrei Klimovich.

"Did you have dinner?" he nodded at the table.

"That's none of your business," said Tamara proudly. "What right have you to shout at me?"

"A member of the Komsomol! Huh! I was a member of the Komsomol in 1918, and I've seen plenty of good-for-nothing ladies the like of you."

"Stop shouting, I tell you! Good-for-nothing! Perhaps I work more than you do."

Tamara turned her shoulder to the visitor. For a second they stared at each other angrily. But Andrei Klimovich suddenly relaxed, spread out his arms and puckered his eyes cunningly.

"All right, I'll ask you nicely: do me, an old partisan, a favour, and wash up!"

A smile peeped out of Tamara's face and instantly took on a haughty expression. She shot a lightning glance at her subdued mother, and another at the dresses lying over the chair.

"What about it? Let's do it together. You can wash and I'll fix the primus. I bet you don't know how to."

Tamara went quickly up to the table and began to pile the plates. Her face was stony. She had even closed her eyes; her beautiful dark lashes were trembling slightly.

Andrei Klimovich opened his mouth in surprise.

"There's a girl!"

"None of your business," whispered Tamara huskily.

"You don't mean to say you'll do it?"

"I'll go and put on my overall," she said in the same low voice, going into the bedroom.

Vera Ignatyevna stared at her visitor and did not recognize him. What had become of Andrei Klimovich, the book-lover, the man with the curly moustache and gentle smile. In the middle of the room stood a stocky, masterful and rather rudely aggressive man, milling-machine operator Stoyanov-Himself. Bear-like yet cunning, he squinted round at the bedroom and grunted, like an old man: "You just watch your step, you young whipper-snapper! Don't shout at her! Wait till I set about you!"

He began to roll up his sleeves. Tamara walked quickly out of the bedroom, in her overall, and glanced challengingly at Stoyanov.

"You think you're the only one who can do things? One of the working class! Fancy that! You can't wash up yourself! At home your wife does it for you, and you play the gentleman too."

"Not so much talking, bring the plates."

Vera Ignatyevna came to her senses and rushed to the table.

"What are you doing! Comrades!"

Stoyanov took her by the hand and sat her down in the armchair. Vera Ignatyevna felt particular respect for his bare hairy arms.

Tamara gathered up the plates, dishes, knives, forks and spoons quickly and neatly. Stoyanov stood watching her with serious eyes. She went out to the kitchen, and he followed her, swinging his hairy arms and looking as if he had come not to wash dishes but to move mountains.

Vera Ignatyevna was left sitting in the armchair. Her fingers felt the cool silk on the arm, but she could no longer think of clothes. Stoyanov filled her mind. She envied him. It was from there, from the milling-machine shop, that people got their iron grip and simple wisdom. There the work was real and the people were different. She seemed to have had a glimpse through a big curtain, and behind it she had seen the blazing field of real battle, compared with which her library work paled to insignificance.

Vera Ignatyevna rose and walked unhurriedly towards the kitchen. She stopped in the hall. Through the half-open door she could see only Stoyanov. He was sitting on a stool, his feet planted wide apart, his hairy arms resting on his knees, a sly grin playing on his face. He was watching. His moustache no longer curled over a gentle smile, it stuck out, and it looked far more like a sharp weapon than a moustache.

"Now then," he was saying, "now I see you working it's pleasant to look at you. Quite a different girl. But when you start chucking dresses about, what are you? A witch, a real witch. Think it's a beautiful sight?"

Tamara said nothing. The plates rattled in the basin.

"There you go, straining your heart out after beauty, and it's such an ugly spectacle I wouldn't waste my spit on it. What do you need all these different fashions for? A black dress, a brown dress, a yellow dress! Why, you're beautiful as it is, and somebody's in for trouble over you anyhow!"

"Perhaps it won't be trouble. Perhaps it'll mean happiness for someone!"

Tamara said this without anger, in a confiding jolly tone. Obviously Stoyanov's talk did not offend her.

"What happiness can you give a man?" said Stoyanov, shrugging his shoulders. "What happiness will he get if you are mean, bad-tempered and stupid!"

"Don't shout at me, I tell you!"

"What an ungrateful bitch you are! Think of your mother.... The whole factory honours your mother. She's got one of the hardest jobs I know.... For all that I'm a hard-working man myself.... Here, do you call this washed? Who's going to wash the other side? The man in the moon?"

"Oh," said Tamara.

"You can say 'oh' all right, but you don't see your mother. Thousands of books, and she's got to know them all, and tell everyone about them, and select something for everyone's taste and for special subjects too. Isn't that hard labour? And when she gets home she's a servant! And for whom? You. Why should she be, just you tell me why? So that you should grow up such a witch to sit on somebody else's neck? Why, you ought to worship the ground she walks on. You ought to give everything, do everything, go everywhere for her, you are young, darn your hide. Just you come to my place and see—my girls are no worse than you, lovely hair, and well educated too, one of them's going to be a historian, the other a doctor."

"All right, I'll come."

"Yes, you come round, it'll do you good. You've a good heart, only you've been spoilt. Do you think my two would let their mother look after them like a servant? Their mother's ... a queen! And you don't know how to wash up, you know. What's this ... swishing the rag about for half an hour, and the grease is still there."

"Where?"

"Look. You have to rub it."

Stoyanov got up from the stool and vanished out of sight. Then Tamara said quietly: "Thank you."

"That's right," responded Stoyanov, "you should say 'thank you.' Gratitude is a very necessary thing."

Vera Ignatyevna walked away on tiptoe into the living-room. She took Tamara's dresses off the chair and put them away in the wardrobe. Then she dusted the crumbs off the table and began to sweep the room.

It made her uncomfortable to think that in the other room a stranger was doing her job of bringing up her daughter. She wanted to know why Tamara listened to him so attentively, without answering back or taking offence, why the teaching proceeded so smoothly and well.

Tamara brought the dishes in out of the kitchen and began to put them away in the sideboard. Stoyanov stood in the doorway. When she closed the doors of the sideboard he stretched out his hand.

"I'll be seeing you, Comrade."

Tamara slapped his hand with her rosy fingers.

"Apologize at once! Apologize for everything you said, all those names you called me: good-for-nothing, witch, slut, hussy, and worse still. Do you think it's right to talk to a girl like that? Call yourself working class! Apologize at once!"

Andrei Klimovich showed his gentle smile.

"Beg pardon, Comrade. It's the last time. I won't do it again. You're right: people ought to be polite to each other in the working class."

Tamara smiled, suddenly flung her arms round Stoyanov's neck and gave him a kiss on the cheek. Then she ran to her mother, performed the same operation and slipped away into the bedroom.

Stoyanov stood in the doorway, stroking his moustache in a business-like manner.

"Nice girl, your daughter, very affectionate! Mustn't spoil her though."

After that evening Vera Ignatyevna began to spend her days in a new way. Tamara threw all her bubbling energy into the work of looking after the house. When Vera Ignatyevna came home she would find everything in apple-pie order. In the evening she would try to do things, but Tamara in her overall swept through the flat like a whirlwind, and it was hard to keep up with her. Rather rudely she would pluck various utensils out of her mother's hands, take her mother by the shoulders and politely push her into the living-room or bedroom. Pavlusha came in for a real reign of terror; at first he protested, then stopped protesting and sought refuge in the street with his comrades. A few days later Tamara announced that she was going to give the flat a complete spring-cleaning, and that Mother had better stay late at the library that evening, or she would be in the way. Vera Ignatyevna raised no objection, but on her way to work she became thoughtful.

She was pleased at the change in her daughter. She felt, perhaps for the first time in her life, the full benefit of having a rest, she had even filled out a little and was looking better; yet something still troubled her mind, and a feeling of alarm that had not been there before grew in her soul. Sometimes it seemed to her that it was wrong and even criminal to weigh down the girl with so much dirty and unrewarding domestic toil. Tamara's hands had spoiled in the past few days. Vera Ignatyevna noticed that Tamara had begun studying harder, too. The wonderful lions with flowery tails were finished, and had vanished from the desk; instead, half the dining-table was taken up by a huge sheet of paper on which Tamara was erecting whole forests of dotted lines, spirals and circles, and which was called a Corinthian Order. All this Vera Ignatyevna considered, and yet she still felt that this was not "it." Her thoughts tunnelled in another direction too. There was not a shadow of doubt that there could be no returning to the former way of life. The Tamara who with a naive greediness had used the life of her mother, who had thrown silk frocks in her mother's face, could not be restored. Vera Ignatyevna now understood well the full enormity of the thoughtless mistake she had been committing all her life. Andrei Klimovich's harsh words about her fostering a potential enemy of the country had struck Vera Ignatyevna as a serious and just accusation. And still, she had made practically no reply to that accusation. She still felt uncomfortable when she remembered how helplessly and passively she had allowed an outsider to deal with her daughter, while she herself had listened like a coward in the corridor, and then crept away from them on tiptoe. And who would bring up her daughter in the future, who would bring up Pavlusha, surely she would not have to appeal again for aid to Andrei Klimovich?

Vera Ignatyevna went over all this with great attention, finding much that was right and important, and yet she still felt that this was not the main thing, not "it." There was something else that she could not grasp at all, and it was this that roused her faint sense of alarm. That new human dignity she had discovered in herself at the last conference, that new Vera Ignatyevna who had come to life on the way back from the dress-maker's, were not yet satisfied.

Still worried by a feeling of alarm, still with a sense of dissatisfaction, Vera Ignatyevna arrived at the library.

The day's work began badly. Dark-eyed Marusya fluttered up and down the step-ladders from shelf to shelf, looking confused, returned to the growing queue of readers, and kept on peering vainly at one and the same index card.

Vera Ignatyevna went up to her.

"What's wrong?"

Marusya looked again at the card, and Vera Ignatyevna guessed what the matter was.

"The card's in place, but where's the book?"

Marusya glanced at Vera Ignatyevna in fright.

"Go and look for it, I'll deal with the queue."

With a guilty look Marusya wandered back to the
shelves. It had now become even more difficult for her to
imagine what strange place she had removed the book
to. She no longer fluttered up and down the step-ladders;
instead she roamed wistfully about the library, fearing to
meet Vera Ignatyevna's eye.

Vera Ignatyevna got through the queue quickly and
was just about to resume her own work when she heard
the alarming sounds of a break-down nearby. In front
of Varya Bunchuk stood a young man in spectacles, with
a high colour and lively manner, expressing loud surprise.

"I can't understand it. Please, once again, give me
some kind of book about Maupassant. Not some begin-
ner-writer, but Maupassant. And you say 'there isn't
one'!"

"There isn't one here. . . ."

Varya Bunchuk, a girl with freckles, stammered out
her "there isn't one" and glanced fearfully at Vera Ignatyevna.

"Varya," said Vera Ignatyevna affectionately, "you
manage here, and I'll see what our comrade wants."

Varya Bunchuk's freckles disappeared in a deep flush
of shame. In changing places she bumped clumsily into
Vera Ignatyevna; this sent the blood rushing into her
neck and ears, and she let out a suppressed: "Oh!" At the
end of the counter Marusya surreptitiously handed over
the refound book at last to the reader, and went back to
the other readers, but now she spoke to them only in
a whisper.

Vera Ignatyevna helped the lover of Maupassant and
went back to her room. Ten minutes later Marusya was

leaning over her desk and saying: "Oh dear, oh dear, Vera Ignatyevna!"

"You must not be so careless, Marusya. Do you realize you might have been looking for that book all day?"

"Vera Ignatyevna, don't be angry, it won't happen again."

Vera Ignatyevna smiled into a pair of eyes that were pleading for a smile, and Marusya ran off happily, ready and willing to achieve any feat of library work.

Half an hour afterwards Varya Bunchuk peeped in at the door and vanished. A few minutes later she peeped in again.

"May I?" she asked.

That meant she was to blame for something. At any other time she would have burst deafeningly into the room.

Vera Ignatyevna realized what Varya Bunchuk wanted.

"Varya, you must read the catalogues," she said severely. "And be able to use them. What a silly thing to say: 'there isn't one'!"

Varya Bunchuk nodded sadly through the half-open door.

"I give you ten days, until the twentieth. Then I shall test what you know about the catalogues."

"Vera Ignatyevna, he frightened me with his spectacles and his big fat face. And the way he kept talking...."

"Do you call that an explanation? Can you only deal with emaciated individuals?"

Varya hastened to promise gladly: "You'll see on the twentieth, Vera Ignatyevna!" She closed the door and her heels clattered merrily away.

Nice girls! At no time had Vera Ignatyevna had to give them a sterner reproof than today; she never had to raise her voice and never remembered their crimes for long. Yet they had the tenderest way of sensing her displeasure and disapproval. And then they would go sour instantly, bear their guilt quietly among the books, and look sadly on the world. They would be desperately in need of a few strict words from her, even if the words themselves had perhaps no practical significance. Without that Marusya could never forgive herself carelessness in arranging the books, and now Varya Bunchuk had already put aside the catalogues to study them that very evening. But one had to give them attention and show respect for their work.

Why was it all so easy and simple here, in the library, among strangers? Why was it so difficult at home, among your own people?

Vera Ignatyevna paused to consider the problem. Making an effort, she tried to analyze and compare her family and business life. In the library there was duty, the joy of labour, and love for her job. In the family there was the joy of labour, and love, and there was also duty. Duty! If the process ended with "fostering an enemy," obviously everything was not well with duty. Why, indeed, was duty so difficult in the family, while here, at work, the problem of duty was simple, so simple that it was almost impossible to distinguish where duty ended and delight in work, the joy of labour, began. Here duty and joy were blended in such gentle harmony.

Joy! What a strange, old-fashioned word. In Pushkin that word rings with such a simple charming beauty, and next to it you are bound to find "sweetness" and "youth." The word for happy poets, for lovers, the word for the family nest. Who before the Revolution would have thought of applying this word to business, to labour, to office work? But now it was to just this sphere that Vera Ignatyevna did apply it, without shame or hesitation, while in her family life it had so little scope.

Like a catalogue Vera Ignatyevna flicked over the pages of her life, and could not discover a single vivid instance of family joy. Yes, there had been, and there still was, love, there could be no doubt of that. This love, apparently, could even make you forget that you had a duty to perform and that there was such a thing as joy in the world.

Vera Ignatyevna rose from her desk and paced several times up and down the room. What rubbish was this: love—the cause of a joyless life! It could not be that!

Vera Ignatyevna halted at the closed door and put her hand to her forehead. How was it? How? Could anyone have loved her children more than she had loved hers. But even this great love of hers she had never expressed. She hesitated to fondle Pavlusha, or kiss Tamara. She could not imagine her love as anything but an unending and joyless martyrdom wrapped in silence and gloom. And in such love, it seemed, there was no joy. Perhaps only for her? No, quite obviously there was no joy for the children either. Yes, everything fitted: temper, greediness, egoism, and an empty heart. "Fostering an enemy"!

Was this all from love? From her great maternal love? From great maternal love.

From ... *blind* maternal love!

Suddenly Vera Ignatyevna saw light. She realized why there was so little joy in her personal life, why her duty as a citizen and a mother was in such danger. It turned out that her love for Marusya and Varya Bunchuk was wiser and more fruitful than her love for her daughter. Here, in the library, she could see through her love to the making of a person; with a word, or glance, or hint, or tone of voice, affectionate or severe, she could help him so quickly and so economically; at home she could only indulge in senseless and pernicious grovelling before a blind zoological instinct.

Vera Ignatyevna could not wait another minute. It was only two in the afternoon. She went out into the lending department and said to Marusya:

"I must go home. Can you manage without me?"

The girls chorused something excitedly.

She hurried home as if an accident had happened there. Only as she got off the tram did she suddenly notice her panic and remember that she must be as calm and confident as at the library.

Vera Ignatyevna smiled at her daughter and asked: "Is Pavlusha back yet?"

"Not yet," answered Tamara and assailed her mother: "What have you come for? I told you not to come at all!"

Vera Ignatyevna put her bag down on the window-sill in the hall and went into the living-room. Tamara stamped her foot and shouted: "What do you mean by it, Mother? I told you not to come! Go back to work!"

Vera Ignatyevna looked round. With a superhuman effort she willed herself to imagine Tamara with the face of Varya Bunchuk. For a second she seemed to succeed. Calmly taking a chair she said in a pleasant but formal tone:

"Take a seat."

"Mother!"

"Sit down!"

Vera Ignatyevna sat down in the armchair and nodded again towards the other chair.

Tamara mumbled something in protest, shrugged her shoulders discontentedly and sat down on the edge of the chair, thus emphasizing the fantastic inappropriateness of any kind of sitting down. But her glance also showed curiosity not unmixed with surprise. Vera Ignatyevna made a further effort to conjure up one of her young assistants on the chair. She wondered doubtfully whether she would be able to control her voice.

"Tamara, explain to me sensibly why I should leave the house."

"Why?! I'm going to do the spring-cleaning."

"Who decided that?"

Tamara halted in amazement at this question. She began to answer but only uttered the first word.

"I...."

Vera Ignatyevna smiled into her eyes, just as she smiled in the library, as an older friend smiles into the eyes of hot-headed, inexperienced youth.

And Tamara meekly answered the smile, answered it with a kind of loving, happy, apologetic embarrassment.

"How then, Mummy?"

"Let's talk it over. I feel you and I are beginning a new life together. Let's make it a sensible life. Do you understand?"

"I understand," whispered Tamara.

"If you understand, how can you order me about like that, and push me out of the house? What is it: a whim, a bad joke, or just obstinacy? I don't suppose you do really understand."

Tamara rose wearily from her chair, took two steps towards the window, and glanced round at her mother.

"Do you really think it was the spring-cleaning I wanted?"

"What did you want, then?"

"I don't know ... something ... good...."

"But you didn't mean to hurt me?"

And after that nothing could stop Tamara. She went up to her mother, clung to her shoulder and turned her face away in happy wonder.

The dress was ready on time. Vera Ignatyevna first put it on at home. Tamara helped her dress, kept stepping back and looking at it from the side, then finally got angry and threw herself on a chair.

"Mummy, you just can't wear those shoes with it!"

Suddenly she jumped up and shouted at the top of her voice: "Oh! What a goof I am!"

She darted to her attaché case, and standing over it kept singing with such inspiration that her feet began to dance: "What a goof! What a goof!"

Finally she pulled a packet of five-ruble notes out of the case and rushed back into the bedroom with them.

"My grant! Take it for your shoes!"

When Pavlusha saw his mother, his golden-blue eyes nearly popped out of his head.

"Phew! Mummy! That's a dress!" he gasped.

"Do you like it, Pavlusha?"

"Don't I just!"

"It was given to me as a prize for good work."

"Oh, you are. . . ."

Pavlusha stared at his mother nearly the whole evening with an almost scared expression, and when she caught his glance he would give a broad happy smile.

"Mummy, you know what?" he said at last, gulping excitedly. "You're so beautiful! So. . . . You should always be like that! So . . . beautiful."

The word came right from the depths of his being—not a word, but pure emotion.

Vera Ignatyevna looked at her son with a severe restrained smile.

"That's good. Perhaps now you won't stay out all the evening skating?"

"Of course, I won't."

The last act of the drama took place late in the evening. When he came home from work Ivan Petrovich saw at the table a beautiful young woman in a cherry-coloured silk frock. Before entering the room he even made a movement to straighten his tie, and only at that moment did he recognize his wife. He smiled condescendingly and went up to her, rubbing his hands.

"Oh! Quite a different thing!"

With a new easy gesture that she had never been aware of before, Vera Ignatyevna tossed back a tress of hair and said gently: "I'm glad you like it."

And that evening Ivan Petrovich did not nibble at the joints of his fingers and stare thoughtfully at the wall, and did not whistle the song of the duke. He joked and laughed, and even made eyes. And his enthusiasm only waned a little when Vera Ignatyevna said calmly:

"By the way, Ivan, I keep forgetting to ask you what salary you are earning these days."

Our mothers are citizens of a socialist country: their lives should be as full and as joyful as the lives of our fathers and children. We do not want people brought up on the silent sacrifices of their mothers, fed by their endless martyrdom.... Children brought up on the sacrifice of their mothers can live only in a society where there is exploitation.

And we should protest against the self-sacrifice of certain mothers that goes on here and there in our country. For lack of other petty tyrants and oppressors these mothers make them themselves out of ... their own children. This anachronistic practice is to a varying degree still with us, particularly in the families of the intelligentsia. *"Everything for the children"* is here given an utterly impermissible formalistic interpretation, and comes to mean everything *possible*, that is to say, both the value of a mother's life, and a mother's blindness. All that for the children! The life and work of our mothers should be guided not by blind love, but by the great forward urge of the Soviet citizen. And such mothers will give us fine, happy people, and themselves will be happy to the end.

Chapter Nine

*A*BOVE a broad shipping river stands a town. It backs on to the river with its busy commercial district of saw-mills, warehouses, endless rows of tar-barrels, and rumbling waggons that grind over the dusty broken paving. And beyond this busy world comes the town proper with its various cultural adornments: granite curb-posts, rows of acacias, the amiable rattle of red, yellow and brown droshky wheels.

The river sweeps past the town in a cheerful vigorous flood, always hurrying and looking ahead, because waiting for it just below the town stands a neat little railway bridge, severe and straight as a ruler. In the water the railway bridge has planted eleven feet clad in granite galoshes, and they stand with their toes always facing the oncoming river. And the river hurries towards them with the natural anxiety of ownership. Its gaze fixed on the bridge, it hastens along, pushing everything aside to the town-side bank: barges, rafts, tugs, boats.

Right by the railway bridge, on the other bank, a settlement has grown up. The settlement takes little interest in the river. It has left only one small house there and run off along the railway embankment to calmer and more peaceful country: to the cherry orchards and rows of poplars and windmills on the horizon. It is not far from the river to the horizon, and beyond the settlement the naked eye can easily perceive a goods-train topping the rise in billowing clouds of white smoke.

Scythians, Tatars and Zaporozhye Cossacks are said to have sailed this river. Perhaps they did. A few years ago some of Denikin's men made the trip in an old cutter armed with an absurd little gun. The town met them in grim silence, because somewhat earlier Cossack forces had been threatening to cut off the town on the north and the defenders had retreated along the railway to deal with them. The Whiteguards had the run of the town, the bridge and the settlement for six months, then abandoned the cutter and its little gun, bundled into a goods-train, and quickly took themselves off south. Two hours later a railway engine rushed over the bridge pushing a truck in front of it: on the truck were a three-inch gun and a couple of dozen cheerful fellows in grey great-coats. The engine steamed cautiously through the settlement station, then got up speed and raced after Denikin's men. The next day it returned with a whole train behind it, having peacefully made friends with the other engine. In the trucks sat the Whiteguards, but now they were rather gloomy and their cheeks were unshaven. At the station the father of Sergei and Timka Minayev jumped down from one of the trucks; he was a factory joiner, a machine-gunner and a Bolshevik.

That was five years ago, perhaps a little more. Vasili Ivanovich Minayev has already begun to forget how a rifle-sling cuts into your shoulder, but he still remembers very well how he and his comrades chased the White-guards all the way from Orel. He often tells his sons about it of an evening. His elder son Sergei listens to him seriously and attentively, the other one, Timka, cannot sit still through a story; he keeps fidgeting on his chair and wanting to ask: what does "beyond Kursk" mean? and what was Voroshilov's sword like? And at night after their father's tales the sons have different dreams. Sergei dreams of burning towns and lines of infantry, his father's battle-hardened comrades who never returned from the war, and the hated enemy scouring the settlement with search-parties. But Timka dreams of Budyonny with his big moustache, riding his horse and waving his sword, of huge cannon belching fire, and of impregnable fortresses with high battlemented walls, like the pictures in the old magazine *Niva*.

Sergei is in his second year at the factory training school, and Timka is in his second year at the labour school. Sergei remembers the time when his father went away with the Red Guards, but Timka got to know his father only after the Civil War. He does not even remember how his mother was called up before counter-intelligence to be questioned, how she did not come home for three nights, and arrived on the fourth day, looking worn and pale, gathered up her things in a bundle in half an hour, and carried off the bundle and Timka to Grandad Pyotr Polikarpovich on the farm. There is much more that Timka does not remember, and what the older folks tell him sounds like a story of a long, long time ago—interesting but not at all frightening.

The sun was shining over the river and the settlement.

The busy, bustling, talkative spring had come. Timka's blue eyes had not seen many springtimes and so they gazed at this one with greedy curiosity, and so much energy flooded into Timka's soul, his legs, his arms and his tongue that he hardly managed to spend it all during the day. And even late in the evening, when his body, tired after the day's exertions, began to go to sleep, his tongue still could not rest and would keep chattering away about something, and his legs would keep on hurrying somewhere in his sleep, and even his fingers would not keep still.

Today Timka had been at work since morning. Life had been very complicated and he had not had time to cope with all its demands, no time even to argue with everybody. When he got home near evening, Sergei was standing at the kitchen-door, talking to Mother.

"Was counter-intelligence really in the Goncharovs' house?"

And at once Timka was on the alert.

"Counter-intelligence?"

Sergei went into the living-room to do his homework, and Timka sat down opposite him.

"Everybody was scared of this counter-intelligence, weren't they?" he began. "They were, weren't they?"

"You must be a fool," said Sergei. "Do you think counter-intelligence is a joke? Do you think you'd find it funny?"

Timka thought only for a second, and answered in a burst of imagination: "Suppose you threw a bomb! You know, a bomb like Dad was talking about? Suppose you threw one! Eh!!"

Sergei grinned.

"What a hero you are indoors. But what if you really had to do it?"

"Well, what if I did?"

"You think it's so easy? Just a matter of swinging your arm?"

"Why not?"

"And they just sit and watch you, I suppose?"

"Let 'em!"

"But they shoot."

"I'd like to see them hit me."

Timka pouted scornfully, but in the back of his mind his imagination was creating unforeseen details: the fierce faces of the capitalists were staring at him and the capitalists were aiming at him with huge guns. Timka looked aside: he was not afraid, of course, but the idea

362

of being shot down by capitalists had certainly not come into his reckoning. The bomb exploit was definitely spoilt, and Timka's sharp eyes went in search of more wholesome experiences. Their gaze rested for a second on the portrait of Budyonny, but now Budyonny refused to mount his horse, and even looked at Timka a little mockingly. Timka glanced to the right. There was a gleam of glass on the sideboard, and through it Timka saw two pies on a plate. The pies lay in silence, but there was something ironic about their appearance, too. Timka transferred his glance to Sergei. Sergei was examining a diagram in a book with the high-sounding title: *Geometry*. Sergei's straight fair hair had grown very long; he combed it back, but it would not yet keep in place and stuck up over his forehead in numerous sharp points. Timka examined his brother's hair style and observed in that, too, the same lofty superiority as in geometry. Sergei was very clever. That was the only reason why today at dinner he had managed to have the last word over the question of the pies.

Timka remembered everything that had happened after that. It had begun with the pies and now here were those pies again.

To start with there had been a lot of pies. Mother had brought in a whole plateful of them and said:

"The pies have turned out well today. Eat up while they are hot."

Father put the newspaper aside and smiled.

"They look as if they're up to the mark! You've had a go at them already, of course, Timka?"

Timka coloured slightly and answered his father with a bright smile. When he had come home from school he actually had run into the kitchen and grabbed one pie off the baking-tray. Even though Mother had brushed him aside she had given him a kindly look.

"Can't you wait for dinner?"

But for all that the pie had not caused much joy in Timka's life: his mouth still felt burnt. The pie had been such a hot one you could not even hold it, and it had been a great deal too hot to eat. In fact, the position had been so hopeless that Timka simply swallowed the pie without any enjoyment at all, just to stop it from burning his fingers any more.

Father cut his first pie in two longwise, exposing a dark moist filling of meat in a white flaky frame of fresh pastry. Father smiled approvingly and began to butter each half. He did this without haste, and even went on talking.

"That's not our water coming down. Our snow was in the sea long ago. This lot comes from up north. Lot of snow there, they say, big wave coming down. Today the water level rose a whole metre."

Father talked, looked at Mother with his severe light-blue eyes, and pointed northwards with his knife, and the halves of pie still lay in front of him with the butter already beginning to go dry.

Timka could not understand his father's queer taste. Perhaps it was nice to eat a buttered pie like that, but what reason could he have for such unwise procrastination? Timka did not rush, of course, he took pies from the dish with awkward care, and Timka's mouth was rather small, too, but the pies were not very big either. They slid so quickly and willingly down your throat that almost as soon as you started one only the tiny hard tip was left in your hand; another second, and that had gone, too, and another pie had taken its place. Before Timka realized what was happening there were only two pies left on the dish, and suddenly he had a feeling that life was not altogether logical. He glanced at his brother: Sergei was chewing and listening to Father. Timka's hand was just approaching the dish again when Sergei grasped his elbow and whispered in his ear:

"Steady on. Leave some for Dad! Don't you think you've had enough?"

Timka had licked his lips and thought to himself that Sergei's interference was uncalled for: obviously Father did not want more anyway.

And after dinner there was a host of events. Father went off to work, and Timka busied himself in the yard and in the street right until dusk. In the yard it was wet. Near the shed a huge puddle had formed. It would have been good to wade in it, but shoes were a hindrance. But the boat Timka had made out of a newspaper would not sail anywhere and stood boringly in one place moored to a stray clump of last year's weed.

Outside the yard there were further troubles that arose from confusion over frontiers and spheres of influence. From the railway embankment just near Timka's yard flowed a mighty torrent. It had carved a deep and complicated channel for itself. A thin bare ledge of ice hung over the torrent making sharp jutted banks; in some places the water ran under this ledge into mysterious enticing shadow. If released from above with the current a paper boat would toss and plunge in the corkscrew waves of the torrent and shoot headlong under this ledge, vanishing out of sight. What happened to it in the mysterious dark cave under the ledge no one could see, but it was pleasant to stand over the flood and wait for the boat to leap out into open water again. And then you had to make your way along the bank to the next cave, and there the same pleasure awaited you.

This was very good fun, but all the most interesting reaches, backwaters, caves and waterfalls were to be found just outside Timka's yard, and here all the other boys in the street assembled. Each brought his own boat, each launched it where he wanted to, each poked his stick into the water, striving to manoeuvre his craft into the most interesting spot. For some time Timka gazed in indignation at this scramble.

"What have you come here for?" he shouted at last. "We don't come to you! Is it your river? You keep to your own part!"

But here, as in other spheres of international life, law and justice rarely triumphed. Freckled, pink-eared, ginger-haired Mitroshka, the son of tailor Grigoryev, stood on the opposite bank and from there poured bellicose scorn on Timka.

"Who do you think you are! Do you think you can show off just because your father's a Bolshevik? Have you bought the river?"

Timka did not answer, he raised his stick, designed for navigational purposes, and brought it down with a crack on Mitroshka's ship, which had run aground on a sand-bank. Dirty water splashed on all sides, and Mitroshka's ship, that was only made out of grey wrapping-paper, flattened out in the water like a wet rag. Having performed this act of international justice, Timka dashed away into the yard. A brickbat clattered on the boards of the gate behind him. Timka's ship was abandoned in midstream, but it had only been a makeshift job out of newspaper anyway.

For about twenty minutes Timka wandered about the yard alone, jumped up and down on a thin crust of ice under the wall of the shed until the ice broke into small pieces. Then Kirik, the owner's son, came out into the yard.

The Minayevs rented their flat from Kirik's father, Bychkov the carpenter. Bychkov was a strange man. He made his living out of building cottages, and his character was fierce and uneven. While he was hewing wood on the ground, you could still have dealings with him and discuss things humanly. He would listen to you in gloomy silence, hacking away with his axe, and only occasionally would he leer sarcastically, then say: "You think things will get better, do you? Well, let's hope they will."

But as soon as he got on the roof and he and his mate began fitting the rafters, or when he was sitting astride the ridge, battening down the roof boards, you could not expect to get a civil word out of him. Whether there was anybody below or not, Bychkov would keep on grumbling and finding fault:

"Nice rule that: eight-hour day! Sits and reads the newspaper, and just ask him who he thinks he is—oh, of course, he's a worker, a Bolshevik! Done his eight hours, and there's your Bolshevik! How many hours do I work?!"

Bychkov lowers his axe and scowls angrily at the ground.

"How many hours do I work, eh, Vasya? How many hours do I work?"

Bychkov turns to his assistant Vasya and watches him not so much with his eyes as with his shaggy eyebrows and shaggy unshaven chin. Vasya taps a rafter into place and does not even look at his master.

"How much do I work?" Bychkov repeats to himself, in deep thought. "Eight hours, eh? No ... Bychkov works twelve hours. Twelve hours! And who's Bychkov, is he a worker or not? That's a question. Perhaps he's a bourgeois? Bah, what a rotten lot of people! But this other fellow, he's a team-leader! Look at him!"

Bychkov goggles his eyes, puffs out his cheeks and makes himself a belly with his hands to show his importance. Then he spits on his fist, picks up his axe and goes on with his work. For about ten minutes he works intently without saying a word, but suddenly he again lowers his axe and again scowls at the ground with a cunning sullen face.

"Nice state of affairs! If a man works and lives by the sweat of his brow, that's not enough for them! Ho no, of course not: some's proletarians, and others, if you please, is handicraftsmen! So I'm a handicraftsman, am I? Think of that? That's what you've come to, Bychkov! That's what you've come to, you old fool! Vasya! What's a handicraftsman?"

Vasya still does not say anything. Bychkov examines Vasya for a few seconds, his moustache twitching. Then he answers himself.

"All right, I know what a handicraftsman is. Small stuff! Nick-nacks, eh! Make baskets, don't they? Whisk, whisk, push it in here, push it out there, make a handle, and there's your basket for you! Two days puffing and blowing, ten miles to market, and sell 'em at fifty kopeks a pair. But do you call this a basket? Is this a basket?"

He points at the trellis of rafters and shakes his head:

"Handicraftsman! May the crabs eat you when you drown! Who built Melnichenko's place? Bychkov. Seroshtan's? Bychkov. Reznikov's? Bychkov. Osip Pavlovich's? Bychkov. Nalivaichenko's, Vasili Yevdokimovich's.... And where is Vasili Yevdokimovich now? Vasya! Where's Vasili Yevdokimovich?"

For some reason Vasya answers this question.

"Chuck that, mate... Vasili Yevdokimovich! He was a real swine, the blood-sucker.... What a fellow to remember!"

Bychkov glares dully at Vasya and scratches his beard near his ear.

"I'm not talking about blood-suckers, I want to know who built his place! And they all try to get a sharper dig at you: handicraftsman!"

Bychkov did not keep company with Minayev, tried not to go into his flat, and sent his wife to settle business matters. But whenever he ran into Minayev he was polite and talked calmly, with a thorough show of loyalty.

"I'm not one of them stall-keepers, I'm a working-man myself."

Kirik Bychkov studied in the same class as Timka. And Bychkov's elder son Lyonya attended the same factory training school as Sergei, only he was a year ahead of the latter. At one time they had not wanted to accept Lyonya at the training school, but he had made such a fuss, shouting and complaining, and going into town about it several times, that he had got his own way in the end.

Timka liked his friend. Kirik was a sweet-tempered boy, had a nice face, and always looked happy and cheerful. And today, when he appeared in the yard, he good-naturedly listened to Timka's heated tale about the conflict on the "river" and said:

"We shouldn't let them come. You know what? Let's dig a canal across this evening and bring this... river ... in here."

"How can we?"

"Like this: we'll dig a canal and change the river's course. Under the gate, right down here. And this'll be a sea."

The boys went over to the sea near the shed. It was a very plausible idea. Timka peeped into the street a few times through a chink in the fence, then glanced behind the shed—it all looked very easy and convenient.

"What if they don't go away?" he asked.

Kirik shrugged his shoulders.

"Oh, they're bound to. They'll go home to bed."

After that the friends went out of the gate and stopped cautiously by the gate-post. About ten boys were engaged in navigation on the stream. Wet through and dirty, Mitroshka, who even had his face splashed with mud, was still messing about with Timka's paper boat. Even by the lowest standards this boat had long ago served its time; it was already quite soggy and showed hardly any signs of seaworthiness. But Mitroshka, puffing and panting, still piloted it on through the dangerous stormy flood. He was so occupied with this wretched task that he did not even notice Timka. The other boys were steering their ships with the same enthusiasm; some of them were of excellent construction. The best-made ship of all was that of Petya Gubenko, the son of the factory watchman. It was built out of a thick piece of bark. Petya's ship had seats, a mast and a sail. It only had one disadvantage: it was too long, and when it got stuck across the river it turned into a bridge. And because of its mast it could not negotiate the river caves.

Timka and Kirik went up to the river. Mitroshka with some foresight picked up his paper hulk and carried it downstream. Petya Gubenko ran up to the embankment and there launched his ship. The light brown craft flew along with the stream, its little rag sail fluttering bravely. It rode freely through the swirling currents, bouncing effortlessly off the banks and diving merrily over the waterfalls. Petya ran alongside, keenly observing the voyage. Right at Timka's feet the happy craft anchored on a stem of old grass and hove to with a jerk. Timka bent down over the stream and picked it up. He was expecting Petya to take offence and start shouting, and was quite ready to make a scornful face, but Petya watched calmly from the other bank and showed no signs of anxiety. In gratitude for this Timka said:

"What a light one!"

"It's made of bark," said Petya.

"Did you cut it out with a penknife?"

"Yes."

"Where did you get the knife from?"

"I've got my own penknife."

"Come on, show us."

Petya trustingly pulled his penknife out of his pocket and offered it to Timka. One of the blades was broken and the other had gone black and lost its edge. But all the same, what a lucky fellow he was to have a penknife!

"Who gave it to you?"

"A sailor."

Timka stared hard.

"What sailor?"

"Last summer: Father and I were out fishing, and there was a sailor there. He gave it me."

"Was he a real sailor? Where is he now?"

Petya found it hard to answer both these questions at once. He shook his head. Petya was wearing an old cap without a peak. His face was pale, thin and sharp-featured, but he had a very trim figure, and a similar trimness in his face: a fine open forehead and well-drawn black brows. Petya smiled.

"He works on the river, he's a sailor on the steamboats. But he's in the town now."

"What did he give you a penknife for?"

"Nothing, we were fishing together. I was digging worms for him and Dad, and he made me a net. Then he said: take this penknife for yourself, I've got another one."

Timka had heard wonderful stories like that before: suddenly a sailor turns up and gives you a penknife. Timka did not believe much in such stories. If you did believe in them, it meant it was easy as anything to get a penknife. And why should this Petya have had such luck all at once? A sailor and a knife!

"Your father's a watchman, isn't he?" said Timka, frowning.

Petya lowered his eyes seriously, then looked up.

"Yes, he is. He guards the factory."

"Well, my father's a team-leader."

Petya was silent.

"My father's a Communist."

Petya stretched out his arm.

"Hand over!"

24·   *371*

"No, wait a minute," said Timka, examining the pen-knife. "Your father isn't a Communist, is he?"

Petya surveyed Timka's face calmly.

"He's not a Communist, but that doesn't make any difference: my father guards the factory."

"Coo! Guards the factory!"

"He does. He guards it with a gun!"

Again Timka stared hard.

"Oh! With a gun! Have you seen it?"

"Yes, I have."

"A real gun?"

"Yes. It's a rifle."

"Why does he come home without a rifle, then?"

"It's not allowed. The rifle belongs to the factory."

"And does he shoot? Who does he shoot at?"

"Who at? At bandits."

"There aren't any bandits now. You make me a boat like this."

Petya gave Timka a quick trusting smile.

"Take that one. I'll make another for myself."

"You don't mean it?"

"Yes, I do. I don't grudge it, don't think that."

Timka felt he wanted to do something for Petya.

"You know what I'll give you? I'll give you a hook for a fishing-rod."

"I've got one already."

"Well, that'll make two. And we'll go fishing together, eh? If only we had a boat!"

"My father's got a boat."

"What? He's got a boat?" burst out Timka in complete amazement.

"Yes."

"A real boat? Where did he get it?"

"He made it himself."

Timka crossed the stream at a bound. There was no doubt about it, this Petya had a marvellous kingdom.

He had a long talk with Petya and grew more and more surprised. Petya's father, a bearded strict-looking man of military bearing, who passed their gate every day in a black great-coat, seemed to be a real magician. The only thing that worried Timka was the faint note of sadness that sounded now and then in Petya's voice. It roused Timka's liking and urged him to make friends with Petya. Timka himself did not attach any importance to his feelings and was sure that the main thing in this acquaintanceship was the real boat that belonged to Petya's father, a boat in which you could sail the river and catch fish.

Timka walked with his friend as far as the embankment, where Petya's father lived in an old cottage.

It was getting dark when Timka reached home. There was no one near the gate, only Kirik was messing about near the stream with a spade. He turned round at the sound of Timka's footsteps.

"Where did you get to? Pushing off like that!"

"What about it?"

"Are we going to change the course of the river?"

Timka remembered the new scheme and had an unpleasant feeling inside. But Kirik went on cheerfully: "It won't be hard at all. Look, you just have to dig here, and dig here. And then fill it in with earth here, and it'll flow straight into the yard. Then we'll have the whole river to ourselves."

Timka was carrying Petya's gift—the boat made of bark. He remembered the sad note in Petya's voice and did not feel like diverting the river from the street.

"The chaps will kick up a row," he said.

"Let 'em kick up all the row they like, what's that to us? We'll have a river and a sea. Why, we'll make a harbour as well! A harbour, understand! And a wharf. At night the ships will lie in harbour."

"Well, all right, as long as Petya Gubenko can play with us. All right?"

Kirik turned up his nose.

"Petya? What do we need him for?"

"He gave me a boat. Look."

For a long time Kirik turned the boat over in his hands.

"Did he make it himself?"

"Yes."

"Let him make me one as well."

Timka made no reply to this. Something twinged inside him. It would be fine fun to have one's own harbour, but he could not hurt Petya.

"When shall we start?"

"When it gets dark. All right?"

"All right."

Many events had happened between dinner and the time when the pies again entered Timka's life.

Timka strolled unhurriedly past the sideboard. He glanced at Sergei. Sergei was still deep in geometry. Timka lingered by the sideboard, then remembered that he must repair the boat made of bark—the sail needed tying on. He sat down beside Sergei and got busy on the overhaul. Mother came in with a lighted lamp. Timka finished his work, put the boat on the window-sill and spent a long time admiring it. The window-pane reflected the whole room and the sideboard. Timka stared with curiosity at the reflection: the sideboard was clearly seen, but the pies were a matter for guess-work. Timka glanced round quickly: no, the pies were still there.

Sergei shut his book and went into the kitchen. Timka remembered that he must go out to make the new river, and sighed. Then he went over to the sideboard, stood on tiptoe and opened one of the doors. His fingers touched the glistening surface of a pie. Timka stretched his fingers, grasped both the pies, clutched them to his chest and softly closed the sideboard. He tiptoed silently past the kitchen and on the first step of the staircase took his first bite of pie. It was a short staircase, not more than ten stairs altogether, but before Timka reached the bottom there were no pies left, only a few crumbs scattered over his chest. Timka made his last swallow hastily, for through the half-open front door he had caught sight of Kirik with a spade. Timka's throat was still contracted in the last efforts of swallowing, but his face already wore an expression of lively interest.

"I'll get a spade, too, eh?"

"You know what," said Timka when he had armed himself with a spade, "let's make a ditch first, then let the water through."

"How else could we do it," answered Kirik, "it'd run all over the yard otherwise."

Darkness fell, but even in the afternoon there had been a moon in the sky, and now it shone straight down into the yard. Timka worked hard and all the time kept thinking how to ask Petya Gubenko to make a boat for Kirik.

"Kirik, suppose Petya won't make a boat?"

"I don't care," said Kirik. "I'll make it myself. It isn't hard. I'll make a boat better than you've ever seen before."

"What'll you make it with?"

"Oh, my dad's got a whole box of tools, I can do it with a chisel, a rasp, a knife, anything you like."

"A rasp! How can you make a boat with a rasp?"

"I won't make it with a rasp. That's just for rounding it off, so that it'll look good."

Timka meditated on the rasp, but again he found himself thinking of the problem of Petya Gubenko. A real boat was linked with the happy days of summer and summer dreams. A boat meant fishing, and camping at night on the islands, and camp-fires, and fish-soup, and sailors who gave out penknives and could make nets. All these delights, except the sailor, of course, were known to Timka from last summer. But last summer his activities had been rather limited because Father had borrowed the boat from Elenich, the electrician, and on the fishing trips there had been Father, and Elenich, and Sergei, and Lyonya Bychkov, and Sergei's friend Abram Roitenberg. As many as that. And everyone had had plans of his own, while Timka had been left to do piffling little jobs like gathering twigs for the camp-fire and dangling a tiny little fishing-line without a float, which was no good for night fishing anyway.

The ditch had already traversed the yard and reached the gate. The boys went out into the street with their spades and set about the most important part of the job. The flood was now foaming along in solitude, and it even made them sorry to think of such a mass of water running away for nothing.

"Won't it be fine!" said Kirik. "Tomorrow they'll come running up here, and we'll have the whole river! And a harbour besides."

But at that moment the tall figure of Father emerged from a hazy patch of moonlight and stepped up to the gate. Minayev crossed the flood and stopped.

"Timka! And who's that? Kirik? What are you doing out here in the dark?"

"Oh, we're digging," answered Timka cheerfully.

He was glad of the chance to boast to his father of such an excellent undertaking.

"Digging? What for?"

"Just look: we've already finished in the yard. Now we'll dig away here, and it'll run right in. It's going to be a river."

"I see! Very good! People drain the water out of their yards, and we do just the opposite—drain it into the yard. What gave you that idea?"

"Because they all come up here," Timka burst out in offended tones. "All of them... with their boats."

"Who?"

"All of them! The whole street. They're sore because we've got a good flow here and a waterfall. So they all come poking their noses in."

"So that's it. But you're fine fellows, you are. So you're going to be the only ones who sail boats?"

Timka noticed something queer in his father's tone, but did not have time to work it out. Besides he was carried away by the very true thought that only he and Kirik would sail boats.

"Oh, yes!" he answered excitedly. "They'll come up here and find the river flowing into our yard."

"Fine! Who was so sharp as to think of that? You don't mean to say it was you?"

"Kirik and me."

Kirik stood holding his spade, listening in some embarrassment to the enthusiastic exclamations of Timka's father. He even ignored Timka's rather impudent violation of his right of authorship, for indeed he alone was the sole inventor of the scheme.

Minayev planted himself astride the flood and looked down at the boys. He seemed to be full of admiration.

"Yes. It's a pity we can't transfer the whole street into your yard."

Timka noted this obviously hyperbolic regret with alarm, and said nothing. Kirik, however, laughed loudly.

"What's the use of the street to us?"

"You'd be able to walk along the street, and others wouldn't. That'd be good, wouldn't it?"

Timka realized that it would be better to take no further part in the debate. But the debate went on in such a vein that there was no need for Timka to take further part in it.

"You young rotters! So that's your idea! Come along home!"

Timka walked in front of his father. He did not notice how he stepped across the new ditch, he did not notice how he reached the room, or how he took off his coat.

Sergei was still sitting over his book, but Timka had no time now for high science. He sat down on a stool, fixed his glance in a corner, and got ready for trouble.

Father came in out of the kitchen with a towel in his hands and said loudly:

"I've got a fine son! He's only fit to live under the bourgeoisie. Even a puddle in the street makes him envious because it's in the street and not in his pocket. Eh? Everybody can look at the puddle and walk past it! That's no good! That will never do! Only Timka can do things like that, others mustn't. That's where greed takes these rotters!"

Timka stared blankly into the corner, and his heart sank under the weight of accusation. His father stood in the middle of the room, straight and firm as a tower, and kept wiping his hands on the towel and speaking in a thunderous bass; his light-blue eyes only glanced occasionally at Timka, most of the time they looked at the towel. His chin and the big folds of his shaven cheeks looked in the same direction. And Timka was struck not so much by the words as by the strength expressed in his voice and stance. Confronted with this overpowering strength Timka felt himself a mere nothing. And that was all he could feel. He could not even think, but there was still room for temper, and Timka got angry with Sergei and his mother. Sergei was looking at Timka with a grin on his face and once or twice had laughed loudly, and Mother was standing beside Father pretending to smile sadly. They were simply glad to see Timka in such a difficult position, to see him turned into such a wretched nobody. Timka even managed to get in a murderous glance at Sergei.

Father went out into the kitchen, and Sergei burst out laughing.

"Did you really want to pinch a puddle all for yourself, Timka?"

Timka jerked his shoulder furiously in protest against Sergei's interference and gave him another glance of menacing scorn, but still did not change his posture and went on staring into the corner. He could not bear humiliating situations and at such times always tried to make up for his loss with the help of fixed gloom. He was even beginning to get a little pleasure out of maintaining his attitude, but suddenly he had to endure a fresh trial, far heavier than the first. Timka had not noticed his mother abandon the pose of a grieved spectator, but suddenly his ears were assailed with terrible words, a blow of incomparable strength.

"Why, he's not only envious about the puddle. He's been after the pies that we left for Father. But perhaps it wasn't him?"

Panic took possession of Timka's brain. He looked round open-mouthed at his mother: she was standing looking at the plate where the pies had once been. An unknown force picked up Timka and hurled him into the next room, wrapped him in a black impenetrable fog and threw him down on the bed. Timka's feet in their wet boots hung down from the bed, and the rest of his body shook with grief. Sergei's explosive laughter reached him through the fog and confusion, but Timka already felt that everything was finished, everything was destroyed, and nothing could be added to his despair.

In half a minute Mother was sitting beside him on the bed, and this made the sobs rush on further until they even reached his feet, which began to kick on the edge of the bed.

Mother laid her hand on Timka's shoulder and said: "There now, dear, don't cry your heart out. It's not worth it over a few pies."

After these words the sobbing seemed to tear through a narrow ravine and flow on further in a broad river. The sobs flowed on thus under his mother's affectionate hand until Father said from the next room:

"Eaten the pies? What pies? The ones that were left for me?"

At this Timka stopped sobbing, not at all because his grief was any the less, but because his father was speaking quietly and as he also happened to be in the other room his words were very difficult to hear. Sergei answered quietly and Father went on:

"Oh, yes, that's right, I only ate one pie at dinner. But did Timka eat them? Perhaps it wasn't him? And he didn't leave any? Impossible! He wouldn't do that! He's always said he's very fond of me. There's a misunderstanding somewhere. I'll never believe it. The mice must have eaten them. They were lying here, were they? Yes, of course it was the mice."

Timka realized that no one was angry with him, but also realized that the talk about the mice was designed to irritate him. And yet two mice did appear in his imagination. They crawled impudently on to the plate, their tails twitching. Then each mouse ate half a pie. This scene only lasted for a second. It was immediately followed by another: Timka was guzzling the pies on the staircase, and with no pleasure at all. Timka let forth another grievous sob. He knew it was too early yet to leave the bed, the situation was still badly spoilt. Mother stroked the back of his head.

"That wasn't a good thing to do, Timka. You can have as many pies as you like, I don't grudge you the pies, but you mustn't just grab them like that, you ought to think of Father. Oughtn't you, dear?"

Timka was silent. Several ideas rushed into his eight-year-old mind, all of them rather like excuses. First, he had thought Father did not want any more pies; second, there had only been two pies, third, perhaps Sergei had eaten more pies than Timka at dinner. Mother went on:

"And fancy doing it without asking. So that nobody should see. That was wrong of you, dear."

Timka could not see his mother's face, but knew very well what it was like at this moment: it was round and tender, her grey eyes were puckered, there was a smile on her full lips, and on the upper one grew a little mole and two hairs.

Timka floated in pleasant thoughtless peace, so pleasant that he suddenly wanted to agree with all his mother said. And just at that moment Mother pulled his head round towards her and looked into his face. She really was smiling, and there was a warm, embracing strength in her smile, that did not humiliate Timka and did not turn him into a nobody.

Timka looked up at his mother with sparkling eyes, well washed by the storm of tears.

"Well, what have you got to say?"

"I won't do it again, Mummy, honest I won't."

"That's a good boy. Get up now, we'll have supper."

She tweaked his ear gently and went away. But it was still impossible to get up: Father's boots could be heard in the other room. If Timka got up Father would be sure to start again about the mice. So Timka lay on his side and stared at the cupboard. But the sound of Father's boots came nearer, and he appeared at the door. Somehow fathers are made so that as soon as you see them everything comes to a standstill inside you and waits for something to happen. Father came nearer the bed, drew up a chair, placed it in front of Timka's nose and sat down. It would have been good to close one's eyes, but Timka's eyes would not close. Father smiled, there was something special about the way he smiled: merry and at the same time fierce. And his hard clean-shaven pink cheeks creased into fierce folds. Father brought his strong wise face closer to Timka.

"Don't you listen to your mother, Timka. If a puddle or a pie turns up again, don't you bother about her, you just grab it quick, or somebody else will, and you'll be left without, won't you?"

Timka understood his father's cunning move, and because he understood, his father became simpler and more accessible. Timka's soul stirred, the cog-wheels clicked round merrily and everything started again, like a watch as soon as a good watchmaker takes hold of it. An honest smile appeared in Timka's blue, still moist eyes, and he answered his father in a whisper.

"No, that's not right...."

"Ah, you're a good lad. I thought you didn't understand anything! Well, what now? Shall we go and have supper?"

Timka spoke more freely, although his voice was still rather croaky because of some pebbles left there by the tears:

"You don't mind then? About the pies?"

"I did at first, but I've stopped minding now."

"Mummy will make some more."

"Yes, I thought of that too."

"And don't be angry."

"Let's leave it at that," said Father.

"Yes, let's," laughed Timka, hopping off the bed and rushing to his father's knee. Father patted him on his tender parts and said:

"They used to use the strap on these parts in such cases. But I think that's unnecessary."

Timka looked up at his father's chin and answered as his father often did.

"Absolutely unnecessary!"

"Come on, let's have supper."

In the living-room Sergei was no longer sitting over his book. He greeted Timka with a meaningful ironic glance. But Timka was so pleased with life that he did not even protest. And as soon as they sat down to table Father said something that abruptly changed the world and showed Timka its lively interesting side:

"Timka and Kirik wanted to bring a little puddle into the yard, but the way things are going now it looks as if we may have the whole river paying us a visit."

"Is that so?"

"The news is very bad. Yesterday the water level rose a whole metre, and today it was up by one point two. Looks like being a real flood."

"What shall we do?" asked Mother.

"They're already doing it. Tonight they start strengthening the dike."

In running away from the river the settlement had not escaped its pranks. Even when the water was at its highest the first little cottage standing right on the bank by the bridge was never flooded, for here the bank was formed by a narrow spur that ran down from the hills on the horizon. A long time ago the settlement had begun to grow up along this spur. But in the course of three centuries, the cottages had spread down the slopes of the spur to the broad marshlands upstream. And it was from here that each spring the flood waters reached the settlement. On the edge of these marshlands, known as Scabland, there were cottages that floated every year, even when the water was at its lowest. They were built with an eye to this troublesome circumstance; all of them stood on long thin legs, and the inmates entered by tall steep ladders.

The railway embankment running from the bridge divided the settlement into two parts: "Little Eden" and "Overbank." Between Scabland and the embankment were scattered many cottages that belonged to the tradespeople of the settlement—carters, ox-drivers, stall-keepers, tailors, market-gardeners. The cottages belonging to them were built on lines that had satisfied life in the time of Tsar Alexei Mikhailovich. Their walls were made of clay and dung on a light wooden framework, fitted with shutters and banked round with earth, but, in keeping with the times, roofed with iron instead of straw. Instead of the traditional clay floors they had proper wooden painted floors. But according to the old tradition the cottages were surrounded by cherry orchards, sunflowers and maize; the fences were fairly high, with sturdy iron-roofed gates opening into the street. On the whole this was a flourishing region, and it was called, rather ambitiously, "Little Eden." In late years the houses here had been built larger, to provide two or three flats, and many of the owners let rooms to the workers and office staff of the nearby agricultural-machinery plant.

The main body of the factory community was concentrated on the other side of the railway embankment. Here there were many two- and three-storied blocks of flats, cobbled roads and even pavements, and a theatre, as well. But here, too, amid the big buildings were scattered some "Little Eden" cottages belonging to the old inhabitants of the settlement.

The high railway embankment dividing the settlement in half also divided its springtime fate: "Overbank" never suffered from flooding. Only in two places, where streets cut through the embankment under little iron bridges, could the water penetrate to the factory, but here it was not difficult to bar its path.

"Little Eden" did not share these advantages. At times of high flood it would turn into a little Venice, and, following that city's example, many of the cottages had been built on piles. True, about twenty years ago, in the time of Mayor Kandyba, whose own house was in "Little Eden," an earthen dike had been built. It stretched magnanimously between "Little Eden" and Scabland, without depriving the Scablanders of their usual spring baths. But since Kandyba this dike had never been repaired; it did only what it could, and that was not very much. . .

The next day was Sunday As soon as Timka had had breakfast he set off for the dike. Everyone was hurrying in that direction, and navigation on the street torrent had been abandoned; the very best ships were lying about unattended. While Timka was on his way to the dike he was joined by a whole company: Mitroshka Grigoryev, and Kirik, and Petya Gubenko, and many others. Today Petya was merry.

"Are you going there?" he asked, coming up to Timka
"Yes."

"So am I."

"What's changed you today?"

"Changed me?"

"Yesterday you were different: thinking all the time."

"Oh, that was nothing," said Petya. "I had had a fight with my sister." Petya smiled awkwardly. "With Natasha. Over an exercise book."

"What Natasha?"

"My sister Natasha. She's in the ninth class."

"A-ah! I know. Natasha Gubenko."

Timka knew Natasha Gubenko well. She was chairman of the school committee and often came into their class to scold the boys for making a mess or stamping chalk on the floor.

Taking advantage of its being Sunday, many people had gathered on the dike. A pleasant April sun looked down from the sky. The dike was firm and solid; it was not yet free of frost. Ahead, in front of the dike, Scabland was afloat; its inhabitants were scurrying about between the houses in their canoes or climbing up and down the high steep steps; the water had risen almost to floor level.

It had not yet reached the dike and lay motionless, calm and dirty, bearing on its surface all the rubbish that had collected in the streets of Scabland in the course of the year: dung, straw, rags and litter. Piles of boards and logs were already strewn over the dry ground in front of the dike; long carts were turning round awkwardly; carpenters were busy. The dike was about a kilometre long, and everywhere the work was afoot; carpenters with hammers and spades were reinforcing the posts and nailing rough, knotty planks to them; on the other side of the dike heavy carts were churning over the soft ground and tipping loads of fresh earth on the embankment.

On the dike itself roamed the settlement folk and the factory workers. Bychkov, wearing a new jacket, was standing talking to Grigoryev the tailor, a feeble little man who instead of a moustache had near the corners of his lips about three hairs that had sprouted in his youth and never grown any more since.

"Look how many people they've brought here! And all for nothing," Bychkov snorted confidently. "Who said there'd be a flood? Who said so? Floods happen every ten years. There was one in seventeen, so there won't be another until twenty seven. This is just to show you how much care they lavishes on us. Look at 'em, with their boards and carts. And there goes the boss marching around. Don't he look just like a boss! But as a matter of fact, he happens to be just Spirka Samokhin. Yesterday he was a stoker, but today he's a Bolshevik. Oh, he understands everything, he does: where the flood's going to be and what kind of dike we need. Marching around with his note-book."

Timka and Petya explored the whole dike; twice they

went right down to the water, threw in a stick and watched to see where it would float. For a long time the stick did not move, then it began to float almost imperceptibly along the bank.

"Where's your boat?" asked Timka.

"Over there, on the river. My uncle works there on the bridge."

This Petya seemed to have all the good things in life. Yesterday it was a sailor, today he had an uncle actually working on the bridge.

"What's his job?"

"He's called chief of the bridge."

Petya said this without boasting, but all the same a sharp pang of jealousy pierced Timka's heart.

"You'll be telling me he's a Bolshevik next?"

"Yes, he is. He's a Party man, a Communist "

"You're lying!"

Petya grinned.

"Why should I?"

"Do you think everyone you see around is a Communist?"

"You nut, he is a Communist, I tell you "

"Why don't you bring the boat over here?"

"Where? To the dike?"

"Just here. Tie it up here. That'd be fine!"

"You couldn't tie it up here. In another three or four days' time the water will be over the dike."

"What, right into 'Little Eden'?"

"Right into these houses."

"Gosh, that would be fine! How do you know?"

"Father said so."

"How does he know?"

"He knows everything. He says it'll be a disaster if they can't stop the water. He says it'll swamp everything."

Petya pointed towards "Little Eden" and glanced at Timka with serious dark eyes

Timka looked in the direction of his arm, and in his imagination he saw cottages, orchards and fences all floating in the water. His eyes glowed with delight.

"Won't it be lovely! Then we'll be able to go there on the boat, won't we?"

Petya frowned.

"Yes, we'll be able to do that. Only I'll be sorry."

"Why should you be sorry?"

"What about the people?"

Timka laughed.

"Oh! The people! Look over there, everything's flooded, but all the people are safe. And they're going on boats Why be sorry? You'll be able to go everywhere by boat! Why, you'll even be able to go under the bridge right to the factory!"

"To the factory? They won't allow that."

"I'll ask. I'll say: just for a minute, just to have a look, and straight back."

"They won't let the water in. Who'd let that happen? And have the factory stop?"

Timka thought hastily.

The factory could not stop—Timka knew that well enough, because to him the factory was the biggest and most significant thing in existence. Every day Father came home from the factory, bringing with him a somehow special, complicated and joyful smell of a real grand life. Timka did not think long.

"Why should it stop?" he conceded. "It's only a matter of blocking up the bridges."

That Sunday, life went on normally, and even gaily The dike was a lively place, girls and young men came out for walks. The creak of the carts was pleasant and peaceful. Spiridon Samokhin paced up and down the dike, glanced at Scabland and efficiently noted down in his book how many boards and cart-loads of earth were brought up. Business-like people came up and talked to him in the same calm manner, unhurriedly turning to look at Scabland or at "Little Eden." Even the Scablanders, who usually had plenty to say for themselves, rowed up to the bank in their canoes and voiced desires that had nothing to do with the threat of flooding.

"Hey there, canary, let's give you a ride in the boat! Oh, it's Katya! Katya, why tire your feet out up there on the dike? Come and have a sit down."

"You'll capsize."

"Now what's the point in my capsizing. Why, I'm an old sailor."

And some of the girls, coquettishly pulling up their skirts, would go down the slope and, with all the care and excitement due to the occasion, set foot in the fragile craft, then waken the marshlands with a shriek, collapsing gracefully into the arms of the gallant boatman. Other boys and girls watching them from the dike would shout:

"Don't believe him, Katya, he's a fox, his boat's got holes in it!"

"You'll spend the night on the roof!"

In engineer Veryovkin's proper big boat there was a company of young people; they were pulling with two pairs of oars, playing an accordion and singing:

Down where the River Volga flows....

And when evening came, bonfires were lighted on the dike, a new batch of workers went on tapping away peacefully with their axes, the carts creaked, and various people gathered round the bonfires, talking quietly and recalling past floods. Occasionally their stories were interrupted by laughter, and not a single tragic incident was related.

As the evening drew on the boys' excitements and worries increased. That day they had had enough running about, sight-seeing, talking and quarrelling to last them a year. And many of them were hungry, too. When it grew dark the mothers came out in search of their over-impressionable sons. Some led them home with quiet tender words to have dinner or supper, here and there a mother had to push her vagabond son home and in doing so would make good use of the conveniently soft slope of the dike. And there were some who searched in vain, and went about asking everybody they met: "You haven't seen Kolya, have you? Well, did you ever! What a terrible boy he is!"

And meanwhile Kolya had got on friendly terms with the driver of a cart and was sitting on the narrow seat, clicking his tongue at the horse and shaking the rope reins.

It was hard to go home, incidents crowded so fast on top of one another you had no time to look at one before the next was upon you. No sooner had a tipsy young man turned over in his canoe, no sooner had he managed to squeeze the dirty water out of his clothes, than there was a shout on the right, and you'd have to rush over there, all eyes to see what had happened. And there they had brought up some sacks, and somewhere else they were unharnessing a horse, and over on the left a lorry had arrived, and over on the right somebody had started playing an accordion, and in the middle there was a smart car with glaring head-lights—the Chairman of the Executive Committee had arrived. And again and again tired legs would go into action, and eager eyes would peer ahead, and again you would pant along, covering enormous distances. And when evening came, besides all these fleeting incidents you had the results of the day to think about. The chief thing was that the water had reached the dike itself. Dirty young Mitroshka was already splashing in the water and shouting to those above: "It's already covered two boards! Two boards are covered!"

The other boys hung over the top of the dike and groaned with envy at Mitroshka, on whom fate had bestowed such rare good fortune—accommodating parents who let him go about all day without any shoes on.

But next morning the scene had changed: Mitroshka could no longer paddle below the dike. In Scabland the water was creeping over the floors, and instead of cruising about in their canoes the Scablanders were carrying their belongings up into the attics. Again the Chairman of the Executive Committee came out and shook his head. He had a lot to worry about: there was a dike ten kilometres long round the town itself.

Another day passed, and another. The water was rising visibly a metre and a half a day. The windows of the Scablanders' cottages were covered. The surface of the water was no longer littered like a dirty puddle; the refuse had all disappeared somewhere. You could see the current now, and here and there little whirlpools had formed, and a faint breeze was already stirring the usual speckled waves. The water was lapping quietly round the dike itself, which had been boarded up right to the top of the posts and filled in with earth. The dike still rose several metres above the level of the water, but the sceptics looked doubtfully at the thin wall: to withstand the pressure of the river it needed to be at least twice as thick. On April 24 the level of the water reached the 1917 level. That evening the factory stopped work and announced that all workers would be mobilized to fight the flood. The schools were closed. Goods-vans were provided at the station for people whose homes were flooded.

On the 25th the Minayevs rose at the crack of dawn. The night before Father had said: "We've been allotted a van, but we'll wait a bit before we go over there. Sergei, get together all our spades and shovels." And turning to Timka: "Don't you come getting in the way, you stay at home, there's no need for you to be on the dike."

But Timka's eyes answered his father with such suffering that his father laughed and waved his hand:

"All right, but you needn't be a spectator; bring a bucket, and you can fill up some sacks."

Timka felt a little offended with his father for the "spectator." Anyone might think he had not helped to make stretchers yesterday.

The dike was divided into three sectors. The left was entrusted to the factory, the centre to the "locals," and the right sector, the most dangerous one, that bordered on the river itself, to a regiment of the Red Army. The Red Army men had been on the job since yesterday. Timka and the boys had run over there but had been unable to get on the dike; it was surrounded by sentries with rifles, who would not even talk to the visitors. The boys sat on a fence for a long time watching the work of the Red Army men from afar. It looked very grim and important. Timka felt this in the belted figures of the commanders, and the quick purposeful movements of the soldiers, in the anxious coming and going of the lorries, and in the two flags mounted on the dike: one blue, the other green. And Father had said last night: "It may be hard on the right, but they'll hold out. Think of it: a regiment of the Red Army! What chance will the river have against them!"

These words even made Timka's mouth open, they were so fine and strong. Now that there was a regiment of the Red Army against it, the river seemed quite different to Timka. He no longer wanted to row about in a boat, he felt he must face the river calmly and sternly as the Red Army men were doing. Timka now saw the river in all its harmful might; he saw the terrible strength and pressure of its movements, the broad sweep of the banks veiled in the mist on the horizon. And he, too, wanted to fight it, and for this reason he began to hate Bychkov.

Yesterday, when Father, Sergei and he had been making stretchers in the shed, Bychkov had come up and stood for a long while watching them work, and then, as was his habit, he bent his shaggy head, fixing his eyes on the ground, and said:

"Why waste your strength, Vasili Ivanovich! They've made you chief of the river, I hear. What do you want with stretchers?"

"I'm not chief of the river, I'm the assistant chief of a sector. And stretchers are needed anyhow."

"Huh! Think you'll stop the river with stretchers! What can you put on a stretcher?"

"A sack of earth," replied Minayev.

"It's too late for that now. The dike ought to have been repaired in the winter. Now, of course, it's grab anything you can lay hands on. And they haven't forced enough of them soldiers here. What's a regiment of Red Army men!"

Minayev was about to reply, but at that moment Lyonya Bychkov appeared in the doorway of the shed. His broad high-cheeked face wore a look of disapproval.

"You may be my father, but you're talking rubbish."

"Oho! Here's a fresh prophet among us! Where did you come from in the name of the Lord!"

"I've been listening to you all the time. 'Forced here'! Saying things like that at your age! They've come here to help you, and you say they're forced to come!"

"To help me be blowed! They forced 'em here, that's why they've come. They were ordered to come, so they came. What's the point in arguing? Everyone knows what a soldier is! And don't you be so free with your remarks to your father, you young booby!"

Bychkov lowered dully at his son. Lyonya stood in the doorway without saying anything, then slammed the door and left the yard. Bychkov put his head out of the shed and stood for a long time looking at the gate through which Lyonya had vanished. Only his ear, as hairy as all the rest of him, paid any attention to the Minayevs. Frowning at Bychkov's ear, Minayev said, as if speaking to his sons:

"Goes about talking. Wasting his time and his breath. What are stretchers for?!"

Bychkov suddenly turned round and jutted his beard. "Do you grudge me my breath, then?"

"Yes, I do."

"It's my own breath, isn't it?"

"Of course, it is."

The boys burst out laughing.

Bychkov looked round the shed and was about to leave without saying anything, but turned back.

"You don't mind wasting my life, do you," he said.

Minayev bit his lip and struck a deafening blow with his hammer on a long nail. With two blows he drove the nail into the wood, then gave the head an even more resounding stroke that echoed right round the yard. And with that he said to Bychkov:

"Go and blather in church!"

Bychkov departed

Timka remembered all this on the road to the dike. This talk, that was so bewildering, and new, and fierce, stirred him strangely. His mind searched hither and thither, and everywhere it encountered a feeling of alarm among men, and there was much that he did not understand.

The bucket clanked faintly as he walked along, similar sounds echoed down the street. The stretchers that people were carrying on their shoulders gleamed white in the dark dawn mist. Beyond the street, over the roofs of the houses and the birch-broom tops of the still bare trees a faint pink glow began to colour the sky. Where the dawn was rising and on the other side, where the river and the dike lay, lingered a strange repelling stillness, but people hurried on towards it. The heads of the people in front and the shovels poised above them melted fast into the remaining darkness. Somewhere very far away dogs were barking and each one could be heard distinctly; they lent a touch of foreboding to the approaching day. Timka ran up to his father and pulled his sleeve.

"Never mind, Timofei, keep your spirits up!" said his father quietly, striding on.

On the factory sector of the dike the shifts were changed at six in the morning and six in the evening. On the 26th, as soon as the sun began to sink, Minayev said to Timka: "Has your relief arrived?"

"Yes, but I'll stay on a bit longer."

"Come with me. We'll have a look over the sector."

Timka handed his bucket to Volodya Soroka and ran off after his father. They walked along the dike. The day had been a successful one. There had been an off-shore breeze, the weather had been warm, the work had gone cheerfully and well. Minayev kept looking at Scabland, of which only the roofs were visible above the water. That morning life-boats had been taking people out of the attics and transporting them to the goods-vans. The Minayevs had also moved the day before. The roofs of Scabland seemed black in the sunset.

The river was level with the dike, like a glass filled to the brim. Below and on the slope of the dike people were scurrying to and fro, while on the beaten trampled ridge above only occasional figures were to be seen.

Timka ran to keep up with his father. He looked at the river in indignant alarm. The water stretched beyond the roofs of Scabland to the sunset in a boundless sea. Now it was hushed and silent, but of course it was only waiting for the chance to pounce down on the settlement whose roofs now showed far below.

At the foot of the dike an argument was in progress. Lyonya Bychkov was shouting.

"To start with, I'm not a local, I'm a factory school trainee, that means I'm a worker."

He was answered by a calm, slightly scornful, nasal-sounding voice.

"But you talk like a local."

"Local, local! The locals are on the dike day and night anyhow!"

"That's because they've got no organization."

"Well, why keep on about my being one of them...."

"Because you talk like one. Go home, I tell you. Your shift's over."

"I won't. I've got the right to stay if I want to, haven't I?"

Minayev ran down off the dike. Timka remained aloft and listened, taken aback at the complexity and seriousness of the situation.

"What's the matter here?" asked Minayev.

In front of the angry Lyonya stood a young turner Golubev, the foreman for that strip. No one answered Minayev's question. Apparently Golubev, too, had his doubts. Minayev glanced round him: among the stretchers, shovels and sacks other men were standing, listening curiously to the argument.

"What are you arguing for? Stopping work...."

"Of course I'm arguing," said Lyonya, almost in tears. "He keeps trying to send me home. He won't leave off."

"That's the order, Lyonya."

Lyonya turned his face away.

"Order! Orders are just for organization. What if I want to do some more work?"

"His cottage is in 'Little Eden,' that's what he's worried about," said a quiet sly voice somewhere aside. Lyonya swung round angrily, bristling all over.

"The blooming cottage can fall down for all I care! Go and live in it yourself, you fool!"

"Yes, that's a foolish thing to say," put in another, deeper voice, also rather sly. "Lyonya isn't working for his cottage."

"Calm down, Lyonya, and go along home," said Minayev evenly.

Lyonya swung his shovel and drove it furiously into the ground.

"I won't go! You've no right to stop me if I want to work!"

"And you've no discipline. For talk like that I could send you away from the dike altogether, if you weren't young...."

"But why?"

"We can't allow it. We don't need your heroism at the moment. There are plenty of heroes like you here. But you seem to want to show off, as if you were better than anyone else."

"Heroism's always necessary...."

"No, not always. All of you here are heroes, you're all ready to go on working without rest, but suppose it's really necessary tomorrow, or the day after, and you're not here, you've collapsed and are no good for anything. What'll happen then?"

"I won't collapse," Lyonya clung obstinately to his shovel.

"Go straight home this minute, do you hear!" Minayev shouted suddenly at him. Timka on top of the dike had a fright, his feet twitched and shuffled. Lyonya jumped aside and threw down the shovel. Then he walked off glumly towards the settlement, but stopped and mumbled:

"Why couldn't you have said that from the start instead of all this stuff about belonging to the settlement!"

Everyone laughed. Minayev climbed up the steep slope and shook his fist smilingly at Lyonya. Lyonya put his hand to the back of his head, then with a wave of his arm wandered off home. Gubenko came up to Minayev, wearing his black belted great-coat. His black beard was ruffled, and expressed anxiety.

"Vasili Ivanovich, I refuse to have any more to do with them. I can't stand it. I've never worked in a madhouse before."

"What, don't they turn up?"

"In the first place, they don't turn up, and second— they work badly. They'll let everybody down."

He paused for a moment, then added:

"The dirty swine!"

"Well, come on, then. And how's the dike?"

"Not too bad so far, holding. But it's weak ... very weak."

Gubenko was as tall as Minayev. Timka had to run to keep up with them.

On the "local" sector the number of people was noticeably less, but Gubenko seemed to have been mistaken. There was a great deal of movement about. Many of the people here were women. They were chattering and shouting at each other, and everyone was making for one particular spot.

"What are you all in a heap for?" asked Gubenko.

A sturdy young woman who had been bending down near the dike straightened up.

"The wet's coming through."

Minayev strode forward. On the steep slope of the dike a patch about a metre long was trickling with water. From behind his father's arm Timka watched the little rivulets trickling down, and could not see anything terrible in them. But Father was obviously worried.

"Very bad! But what are you piling sacks on it for? They're bound to fall down. They've got nothing to support them. And where are all your people?"

The women were silent.

"Where's Bychkov?"

"Bychkov wasn't here yesterday either," answered Gubenko.

"Bychkov is building a cottage for Rakityansky," said one of the women.

"A cottage? In Overbank?"

"No, in 'Little Eden.'"

"Damn the idiots!" Minayev got angry. "And Zakharchenko, and Volonchuk? And that ... Grigoryev?"

"Volonchuk came here, but he'd got himself all wet. Been drowning his sorrows, he said. And Zakharchenko was here yesterday, but today he's gone into town for something."

"I see.... Well, all right, start from the bottom...."

"Take me off this job, I can't answer for them..." began Gubenko.

"Why should you answer for them? You deal with this hole, and I'll run and see about getting help. Timka, go home, I'll be back later."

Next morning when the new shift arrived nobody thought of going home to rest. When Timka arrived with Petya he could not recognize the dike. Bad weather hid both Scabland and the river from view. Drizzling rain was falling in sharp cold gusts. A strong wind blew from the river, whipping up clouds of spray. White-topped waves heaved on the river. Almost incessantly tongues of water splashed over the edge of the dike, flooded the ridge and trickled down in a delicate pattern of foam. People were stumbling and falling on the slope.

Timka, Petya, Volodya and the other boys had no time to fill the empty sacks with earth. The earth had become muddy and stubborn. It stuck to the buckets and to their hands, and would not fall into the sacks. Golubev told them to take earth from the sheds of the nearby cottages, but no sooner had the boys run over there than Minayev, drenched and muddy, galloped up on a bare-backed horse.

"Golubev," he shouted, "take all the Komsomols and go to the centre. They can scarcely hold it there!"

The youngsters rushed for the centre. Timka glanced round hesitantly. His father looked at him with unseeing eyes and galloped on. Timka grabbed his bucket and ran after the Komsomol boys. Ahead, kicking up the mud with his heels, ran Petya. Minayev overtook them at a gallop.

When Timka reached the centre all the Komsomols had arrived. The women were retreating in confusion. Grigoryev was stamping about, groaning. In front of Timka's nose Lyonya Bychkov crashed down a heavy sack on a strangely bubbling cauldron of mud at the very foot of the dike, and shouted:

"Sacks!!! More sacks quick!!"

Timka dodged a wave of people with sacks and made a dive for the first comparatively dry mound of earth. Several people dived with him, and others rushed in their direction with empty sacks. Someone snatched the bucket out of Timka's hands and he worked with bare hands. Petya appeared on his right, plying his shovel furiously and whispering: "Any minute now ... it'll all be over...."

Timka looked up. The slope of the dike towered high above him, and all over it, running, crawling and sliding, the Komsomols were ramming heavy sacks of earth into the oozing mass. Lyonya rushed up to Timka, his face black with mud, and panted hoarsely:

"Come on, lads, give us some more!"

"Oh!" someone shouted in front, and everybody dashed there. Timka watched in horror as a whole batch of sacks on the slope seemed to gasp and heave up. Suddenly a shining black dome burst through them and flooded outwards. Several sacks slid down heavily, and in their place an unexpectedly clean fountain of water gushed forth. Lyonya jumped towards it with a sack and suddenly sank in up to his waist. Father's voice rang out sharply over Timka's head:

"Up here everyone! Get away from there! Scatter along the dike!"

Timka saw his father only for a second. He was a blurred dot in the general turmoil. A cold wave of water struck Timka's knees, then his chest, knocking him down. As he fell, Timka clutched at Petya's shoulder, but Petya fell too.... Right in front of Timka's face loomed the leg of a horse.

"Grab him!" said a calm voice.

It sounded like Father. Timka somersaulted upwards and came to himself only when he felt a strange wet brush on his cheek. He opened his eyes and saw Gubenko's face terribly close. Timka brushed Gubenko's beard out of his eyes, and said:

"I'm all right ... I'm getting up. Where's Petya?"

"Wait a bit before you get up," said Gubenko.

He heaved himself up the slope. On the ridge Minayev was sitting astride his horse, holding Petya in his arms.

Timka looked round: people were running along the dike. Down below, the water was already swamping everywhere. It was tearing through the gap in a crested wave and beating frantically on the wall of the nearest cottage. The cottage heeled over under the blows, its roof lifted slightly along one edge, then suddenly collapsed.

"That's that," said Father. "We seem to have changed sons."

Gubenko put Timka down on the dike.

"We'll sort them out."

A boat was cruising down a street in "Little Eden." In the boat sat Timka's father, Gubenko, Petya and Timka. Timka could not recognize his street—only the upper parts of the walls showed above the water, and the roofs hung over them like tents. On one of the roofs sat Bychkov.

"A-ah! Out boating, are you?" he shouted. "You can sail your boat. What about me? Taken my house away, and my son!"

He struck his chest with his fist.

"Taken my son away!"

"Been drinking?" asked Minayev calmly.

Bychkov's eyes bulged.

"Yes, I have. What about it? I suppose I mustn't drink now? You're drowners, that's what you are! Drowners! You've taken my son!"

Gubenko burst out laughing.

"Who needs a father like you? Rubbish! Lyonya did the right thing. What's the use of a father like you to him?"

"So I'm no use to him, eh? No use to my own son?"

The boat was already far away, but Bychkov still went on shouting.

Timka told Petya in a whisper that Lyonya had disowned his father and was now living in the hostel at the factory training school.

"He says, 'I'm a worker and he's no father for me,'" said Timka, his eyes wide. "He says he's a self-seeker. Do you understand?"

Petya nodded.

"He's right, too."

And Timka nodded.

"Of course, he is. All this trouble going on, and he goes away and builds a cottage. Thinks he'll make himself some more money! Just grabs everything for himself all the time, doesn't he?"

Zhora, aged two, looks with scorn at a cup of milk, waves his little hand at it and turns away. Zhora is full up and has no desire for milk. This young man-to-be experiences no gaps in the sphere of feeding. But very likely there are other spheres where his needs are not fully satisfied. Perhaps he has a need to feel sympathy for other people or, at least, for other creatures. And if Zhora has no such need yet, perhaps it should be created?

Mother looks at Zhora fondly, but for some reason these questions are of no interest to her. They are of no interest to the brood-hen or any other mother in the zoological kingdom.

Where life is guided by instinct the mother has only one aim—to feed her young. And the mothers of the animal world carry out this task with noble simplicity; they stuff into open beaks and mouths all the food they succeed in catching and bringing back to the nest, and they go on stuffing until the satisfied offspring simply shut their mouths. After that the animal mother can take a rest and attend to her own personal needs.

Mother nature has been extremely thoughtful in providing animal mothers with very wise conditions. In the first place, to feed their young, sparrows and swallows have to make several dozen, or perhaps several hundred, journeys by air in the course of a single working-day. Each little insect that carries about a hundredth of a calory in its body requires a separate journey, and often the journey is unsuccessful. Secondly, animal mothers have no command of articulate speech. This achievement belongs only to man.

It would seem that human mothers are placed in far better conditions. But these favourable conditions constantly become a danger to the upbringing of human children. . . .

Man is ruled by the laws of human society, as well as the laws of nature. The laws of social life work with far greater accuracy, far greater convenience and far greater logic than the laws of nature. But they impose on man far sterner demands of discipline than Mother

Nature, and for breaches of this discipline they punish very severely.

It often happens that a human mother shows a tendency to obey only the laws of nature, but at the same time does not renounce the benefits of human culture. What name can one give to such conduct? Surely, it is nothing but double-dealing. And for this crime of the mother against the lofty nature of man the children suffer a fierce revenge: they grow up into inferior members of human society.

Our mothers do not have to spend so much energy on feeding their children. Human ingenuity has invented markets, shops and well-organized food supplies. And therefore the passion for stuffing food into the mouths of children becomes fatally unnecessary. And it is all the more dangerous to use such a complicated device as human speech for this purpose.

Zhora looks with scorn at the cup of milk. Zhora is full up. But Mother *says* to Zhora:

"Pussy wants to have the milk. Pussy's looking at the milk. No! We won't give it to pussy! Zhora will drink it up! Go away, pussy!"

Mother's words seem to be true. Pussy is looking at the milk, and he would not mind having some breakfast. Zhora looks at pussy suspiciously. And Mother Nature triumphs: Zhora cannot let pussy have his milk.

Such trifles breed egoists.

> **"I am not an ascetic, but the feelings should develop dialectically."**
>
> FELIX DZERZHINSKY

Perhaps all the failures in upbringing can be reduced to a single formula: "the cultivation of greed." The ever-alert and tireless desire to consume can find expression in the most varied forms, very often not at all unpleasant on the outside: This desire starts developing in the very first months of life. Were there nothing else but this desire, social life and human culture would be impossible. But side by side with this desire our knowledge of life grows and develops, and, above all, so does our knowledge of the limits to greed.

In bourgeois society greed is regulated by competition. The scope of one man's desires is limited by the scope of the other's. It is like the swinging of millions of pendulums crammed together in a confined space. They work in various directions and on various planes, they hook together, they knock together, they scratch and grind together. In this world it is profitable to gather in oneself the energy of a metal mass and swing as hard as possible to knock down and destroy one's neighbours. But in this world it is also important to know the strength of a neighbour's resistance, so as not to shatter oneself by making a rash movement. The morality of the bourgeois world is the morality of greed adapted to greed.

In human desire itself there is no greed. If a man coming from a smoky town arrives in a pine-wood and delights in breathing his fill of the fresh air, no one will accuse him of consuming oxygen too greedily. Greed begins where the need of one man clashes with the need of another, where joy or satisfaction must be taken from a neighbour by force, cunning or theft.

Our programme includes neither the abnegation of desires, nor hungry isolation, nor beggarly kneeling to the greed of others.

We are living on the summit of the greatest pass in history, our day has seen the beginning of a new order in human relations, a new morality, a new law, the foundation of which is the victorious idea of human solidarity. The pendulums of our desires have been given room for a great swing. The road now lies open before every man to achieve his desires, his happiness and his well-being. But he is tragically mistaken if on this broad open road he

405

falls into the old habit of using his elbows, for now even a Young Pioneer knows very well that man was given elbows to feel his neighbour, not to make a road for himself with them. Aggressive elbow-work in our times is an action that is more stupid than immoral.

In socialist society, based on the reasonable idea of solidarity, the moral action is simultaneously the wisest one. This is a very important fact that every parent and educator should know.

Imagine a crowd of hungry people lost in a desert. Imagine that these people have no organization and no feeling of solidarity. These people, each at his own risk, each to the measure of his own strength, are searching for food. And then they find some and pounce on it in a general wild struggle, destroying each other and destroying the food. And if there is one man in this crowd who does not enter the struggle, who condemns himself to death by starvation but refuses to take another man by the throat, he will, of course, attract the attention of all the others. They will watch him expire, their eyes wide with wonder. Some of these spectators will call him a devotee and a moral hero, others will call him a fool. And between these two judgements there will be no contradiction.

Now imagine another case: an organized detachment of people find themselves in the same situation. They are united by the conscious conviction that their interests are mutual, by good discipline, and by faith in their leaders. Such a detachment will keep a strict march to the discovered supplies of food and will halt some yards before the spot, at the stern word of command of one man alone. And if there happens to be someone in this detachment whose feeling of solidarity fails, who shouts and snarls and throws himself forward to grab the supplies for himself alone, the others will take him quietly by the collar and say:

"You're a scoundrel and a fool."

But who in this detachment will be the perfect example of morality?

All the rest.

In the old world, moral excellence was the lot of rare devotees, who were extremely few and far between, and so a supercilious attitude to moral perfection soon became accepted as the standard of social morality. As a matter of fact there were two standards. One a show standard, for moral sermons and for the professional devotees, the other for everyday life and for the "wise." According to the first standard, one had to give one's last shirt to the poor, one had to give away one's estate, one had always to turn the other cheek. By the second standard none of these things were required, in fact nothing sacred was required. Here the yardstick of morality was not moral excellence but common everyday sinfulness. People already thought of it in that way: everybody sins and you can't do anything about it. To sin in moderation was the normal thing. For the sake of respectability it was necessary once a year to add up all one's sins during that period, do a bit of fasting somehow, listen for a few hours to the nasal singing of the sextons, duck under the greasy stole of the priest for a minute ... and "write off" all one's misdeeds. Everyday morality did not venture further than moderate sin, sin that was not serious enough to be called a crime, and not feeble enough to deserve the accusation of simplicity, which, as everyone knows, is "worse than stealing."

In socialist society the demands of morality apply to everybody, and everybody must respond to them. We have no show standards of holiness, and our moral achievements are expressed in the conduct of the masses.

Yes, we do have Heroes of the Soviet Union, but, when it sends them to perform a feat of heroism, our government has not put them through a special examination. It chooses them from the general mass of citizens. Tomorrow it may send millions of people to perform similar feats, and it will have no doubt that these millions will display the same moral excellence. In the people's respect and love for our heroes the rarest element is moral surprise. We love them because we feel united with them—in their feat we see a practical example that we must apply to our own conduct.

Our morality grows up out of the real solidarity of the working people.

Communist morality, simply because it is built up on the idea of solidarity, cannot be a morality of abstention. In demanding from the individual the abolition of greed, and respect for the interests and life of his comrades, communist morality demands solidarity in everything else, especially in struggle. If extended to make a philosophical generalization, the idea of solidarity embraces all spheres of life: life is a struggle for every tomorrow, a struggle with nature, with ignorance, with backwardness, with zoological atavism, with the survivals of barbarism; life is a struggle for mastery over the inexhaustible forces of earth and sky.

Success in this struggle will be directly proportional to the greatness of human solidarity.

We have lived for only twenty years in this new moral atmosphere, and how many great changes have we already experienced in the moral nature of men.

We cannot yet say that we have finally mastered the dialectics of communist morality. To a considerable extent we are guided in our educational activities by intuition; we rely more on our feelings than on precise thinking.

There still exist within us many survivals of the old life, old relations, old, habitual moral assumptions. Without noticing it ourselves, we still repeat in our practical life many of the mistakes and falsifications that have

408

already been made in the history of mankind. Many of us unconsciously exaggerate the importance of what is called love, others parade a faith in so-called freedom, very often without noticing that instead of love we are fostering sentimentality, and instead of freedom—licence.

Solidarity of interests gives us the idea of duty, but it does not give us the actual fulfilment of duty. And therefore solidarity of interests is not yet a moral phenomenon. The latter comes only when we have solidarity of conduct. In the history of mankind solidarity of interests has always existed among the toilers, but a united successful struggle became possible only as the culmination of our historical experience, perfected by the energy and thought of the great leaders of the workers' movement.

Conduct is a very complex result not only of consciousness, but of knowledge, strength, habit, skill, fitness, courage, health and, most important of all—social experience.

From the child's very earliest years the Soviet family should foster this experience; it should exercise the child in the most varied kinds of solidary conduct, in the surmounting of obstacles, in the very difficult process of collective growth. It is particularly important that a boy's or girl's feeling of solidarity should not be based only on the narrow pattern of the family; it should extend beyond the boundaries of the family into the broad sphere of Soviet life and the life of mankind in general.

As I finish the first volume of *A Book for Parents,* I should like to hope that the book will do some good. I hope mainly that the reader will find in it useful starting points for his own active thinking about education and upbringing. I cannot count on more than that. Every family has its own peculiar features and conditions of life, every family must solve independently many educational problems, not by using ready-made recipes picked up here and there, but by relying exclusively on the general principles of Soviet life and communist morality.

In this first volume I have managed to touch only on the basic problems connected with the structure of the Soviet family as a collective body. In the future I plan to go on with the problems of the spiritual and material culture of the family and of aesthetic education. It would be a good thing if the second volume were written not only on the basis of my own personal experience, but on that of other people as well. Therefore I shall be very grateful to any parents who will write me about their thoughts, difficulties and discoveries. Such communication between the reader and the author will be the best expression of our solidarity.

www.ingramcontent.com/pod-product-compliance
Lightning Source LLC
Chambersburg PA
CBHW010854090426
42737CB00019B/3365